Ingerland

Ingerland

Travels With a Football Nation

Mark Perryman

SIMON &
SCHUSTER

London · New York · Sydney · Toronto

A CBS COMPANY

First published in Great Britain by Simon & Schuster UK Ltd, 2006
A CBS COMPANY

3 5 7 9 10 8 6 4 2

Simon & Schuster UK Ltd
Africa House
64-78 Kingsway
London WC2B 6AH

www.simonsays.co.uk

Simon & Schuster Australia
Sydney

A CIP catalogue record for this book is available
from the British Library

ISBN 0-7432-6873-3
EAN 9 780743 268738

Typeset in Times by M Rules
Printed and bound in Great Britain by
The Bath Press, Bath

*For all the fans who – win, lose or draw – still believe
in an England everybody can be proud of.*

Mark Perryman

Mark Perryman has followed England home and away for the past ten years through qualifying campaigns and tournaments from Euro 96 to World Cup 2006. He is one of the main organizers of supporter-led efforts towards creating and maintaining a positive England fan culture; these include the 'Raise the Flag' initiative at home games and, on away trips, fan-friendly events bringing together our own and opposition supporters. In between all this he chairs the independent LondonEnglandFans group fan forums.

A regular commentator on England fan issues for BBC TV News, Sky Sports, Radio Five Live, TalkSPORT and local radio, he is also the editor of *The Ingerland Factor* and *Going Oriental: Football after World Cup 2002*. In 2002 Mark wrote the influential report 'Ingerland Expects: Football, National Identity and the World Cup' for the think-tank The Institute for Public Policy Research. He is a part-time research fellow in sport and leisure culture at The Chelsea School, University of Brighton and serves on the Home Office working group on football and public disorder.

In 1994 Mark co-founded www.philosophyfootball.com, self-styled 'sporting outfitters of intellectual distinction', the people who put quotes about the beautiful game from Camus, Cruyff, Cantona and Sartre on a T-shirt, with name and squad number on the back.

England supporter, fan activist, media pundit, author, academic and T-shirt entrepreneur Mark Perryman is uniquely placed to write a book that no one else has ever written. The story of how the pride and the passion of Ingerland can help create a football nation all would be proud to support.

Contents

Assists, Late Tackles and Saves

It is thanks to the hundreds of supporters I have come to know through LondonEnglandFans, Raise the Flag and fan-friendly events that I was convinced that the story of what it means to be an England fan was one worth telling.

Thanks in particular to Pete Nicholas and Anne-Marie Mockridge of NorthWestEnglandFans, Martin O'Hara of Yorkshire England Supporters, Dave Finn and Richard Stiff of EasternEnglandFans, Neil Shenton of MidlandsEnglandFans, Joe Summerell of SouthWestEnglandFans, Tim Murray of SouthCoastEnglandFans, Ian Potter, Olivia Platt and Alan Lee of 4England. And from LondonEnglandFans, some special mentions: Peter John-Baptiste for the website www.londonenglandfans.co.uk and the photos; Julie Nerney, Lynda Copson and Jess Mortimer for the meeting reports; Simon Copson for organizing the raffle draws. Thanks also to Damien Devine, Lorcan Devine and Richard Kay for the hospitality at The Offside Bar.

Ingerland is about the fans but it is also about our relationship with organizations responsible for us. The FA's Ian Murphy, Nicola Jones and Jamie Craig have listened to complaints, borne the brunt of criticisms and responded positively to many of my ideas. Susan Warrilow and Rachel Ely have endured my detailed checklists for countless Raise the Flag preparations.

David Bohannan and Martin Gooday at the Home Office, David Swift from the Association of Chief Police Officers, Andy Brame, Bryan Drew and Tony Conniford at the Football Policing Unit, have allowed me to acquire an insight into what they are doing while recognizing that on occasion we might disagree over the detail of their methods.

Dame Glynn Evans and Gary Fisher at the British Embassy in Portugal, Andy Battson at the British Embassy in Germany and Stephen Durrant of the Consular Directorate have invited me to take part in valuable discussions with host countries' authorities.

Thank you to the following British Council staff: Rohini Naidoo in South Africa, Rosemary Hilhorst in Portugal, Paul Fairclough in Poland, Paul Hilder in Azerbaijan, David Alderdice in Holland, Michael Sorensen-Jones in Denmark, Colm McGivern in Northern Ireland, Caroline Morrissey in Switzerland, Frauke Kegel and Elke Ritt in Germany, and Andy Hansen and James Schone in London. You have all supported fan-friendly events I have organized and helped thousands of supporters to do something to make others feel good about England.

Thanks also to those who have put me up during the course of writing this book: Ana Pereirinha, Antonino Solmer and Felipe Caetano in Portugal, Hannes Schneeberger in Austria, Robert Strupiechowski in Poland, Ben Forgey and John Burke in the USA, Christian Moeller in Denmark, Elaine Moore in Wales, Simon Murray in Northern Ireland and Jeff Turner in Switzerland.

Brian Young has organized some great away trips. Philip Cornwall has been an irregular travelling companion, his presence always welcome both as a friend but also an unrivalled source of tactical insight.

My students at The Chelsea School, University of Brighton have provided feedback on the ideas in *Ingerland*. Departmental colleagues Steve Redhead, Dan Burdsey, Alan Tomlinson and John

Sugden have tested my opinions. Elsewhere Stephen Parrott and Sean Hamil at Birkbeck College, Dasa Sephton and the British Council in Prague, Can Ozgun and the British Council in Istanbul, have all invited me to give talks about England fans.

Literary agent David Luxton responded positively when I first tried to sell him the idea of this book. Andrew Gordon at Simon & Schuster gave the proposal a fair hearing and has backed it enthusiastically ever since. Kerri Sharp and Ian Allen have done a magnificent job in improving my original manuscript. Sports photographer Mark Leech provided the perfect pictures for the cover.

Ken Jackson and Paul Jonson are my two oldest friends. Your support, understanding and patience have been unstoppable. My sister Penelope Cattaneo and her family provide the sofa view of England while I'm abroad at a Euro or World Cup. My youngest niece Katie, with boyfriend Simon, have become England regulars at home matches; their questions about my away trips helped me think through what I needed to write about to convey the experience for readers who haven't been there, done that.

Football and Englishness . . . I could quite easily become an insufferable bore talking about them. Preventing a decline into unsociability is my partner Anne Coddington. Without her, following England wouldn't be half the fun. Not another night under canvas is part of the deal after I pitched the tent on the edge of a French village's cesspit following our defeat to Romania in Toulouse. I remember the score, she's never forgotten the early-morning stench we woke up to. Anne rounds off the rougher edges of these privations for the cause and does it all with love in unimaginable quantity.

Becks, Rooney and Lamps. Without them, their team-mates and Sven none of what I've written about would matter a jot. I'd like to think there's a chance they might read my book. Just to help them understand what they do with a ball means to those of us in the stands and watching back home. Meticulous in their preparations, the FA will pack up a consignment of paperbacks to take for the World Cup squad to read and stave off any unwelcome distractions. If they include this one along with the latest blockbuster from Andy McNab, I'll be a very happy author.

Ingerland

Introduction: This Ingerland of Mine

This book was inspired by the fans who follow England home and away, but particularly away. Add all those who attend England internationals in this country to the thousands who travel round Europe to support the team through a qualifying campaign, then chuck in the tens, or hundreds of thousands who will catch a flight, train or ferry to cheer on England at a European Championship or World Cup. If you then include those who sit in front of the TV for the duration of the tournament watching the games, wishing they were there and deciding next time they will be, England's *active* support must number many hundreds of thousands. What I found strange, then, was that there was no book that tried to explain what it means to be an England fan.

Since Nick Hornby's *Fever Pitch* was published in 1992 there's been an avalanche of books, some good, others awful, telling readers what it is like to support the author's chosen team. On my bookshelves, being an open-minded sort, apart from those by fans of my own club, Spurs, I've got some of the best of these. Fans' tales of supporting Barnsley, Celtic, Charlton, Leeds, Liverpool, Man City, Man United, Norwich, Sheffield United, Stoke and West Ham, and even a rather brilliant one by a Cowdenbeath supporter. But, apart from books which concentrate on the story of how England have done on the pitch at a particular World Cup, or the hooligan confessionals I've collected to keep me awake at night, there's scarcely anything about the experience of supporting England.

Ingerland is not my story. I've followed England for ten years, missing just one home match and a handful of away ones in that time. I'm not sure if that now makes me an old hand, or still a new fan. That's for others to decide. But I certainly don't believe that what I've got up to following England would amount on its own to a particularly fascinating or necessary tale to tell. I was much more interested in gathering together as many different experiences to record as would fit in a book of reasonable length: fans who had followed England much longer than me, and some who had only just started; women, some who went on their own or with other women, others as mums, girlfriends, wives or sisters; families, dads with daughters, sons with dads, single parents; black and Asian fans, first, second and third generation, those who have experienced racism at England games but refuse to be turned away, and want others to hear that the good times far outweigh the bad.

My experiences are in here too. I couldn't have written the book if I hadn't been at the matches, sometimes seen trouble (though mostly there wasn't any to see), and had to put up with the way we're often mistreated and misrepresented. There's no way I'm going to try and pretend I'm a neutral observer in all of this. C'mon, this is England I'm writing about.

The fans whose stories I tell are from all over England. I've travelled to Manchester, Ambleside, Birmingham, Worcester, Taunton, Bath, Eastleigh, High Wycombe, Brighton, Harrow, Doncaster, Newcastle, Derby, Rotherham and elsewhere to meet them. None, as far as I know, are convicted hooligans. Not because I have any qualms about interviewing those with a violent past, or present, but because this book is about those England fans who don't get written about, the ones who don't cause any trouble.

Introduction: This Ingerland of Mine

And increasingly it is they who form the majority, often actively involved in developing a fan-friendly culture around supporting England. Representative? I can't prove it; that would be a different sort of book, demanding all sorts of surveys and questionnaires. But everything I know about England fans, have seen with my own eyes, and come to believe in with a faith that sometimes comes close to missionary zeal, convinces me that these hundred or so fans whose stories I recount represent more about England than many who write about us realize. Add the thousands more I've met at fan forums or Raise the Flag set-ups, swapped emails with, or seen at a fan-friendly event abroad and it is this certainty that started me writing.

Get any group of England fans together and in a very short space of time we'd be complaining about not getting our tickets, the way we're policed, and what's been written about us. I make this claim with some authority, having chaired the LondonEnglandFans forums for the past five years. *Ingerland* seeks to find out how the FA manages its relationship with England supporters. The book investigates the way the media works at a major tournament and why the fans' story gets told in a particular way. Readers may be surprised, or feel they've been short-changed even, that there is no chapter providing the gruesome, scarcely believable accounts of beating up foreigners and gory last stands in some foreign bar as the windows shattered and the last empty glass was chucked. This is partly because this isn't what following England is like for most of us, but also because the story of how we're policed and why this is so important too often gets lost in the glamorous subculture of hoolie-lit. *Ingerland* provides a rare insight into policing strategy, football intelligence and crowd management to discover whether England's drift away from its hooligan past is irreversible, tragically temporary or somewhere in between.

Ten years, 1996 to 2006: three European Championships and the same number of World Cups; qualifying campaigns and friendlies too. There have been some changes during this period. Whether we believe there are two sides of a story or not, for the first four years, until Euro 2000 at least, we were still staggering under the unwanted reputation of the least welcome guests at any tournament. In late 2005, when Ian Murphy and Nicola Jones from the FA invited fans to the organization's Soho Square headquarters for a discussion about World Cup 2006, one of those changes was very evident. These weren't hand-picked individuals, lonesome maverick voices speaking for nobody but themselves. No, this was the beginning of a national network of independent regional England fan groups, some bigger and involving more fans than others, but all bottom-up, run by the fans themselves and full of ideas to help ensure England's support in Germany might be a credit to the nation.

Our rapidly improving reputation is at last receiving the recognition it deserves. When England played Argentina in Geneva, November 2005, two hundred fans travelled out to Nyon on match day to play friendly matches. Kids played against a Swiss side, while the seniors and veterans took on the UEFA staff side. When they heard how keen we were on promoting some goodwill, UEFA took the extraordinary step of inviting us all into their HQ, also in Nyon, for a reception. Alex Phillips, head of professional football services at UEFA, welcomed us. He explained this was the first time a fans group had been invited into their building on anything like this scale, and admitted how surprised but impressed they were by what we were trying to do. There was nothing particularly out of the ordinary about the group who went. Blokes in their twenties, thirties or forties, some for whom this was their first England away match, and some who had been going for decades. There were mums and dads with their kids, a few women fans. I recognized familiar faces who had taken part in previous fan-friendly events, but many were new faces – they had read about this effort on the englandfans website and decided this time they'd join in. Just by being there everybody was actively contributing to this turnaround being welcomed by UEFA. Only five years previously, rightly or wrongly, the same organization had been on the verge of kicking England out of Euro 2000 because of hooligan behaviour.

Others have noticed the changes and the conditions required to keep things moving in the right direction. Henry Winter in the *Daily Telegraph* was one of the few journalists to report on the atrocious stadium mismanagement in Geneva for the match against Argentina: 'England fans need treating properly, not herding into unsafe corridors like animals. Otherwise, some will get hurt, or others will fight back.' Sensible, fair-minded words which recognize how important it is to ensure supporters' safety and security. When this is done properly it becomes easier to persuade increasing numbers of England fans of our responsibility to represent our nation positively off the pitch and in the streets. *Ingerland* examines the factors that determine positive and negative expressions of our support for England, records the process of change towards a better England and traces developments that have changed the face of England's support.

Ingerland is about a football nation too. National identity cannot be reduced simply to what a football team and its supporters get up to. Yet it is impossible to deny that more St George Cross flags are seen around the country when England are playing in a Euro or World Cup than at any other time. This book tries to uncover any deeper meaning for this curious collision of eleven blokes, a ball making its way towards the back of a net, and nationhood. When we sing in joyful defiance as Joe Cole pops up and scores against the Welsh at Cardiff's Millennium Stadium, 'You're just a small town near England', is it just another wind-up or a more menacing greater English nationalism? Four days later and David Healy puts away a scorcher to record Northern Ireland's best performance since beating Spain in 1982, this time at our expense. The Northern Ireland fans sing at us, 'You'll win fuck all again'. To a man, and the odd woman, the entire England end in Belfast that night, all fifteen hundred of us, retort, 'We'll win fuck all again'.

Has magnanimity and humility been added to that more bullish and cocksure identity on parade in Cardiff? Two months after that game a big part of the England end is singing at the start of the game against Argentina, 'What's it like to lose a war?' By the end, after Owen's thrilling ninetieth-minute winner, we're all joining in with 'Eaz-ee! Eaz-ee!' Does this mean the dragging in of matters not much to do with football wasn't as important as some feared? That if only England always won the other less savoury stuff would fade away? Who knows, but the home truths football tells us about Englishness are not to be lightly dismissed. With no parliament, no proper borders, not even an anthem to call our own, football provides us with the occasion to fly our flag and, arguably, wear our national dress too. A football shirt which, since the 2002-vintage red stripe down the front, has carried St George on chest, shoulders or some other part of the design ever since.

In this book there are no footnotes but, at the end, if *Ingerland* has sparked an interest to find out more, there is a brief guide to further reading on many of the subjects I cover, useful websites, contacts and details on how to join the England supporters club, englandfans, or get involved with one of the regional independent groups of England fans. I must warn you, though, such enthusiasm could affect your reading habits, holiday plans and bank balance dramatically. I know all three of mine have never been the same since that first away trip to Moldova in September 1996.

And *Ingerland*, why I-N-G-E-R-L-A-N-D? Is it because we're

so gormless and lacking in diction we can't even pronounce our own country's name properly? Anything but. I would hazard a well-founded guess that England fans have more sense of what their country means to them than most, and we certainly know how to both spell it and say it, thank you very much. It just sounds better shouted, chanted or sung with that extra syllable. It's not entirely original – those wonderful Northern Ireland fans who showed us how to party in defeat when losing to us 4–0 at Old Trafford in March 2005, and then celebrated with such friendly abandon when they beat us at Windsor Park six months later, cheerfully print 'Nor'rn Iron' on their shirts, flags and scarves. They take the piss out of their occasionally impenetrable accents and remove a syllable or two to come up with their own green-and-white football army.

We're just doing the same, except we're adding a syllable, not taking one away, and ours is red and white, with a gold star for that trophy we won way back in '66. If others don't get the meaning of it, that's their problem, but the fact that I-N-G-E-R-L-A-N-D has acquired that extra syllable means the world to us fans. This is our football nation, and *Ingerland* is our story of how we made it.

1

Something to Declare

We wear the same shirt, fly the same flag, cheer for the same team.
And for most of us you can tick at least one of the other four distinguishing marks of I-N-G-E-R-L-A-N-D: closely cropped hair, beer belly, tattoos and a variety of designer labels. People think they know us; not much good, mainly bad, and likely to turn ugly. And when we're in town it's a dangerous place to be. Bars shut down, the local toughs looking out for us, and armour-plated police everywhere. It's been like this for more years than I care to forget. But what do they know of I-N-G-E-R-L-A-N-D who only this England knows?

Marseilles, summer 1998, the venue of England's opening World Cup match versus Tunisia. The city is an urban sprawl that has had more than its unfair share of racial tension in recent years, particularly between a resurgent fascist Front National and the local Arab youth. The day before the England match, myself and my partner Anne took a look around the beach area, where a huge screen had been set up for the large numbers of English holiday-makers who would venture into Marseilles ticketless but eager to be part of the World Cup buzz. Across the road security guards with Alsatian dogs patrolled the aisles of the local supermarket. This is an area with a high level of street crime, which was likely to rise with the influx of football tourists. Further into town we skirted around the old port area after being warned by the volunteers staffing the supporters' Fans Embassy that a mobile-phone call there was an open invitation to robbery or worse. These two areas on match day would be a potent mix of criminality, racism and violence, in other words places to avoid.

The I-N-G-E-R-L-A-N-D reputation had arrived before us. The young Arab immigrants fancied their chances of taking the English on, and the beach and the bars facing the harbour would be where any battles would commence. Large chunks of the 25,000-plus England fans in the city sensibly ignored these obvious flash-points. Instead we soaked up the sun in the many parts of the city that supplied a more hospitable welcome. We made our way to the match, enjoyed enormously England's opening victory, and left the city that evening dreaming of maybe some glory coming our way at last.

As the match finished I had popped into a phone kiosk, having arranged to do a phone report for my local radio station, BBC London 94.9. I was full of Paul Scholes' brilliant goal, the searing heat inside the stadium, the noise of the supporters' band standing in front of me, the sight of England flags in every part of the stadium and, having avoided those two trouble spots, the complete absence of trouble.

'No trouble? But it was everywhere,' was the presenter's incredulous retort to my upbeat account. Marseilles had been a nasty, violent and vengeful place in two parts of the city, and on the English side the fighting had involved possibly upwards of five hundred people. Imagine that number in a town square, any town square, ready to throw a punch or chuck a bottle without a care for their or anybody else's safety and security. Then add row after row of TV crews and long-lens cameras, reinforced by instant-response experts primed to provide a running commentary.

The morning after the night before, former Metropolitan Police Deputy Commissioner Sir Brian Hayes was on TV in his capacity as the FA's chief security adviser, condemning the English hooligans. He made points most right-thinking fans would agree with, but he was an establishment voice who lacked credibility. Dressed in his immaculate suit, his tie neatly knotted in the face of the ferociously hot combination of Mediterranean sun and banks of TV lights, he just didn't look like one of us.

In the aftermath of the violence I felt a sense of both shame and absolute powerlessness. Like the overwhelming proportion of England fans, I had not caused, witnessed nor been a victim of the violence that was splashed across the front pages of all the papers, and dominated the day's TV and radio bulletins. What had any of this to do with me? Not a lot. But while we could argue the toss over the cause of the violence, and compare the numbers actually involved with the vast majority who took no part in it, it was the effect on our reputation that really mattered. If we allowed this I-N-G-E-R-L-A-N-D to represent something we were ashamed of, what kind of patriotism was that? That day, though, there was very little any of us could do about it, except be polite, remember to say *Merci* and *S'il vous plaît* and, if anybody asked, reply, 'It wasn't us, guv.'

Mark Shore is a big bloke, square-shouldered, chest stuck out and six-foot-something, and when he speaks he is hard to ignore. He feels fans like him have been mistreated, misrepresented and misunderstood for long enough. Mark is at a meeting of the independent supporters' group, LondonEnglandFans, after Euro 2004. He is a regular at these gatherings, always ready to tell those who come along to listen to our point of view – the FA, the police, journalists, even mild-mannered Trevor Brooking – exactly what he thinks of them. Jonathan Arana, the smooth-talking FA customer relations manager, is steadying himself in his seat, getting ready to defend what the FA has done for fans as Mark prepares to deliver what we're all sure will be another of his angrily stinging rebukes. But instead Mark has come to celebrate the achievement at Euro 2004 of England fans being feted for our performance off the pitch. 'We can't do this on our own. But with you lot backing us, the FA, the government, then we've got a chance. You've done well.' Then, realizing that maybe he'd gone too far with this rare moment of praise, he adds, 'Well, not bad anyway.'

Mark is anything but a new fan. He would rather his face was covered in unsightly spots than paint the St George Cross on it. He doesn't have much time for England's brass band either. 'Why do you need a band to start singing?' And as for Mexican waves, I've got a good idea where he'd like to stick those, too. Mark is old school. His first away game was Denmark in 1978 and he's been on enough trips since then to bear reliable witness to the changes.

'Back then hardly any women travelled, and no kids, all young working-class blokes. Three-quarters of those who went would be involved in trouble, if not actually fighting themselves then running with those who were. Plenty of thieving, too. Half of them were there just for that, filling up their bags and back home with the stuff they'd nicked before the game had even kicked off.'

Nearly thirty years later, 40,000 England fans would be seated in the Estadio da Luz for England's match against France at Euro 2004, with estimates of up to another 40,000 scattered around Portugal, just there for the experience. Mark is certain the hooligan numbers have fallen as the numbers of fans has risen: 'How many were in Portugal looking for trouble, serious trouble? A few hundred?'

This is a change few would hesitate to welcome. Those who have suffered most from I-N-G-E-R-L-A-N-D spelling trouble are England's long-suffering support. We are treated as guilty until proven innocent wherever we travel. We're always the sinners, never sinned against, unwelcome and uncared for. But Mark is anxious that in ditching the negative reputation for trouble we don't lose something else.

'Football needs an edge. There has to be a rivalry. There's an excitement in being there, the dangerous times as well as the good times.' It is football's ugly inside. With it you get trouble. Without it you lose the passion and the loyalty that gives England's fan culture its badge of distinction. Nowadays Mark takes his daughter Emma with him on his England trips. Back in the '70s and '80s he freely admits he couldn't have imagined taking her. Security for them both is what he expects, and he isn't backward in demanding it from those he thinks should provide it. But while not glorifying the past, at the same time he doesn't want a smothering of the unruly emotions that attracted him, and Emma too, to football in the first place.

Gary Armstrong neatly sums up this dilemma in his book *Football Hooligans* and adds some much-needed context. 'How risk-taking is chosen is often dependent on economic resources, or what is locally or socially available. Some climb mountains, some take white-water canoe holidays, some go off-piste skiing.' And, of course, like Mark and Emma, some follow England, with all the attendant risks.

Taking risks, though, wasn't what Ken Jackson and his wife Nicola had in mind when they started planning their trip to Euro 2004. It was their first venture abroad following England, having previously only been to home matches. By disposition Ken is a worrier. I've known him since our schooldays, so I took him through the sensible precautions many England fans take as a matter of course. Have a listen and look before you choose your bar to drink in or square to sit in. Learn to distinguish between the boisterous and the intimidatory. Get to the ground early to avoid the last-minute crush – which, in fact, is anything but last minute, more like two hours before kick off. Find your seat and, if you don't like the look of those around you, do what you can to move to sit with a less aggressive group.

As I reeled these off down the phone, Ken jotted them down as his Portugal dos and don'ts. But none of this was going to put him off, nor should it have. Ken remembers the radio news the week before they travelled 'was full of tales of muggings and robberies in Lisbon, but then I realized the same stories could be told of London and it doesn't stop me going there, does it?' Ken and Nicola's trip proved to be hugely enjoyable. Seeing England thrash Croatia 4–2 in the vital third group match helped, and they had a great vantage point. 'When we found our seats we realized we were in the front row by the touchline at the end where the Croatia goal was, so every time Beckham jogged over to take a corner, there we were on the TV back home with our big cheesy grins.'

In the tiny Lincolnshire village of Friskney a cheer went up at The Anchor when they appeared on screen. The pair of them returned home as fifteen-minute local celebrities. And as for Ken's nervousness? He ended up feeling a quite different set of emotions to the ones he expected. 'The trip meant there was something more going on than just the game. This isn't something you experience at home. The biggest thrill was this feeling of community. Only one team can win but, for a few weeks, sixteen nations come together.'

Their flight home clashed with the first half of England's quarterfinal with Portugal. The pair of them dashed through arrivals to catch extra time and penalties at an airport bar. 'The bloke behind me was mouthing off about how all the Portuguese hated the English, that there would be trouble all over Lisbon that night.' Ken knew different, though. He'd been there and experienced the hospitality, friendship and sense of pride in such a small country hosting such a big tournament; emotions that were returned in kind by the vast majority of the English.

Ken and Nicola, like so many other first-time England fans, took a risk following the team away from home and ended up thanking themselves a thousand times over that they had. But plenty of commentators do their damnedest to persuade them their fate will be something fearsome and not worth the effort. Brian Glanville is one of the grand old men of football journalism in this country. In his December 2003 column for *World Soccer* Glanville looked forward to England's presence at the European Championships the following summer: 'Since there is no hope of anything but hooligan violence by the usual suspects, the so-called minority of England supporters, the Football Association should start thinking about it now and impose a ban similar to the one put in place for the game against Turkey in Istanbul in October.' And he added, just in case we missed his drift, 'Otherwise, it is as inevitable as the sun rising in the east that we shall see a reprise of what happened in Charleroi, Marseilles or in Sunderland when Turkey came to play there.'

Like Brian Glanville, David Lacey is a veteran football writer and, as 2003 came to a close, he also wrote a piece speculating on the likely impact of England's support at Euro 2004. 'As the tournament approaches, with hopes of what could be accomplished on the field tempered by fears of what may happen off it, English football would do better to heed: Lest we Forget.' Sound advice from a commentator who has been covering England at World Cups and European Championships stretching back over three decades. It was a pity, though, that he could not see any grounds for optimism on the back of the fans' good behaviour in Japan, adding the fatalistic comment, 'England's hooligan strain runs too deep for there to be a reversal.' When it comes to England fans, Lacey, and many other journalists, tend to be forgetful when we actually do something right.

After the 2002 World Cup, co-hosted by Korea and Japan, though England played all their matches in Japan, we had been widely applauded for our presence off the pitch. Lennart Johansson, in his capacity as the chair of FIFA's 2002 World Cup Organizing Committee, singled out England fans for praise. 'We always hear quickly and loudly enough when fans do not behave. So let's make plenty of noise this time that their behaviour has been perfect. They showed that real football fans know how to enjoy the game, support their team, celebrate when they win and take defeat when they lose.'

These were strong sentiments, and plenty shared them. The musician Fat Boy Slim was out in Japan, mixing with the fans. 'For the first time I felt proud to be English,' was how he described the experience.

Of course, nobody in their right minds would discount the probability of trouble when England's sizeable support jets off to foreign parts. Measures to reduce any risk of crowd violence have to be taken. They help to ensure the security and safety of both the host country and, let us not forget, our own fans too. I have no desire to sit next to somebody at an England match who in the past couple of years has been convicted for a violent offence. If that individual and others like him can be prevented from going to England games by a banning order, good. These kinds of restrictions are widely supported by England fans, and on countless occasions I've heard fans demanding their full and effective enforcement, supporting the vetting we submit ourselves to as members of the FA supporters' club, englandfans. And we expect the police to ensure the banning orders, providing they have been reasonably applied, are complied with. Today's England fans are performing that awkward balancing act, of rights with responsibilities.

There is a growing community of England fans who believe something has be done about the reputation we now have, whether deserved or otherwise. Adrian Clarke is one of these. For Euro 2004 Adrian was staying in Ericeira, a coastal resort not too far from Lisbon. He had no idea whether any other fans had plumped for the same spot so he thought he'd find out. Within a week of posting an invite to join him for a spot of beach football on the englandfans website he had received more than fifty replies, and an idea began to take shape.

The result was 'Huge in Ericeira', thirty teams, including several local Portuguese teams, taking part in a five-a-side tournament. A charity auction raised thousands of pounds for a leukaemia charity, with England fan and professional livestock auctioneer Ian Potter taking bids for the shirt off Beckham's back rather than his more usual fare. The day rounded off with an enormous crowd of English and Portuguese packed into a marquee erected on the beach to watch Portugal play Spain.

Ericeira in 2004 was one of the good times, but it could hardly have happened without the huge shift England fans had effected in Japan two years previously. I met Chris Hewitt stumbling around the Sapporo Dome in something resembling delirium. England had just beaten Argentina 1–0, reason enough for a big grin on Chris's face, but he had another good cause to smile too. 'The scum aren't here, that's what has made this trip so great.' England fans are used to being written off by others, but this was one of our own. 'They should stay away for good, we don't need them.' Chris knew exactly which ones he was so glad hadn't made it out to Japan. 'Not just the hardcore hooligans but the ones who go along with them, that lot who think "No surrender" is the done thing. Well, it's not as far as I'm concerned.'

Chris was glad to see the back of them. They had been there, far too many for his liking, ever since he started following England away with a trip to Sweden in 1986. 'On the trip there were four hundred committed hooligans and most of the rest went along with them.' Chris added, contemptuously, 'Sheep, that's what they are.'

Chris is no shrinking violet. He likes to cheer, stand, and have a drink or three. He effs and blinds, yet he knows what it should mean to follow your country abroad. 'Of course football is all about banter, winding up the other lot. But when we go overseas we're guests of somebody else's country. If someone opens the door to you, you don't slag them off, do you?'

Japan represented a huge and vital break with what was perceived as England's past. Now we finally had a present, and perhaps a future, to be proud of.

In Japan we learned that it was more pleasurable to be loved than to be loathed – a big change from the 'no one likes us we don't care' attitude. But such a shift was only possible by defining ourselves against another England. This is precisely how those who have trademarked the title 'friendliest fans in the world', the Scots' Tartan Army, ditched their own fearsome hooligan reputation in the early '80s. In his book *Football: A Sociology of the Global Game*, Richard Giulianotti studies the culture of Scotland fans and makes the argument that 'A vital part of the Tartan Army's repertoire involves establishing their national identity through a differentiation from England and "Englishness". By presenting themselves as "anti-English", the Scots play upon the international stereotype that "English fans are hooligans"; hence, the Scottish fans are also "anti-hooli-gan".'

Richard is generous enough to recognize that describing all England fans as hooligans is a stereotype rather than an accurate description. Nevertheless, equipped with that stereotype safely stowed away in their sporrans, the Tartan Army go on their mainly merry way defining themselves as anything but English hooligans. So who could the English define themselves against? Chris Hewitt and thousands more like him found the answer in Japan – those who weren't out there spoiling our fun.

Those who wrote off the England fans' positive impact in Japan at World Cup 2002 as unique came up with various reasons why it would never again be repeated. They cited the distance, the expense, the friendly Japanese reception. But this misread the nature of England's support. England's committed away fans will sacrifice everything to ensure they are there to cheer the team on. For four years we had known that the next World Cup destination was the Far East. We checked out cheap flight options, bargain places to stay. We are the supporters who trekked around Europe through a World Cup qualifying campaign to Albania, Greece, Finland and Germany, we weren't now going to miss out on the finals. And the FA's particular method of distributing tickets confirms this: the bulk of the tickets are made available on a loyalty basis. Fans who follow England through a qualifying campaign and to previous tournaments stand at the front of the queue when the tickets are dished out. The numbers too – 10,000 or thereabouts – were still sufficient to cause trouble if the fancy took them. But eleven arrests was the total, not a single incident of violence either, just the odd bit of shoplifting or doing a runner from a sushi bar.

The friendly reception is a better candidate for explaining why Japan was different. How can you get all bitter and twisted in

Tokyo when you are surrounded by smiling Japanese wearing your shirt, flying your flag and supporting your team? It would take a hard-faced psychopath to do anything but smile appreciably. Surely this at least was unrepeatable? Possibly, but we often under-estimate other countries' affection for England and the English. Japan had all the components for friction rather than friendliness. With 'Colonel Bogey' from *The Bridge on the River Kwai* replac-ing *The Great Escape* as our theme tune, the Second World War to drag up, plus a racial element and antipathy to all things oriental, and Japan 2002 could have had a very different ending. But it was a night in Niigata that proved to be my abiding memory, not any of this other nonsense that thankfully never came to pass: in the pouring rain, England 3–0 up against Denmark and cruising towards a quarterfinal, with another week at least out in this footballing paradise to look forward to, and hundreds of England fans form a conga in the stands singing 'Let's go oriental, la-la-la' as they pick their way between the seats and up and down the gangways.

Japan wasn't just about the very obvious lack of trouble. There was also a sort of settling of accounts with a conservatism that has dominated England's fan culture in general for far too long. First, there was the barely disguised antipathy to new fans, which is frankly ludicrous. Apart from those born into an England babygro, we all start our fandom some time in adolescence or adulthood. All old fans were new fans once. Chip away at this antipathy and underneath there is more often than not a resent-ment that these new fans aren't quite the same as those already secure in their fandom thanks to their gender, race, and sense of class certainty.

Secondly, there is the inclination in the face of adversity for England fans to blame everyone else for our predicament without taking any responsibility ourselves. The god-awful reputation we have may or may not be deserved. The vivid reality is that we've been stuck with it for more years than most of us care to remember.

Japan began to transform both of these conservative tendencies. The support was more diverse than ever before, while the friendly reception provoked the England fans' exuberantly positive response. With no more need to blame anybody else we simply celebrated our presence and embraced the Japanese who joined in with us too.

Raj Dodhia is one of a small but significant group of black and Asian fans who travel with England away. When a mate explained how easy it was to get tickets for the World Cup in Japan via the FIFA website, Raj didn't need any convincing. England's opening World Cup encounter with Sweden in Saitama was his first ever England game. Raj described the mood in the stands: 'It was one big party, quite laid-back really, lots of happy people, welcoming too.' And everywhere he wore his England shirt he found the response just as positive. 'It was like a ticket to a conversation. The Japanese went mad every time they saw us in our shirts.'

But what about his colour, and the fact that even though there was a marked increase in the number of black and Asian fans following England at Japan in 2002, he was still part of a tiny minority? 'I didn't even think about it. Being in an Asian country, which is what Japan is, however Westernized some parts of it are, might have helped because you couldn't ignore the Oriental feel about the place.'

After returning from Japan Raj decided to travel again, this time to Bratislava in Slovakia for England's first away match of the Euro 2004 qualifying campaign. Three experiences on this trip made Raj realize England away wasn't always going to be like the fan carnival he'd been a part of in Japan.

'First, on the coach from the city centre to the stadium there were guys singing, "I'd rather be a Paki than a Turk". I started to wonder what was going on. What had this got to do with the match we were all going to? Second, at the ground it was a huge crush to get in, there was no proper stadium management, the most basic safety regulations weren't observed, and all I could think of was the reports I'd read about the Hillsborough disaster. Third, when the match started it kicked off between the Slovak riot police and some of our lads. This woman beside me was screaming, "My kids, get my kids out of here." She escaped, as I did, pulled to the safety of an upper tier by other fans.'

It was a rude awakening but Raj wasn't put off. 'I was on a day trip. Going to the match, there and back, took thirty-six hours. For maybe thirty-five of those hours I had a great time, nice people – the Slovaks were decent hosts too. Apart from those three moments I enjoyed myself.' And when he got home Raj promptly booked himself up for the next England away trip.

Raj's realism and gutsy determination not to be excluded is founded on this mix of experiences he has had as an England fan. 'There is a nasty element to our support. Massed together in large numbers it can be volatile, aggressive and violent. After Bratislava I realized this was a part of what you unfortunately have to put up with following England. You can't blind yourself to what's going on, and sometimes you question whether it is worth going again.'

The answer for Raj is a fan culture that avoids polarization. 'Me, and other fans like me, we have every right to be at an England game,' he insists. It is a sentiment Raj genuinely feels is widely felt but needs expressing over and over again, and not just in racial terms either, adding, 'England for all, that's the big opportunity we should all be pushing.' Such an England won't be the same for everyone. While demanding recognition for the positive experiences that many of those black and Asian fans who follow

England have had, Raj isn't covering up the negatives. But he is arguing for the issues to be seen in context. 'There's some bars full of a certain sort of bloke at an England match that I avoid, but that's the same whether it's at football or not. The heavy-drinking culture is a very white-English thing, it just doesn't appeal to a lot of Asians.'

Sometimes England is for all, and sometimes it is not. The elements that are welcoming within our support can coexist with those who would exclude and intimidate. Amongst the very necessary condemnations of outbreaks of England crowd trouble at Euro 2000, the *Observer* passed comment on England fans in more measured tones. 'Stop off for a beer or a coffee in Tilburg, or Breda, or Antwerp or Ghent, and you'll bump into friendly, knowledgeable English fans who will help with tickets and advice on restaurants and accommodation. It was the same in France 98. But this is no surprise. The English watch football, and love watching football, like no other nation. Yes, England has the worst football fans in the world. But it also has the best.'

Pride, hope and commitment help construct a fan culture consisting of extremes of both positivism and negativism. Effecting the shift from one to the other depends almost entirely on the fans themselves. Lynda Copson and her husband Simon are typical of those seeking to make sure this shift keeps going in the right direction. Lynda was one of a number of fan representatives who visited Lisbon in October 2003 to plan how our supporters would be received at Euro 2004. Lynda describes how the meetings went: 'The authorities were prepared to listen to us as fans. Of course their agenda is different to ours but that doesn't mean they can't understand what this passion means to us.'

Simon explains how this kind of consultation can impact on other fans: 'The vast majority just want to watch the team play. No one is under any obligation to take that commitment any further, nor should they be. We don't want a hierarchy of fans, but if there's groups and initiatives taking this fan-friendly business further, that's got to be good, and most will support the effort.'

Mark Knapper went to Portugal with a bunch of his mates from his local pub The Goat, near Welwyn Garden City. One of them, Dom Withey, had spotted on the englandfans website a goodwill visit on the morning of the England–Croatia game to a Lisbon school, and despite never having done anything like this before Mark decided to join in. 'On paper it looked like a brilliant idea, though to be fair I didn't quite know what to expect.' Mark recounts what he got up to: 'We were introduced to this class of teenagers, and they were a bit nervous so I told them about my family, where I was from, and so on. The conversation class soon got going after that, the kids were practising their English, and I was talking football.' After the class was over Mark joined the rest of the fans in the school playground. 'It was great, all these kids pointing at us, asking for our autographs. We told them we weren't famous but it didn't have any effect, they were just so happy to be part of the tournament.'

The British Council is an organization responsible for promoting good relations with Britain abroad. The arts play a big part in the Council's work, and until recently this has meant anything but football. Rosemary Hilhorst was appointed to the post of director of the British Council office in Portugal in autumn 2003. She was determined to make use of Euro 2004 as a way of exploring how football can impact on the relationship between the two countries. Rosemary details the scale of her ambition: 'As a cultural relations institution, the British Council has to understand why football is so important to how cultures interact. This isn't an optional extra – it's central. Everyone is affected by it.'

The school trip Mark Knapper took part in was organized by England fans, but was supported and facilitated by the British

Council. The Council supported similar events in Porto, Coimbra, Cascais and Albufeira. The initiatives were all fan-led, and Rosemary admits this led to certain anxieties. 'This was a very different group to the kind the British Council was used to working with, but we knew it was the fans themselves who had the greatest potential to be ambassadors for England. There were risks, but if this was to work we had to be willing to take them.'

By the end of the tournament Rosemary was able to report on the impact of the events the Council had helped fans put on, describing it as 'Huge, very positive. It's all about perceptions. If people remember one of these events rather than the pictures they have seen another day from Albufeira then it makes a big difference.' Rosemary puts a lot of the success down to the commitment to fan-led activities. 'The tendency of an organization like ours is to control and lead,' she explains. 'We have to give this up. It is the fans' own reputations which are at stake here. We can't paint a picture for them, it has to be true to their own reality. This is high risk for institutions like ours, but help and facilitation is the way forward.'

Oliver Holt of the *Daily Mirror* had joined the fans on the school visit, and two days later he devoted his column to reporting it. Headlined 'English fans give a lesson in just how to behave' he wrote, 'Everyone knows Beckham is a good ambassador for our game. No one ever says that about our fans. But then no one really ever sees things like the school visit to Nuno Goncalves. No one sees the good work that is slowly but surely starting to repair the tattered image of the England football fan.'

Back home at Mark Knapper's local, the report of the school visit that the *Daily Mirror* published, complete with picture of Mark, was proudly pinned up. 'My mates were both impressed and interested to hear that stuff like this goes on,' he says. Mark is glad he took part, and even more proud of the difference it made. 'It's remarkable how just one small event can change people's views of what it means to be an England fan,' he concludes.

Writing a week earlier Mick Dennis in the *Daily Express* pleaded for some sober thought about the rioting in Albufeira that had followed England's opening match against France, then leading the news bulletins. 'I do not pretend there are no hooligans. And I am not excusing trouble out here. But I know that you didn't all go out rioting in England after the France game, so please don't believe glib generalizations and simplifications if there is trouble out here. Most of us are here for the football.'

The helpful understanding in these two tabloid reports was very welcome. Over the years England fans have become more used to being described by the likes of Steven Howard in the *Sun* as 'the base, sordid pond-life that accompanies England everywhere they travel'.

After Euro 2000 the Foreign Office, like other government agencies, caught up with the huge impact that fifteen minutes of madness in Charleroi town square could have on Britain's standing around the world. The few hundred people involved in the rioting made the government look stupid, and the country far worse. Gary Fisher, a career civil servant in the Foreign Office, was posted to Portugal in autumn 2003 as the British Embassy's rather grandly titled 'Football Liaison Officer'. His job was to do what he could to change things for the better at Euro 2004.

Gary describes the approach the Embassy adopted: 'From the outset we concentrated on preparations: security was one issue, but so was the safety of fans, transport to and from matches, and fair and efficient ticket distribution.' This was a definite break from previous law-and-order dominated approaches. Gary visited the cities where England would play, identified the areas where fans would be likely to congregate, and assessed the facilities available. 'It was a change from past practice when we would be purely reactive, dealing with lost passports, imprisoned fans and the like. This time we were being proactive, preparing for the best as well as the worst eventualities.' Once in his post Gary flew back and forth to England to meet fan groups, commenting, 'At the start I did wonder how representative they were, but pretty soon I began to appreciate that those seventy or so fans I was talking with, listening to, were in touch with many hundreds more through formal and informal channels.'

Japan was treated by many observers and commentators as a geographically determined exception to the unrivalled ability for I-N-G-E-R-L-A-N-D to spell trouble. The positive, peaceful presence of England fans in such huge numbers in Portugal for Euro 2004 could not be discounted in the same easy manner. Though according to Gary there were a set of factors that contributed to the welcome outcome: 'The weather, the holiday-destination location, the fighting in Albufeira being hundreds of miles from where England were playing, all of that certainly helped.' The conditions may have been particularly favourable but Gary remains relieved that the impact on the Portuguese of our fans' presence was so definitive: 'Entirely positive. There is no doubt the Portuguese were nervous beforehand. But after the tournament relations were *better* not worse. I never thought in a million years that would happen . . . the power of football, eh?' As an official at the British Embassy Gary had a seat very close to the VIP area at the Portugal–England quarterfinal: 'It's my abiding memory of Euro 2004. Ricardo puts away Portugal's winning penalty. The Portuguese Interior Minister is cheering, out of his seat, and he catches my eye. He vaults over the barrier and hugs me. He was shouting in my ear, "Wonderful! Wonderful!" OK, Portugal had won, but we both knew what he meant. Our fans, both sets of them, Portuguese and English had made the match such a special and joyful occasion.'

Both Portugal and, particularly, Japan might have had special factors that helped to lessen the potential for trouble. But these tournaments did not exist in a vacuum. The changes they witnessed amongst our support were part of an ongoing process that began long before Sol Campbell's opening goal against Sweden in Saitama. And they have an endurance long after the final, fateful, Portuguese penalty was put past David James in Lisbon. In large part this was about England fans taking a collective responsibility for our reputation. The political commentator and author Madeleine Bunting describes the strong counterpressures that seek to prevail against a community coming together as 'A self-referential narcissism, which finds ample reinforcement in the self-revelatory media; we are all restlessly, obsessively, looking for ourselves, and this purpose usually nudges aside any wider, more collective goal.' Could I-N-G-E-R-L-A-N-D spell not only private pleasure but public good too?

England's reputation is undoubtedly improving, but as soon as it takes another turn for the worse the same tired pleas borne out of self-hatred and cultural misunderstanding will be trotted out. Why can't the English be more like the Scots, the Dutch or the Irish? Well, we can't and we won't. We want to be like the English because that's the way we are.

There are different ways of doing Englishness. Travelling to his first tournament with England in 2002, Mel Kenny and his mate Matt Wyatt bought into the whole idea of having a good time with a most unusual idea. 'We wanted to guarantee we'd have a right laugh and maybe help others to enjoy themselves too,' says Mel. Many others would journey to Japan with the same emotions, but not many would dress themselves as the 'Seaman Twins'. I can remember sitting beside this pair of lookalikes in the Saitama stadium for England's first match, while down below us the real thing stood guard in our goal. Mel and Matt looked a picture: 'Ponytail wigs, stuck on 'taches, huge outsized gloves, and full England goalie's kits. We wore the lot.'

And not only did they look a picture, the Japanese would queue up to have their photos taken with them to complete this weird and wonderful scene. 'We thought it would be fun but we had no idea just how popular we'd prove to be. First the Japanese, then the media started picking up on us. Page three of the *Sun* – now that's one place I never imagined appearing!' Fully clothed, Mel asks me to add.

And they weren't the only ones: blokes in kimonos, Elvis wigs, Queen Elizabeth fancy dress, crusaders, and the extrovert rest. It reminded me of St Etienne, the car park before the game against Argentina at France 98. For two weeks or so the only pictures of England fans were of those causing trouble. Then before this most tense of matches at one end of the car park our band were giving it their musical all in a contest with the Argentines' samba orchestra. To add to this, from the other end came three England fans dressed head-to-toe in lion costumes, bringing our team's badge to life. The photographers didn't know which way to point their cameras. Spoiled for choice, with the kind of pictures they weren't used to taking, they clicked off reel after reel of film that afternoon.

Mel is only too aware of what he was getting up to in his fancy dress. 'If we can make our contribution to changing the face of England fans we're happy to do so. We'll make it easy for the press. They love contrasts. There's the dark side of violence. If we can give them an alternative, a colourful one, then that might just make a difference.' His only regret is that after Seaman's retirement and the sacking of David James, whom they dressed up as in Portugal, the current number one, Paul Robinson, lacks any distinguishing features. Mel is currently considering his future fancy-dress options with a careful eye on the sartorial, tonsorial and facial features of Sven's team selection.

Ingerland

Of course most fans don't dress up in anything fancier than a replica England shirt. They get on with being English in ways less noticeable than Mel and Matt, yet too often find themselves being written up as plankton and pondlife (where the aquatic references come from, I have no idea). Jacky Hawes and her husband Steve have had to put up with the bad times as well as the good over the years they have followed England. 'But if we all stopped going, the hooligans will have won,' is how Jacky describes her persistence. 'I like the football, but for Steve it is a passion. It's the places we go to, the sights we see, the people we meet – this is what makes it all so special for both of us.' Jacky adds, 'Travel and football, they're my two favourite things, so England away give me both.' And the hooligans? 'Now things are getting better my two daughters have started coming too,' she says.

This is how the shift from violence to friendliness is affecting those who might follow England. Steve, like many travelling England fans, is a supporter of a lower-division side, Scunthorpe United. 'Our moments of glory are fairly few and far between,' he admits. 'We have the odd decent match rather than entire good seasons. Following England is passion on a completely different scale.' And, like Jacky, it is the travel that helps make it so special. 'It's an adventure – we book the hotels and flights ourselves, this is almost half the attraction. And during a qualifying campaign you get to go to places you would never dream of going to, simply because if England are drawn in Azerbaijan, Poland, Northern Ireland or wherever, we go there.'

With England in town a huge crowd of our fans gathered in Lisbon's Rossio Square. A few thousand were there at least, their flags hung from lampposts, balconies and railings, all singing and drinking – shirts off, tattoos out. If you knew what was going on it was easy enough to differentiate the boisterous from the threatening and move on when one turned to the other. The TV crews and long-lens photographers were out in force too. This was the picture they would project back home, not negative necessarily, but highly unrepresentative of the bulk of England's support. The reporters and cameramen rarely took off down the back streets, climbed up the hill to the castle or took the funicular train to old Lisbon. If they had they would have found ten times or more the numbers of fans in Rossio Square wandering around, taking in the scenery, meeting up with old mates and mixing with the locals. Like Jacky and Steve, this is England's invisible support.

Ana Pereirinha is Portuguese with a liking for the English. 'When I was growing up TV was very important to me and my elder brother. We were big fans of *Monty Python's Flying Circus*. It was the most fantastic thing we had ever seen. It was total nonsense, there was nothing in Portugal we could compare it to.' Ana can still recite plenty of the most famous scenes word for word – the dead parrot sketch unsurprisingly remains her favourite. 'John Cleese to me represented a collision between absurdity and reserve that characterizes the English. This was so different to the manufactured and formulaic American humour we were used to.' This liking for the English is something that our fans abroad often seriously undervalue. For Ana, 'and now for something completely different' has as much meaning, perhaps more, as a catch-phrase as it does for *Python* buffs in England. She reels off her other favourites: '*Blackadder, Some Mothers Do 'Ave 'Em, 'Allo, 'Allo*'.

Weighed down by a martial and imperial history that turned a Euro 96 quarterfinal with Spain into a rerun of Drake seeing off the Spanish Armada, and sees any encounter with Germany dragging up 'Two World Wars and one World Cup', it is too easy to forget the cultural impact of Englishness abroad. The humour of *Monty Python*, the music of the Beatles and most of all the English Premiership creates a connection far more enduring than the memories of some far-off war or imperial adventure. These are the connections of today that come alive in bars, cafés and hotels at a European Championship or World Cup, as the likes of Ana mix with the English.

When Portugal beat Spain the England fans could only stand back and admire the scale and intensity of the Portuguese celebrations. For Ana it brought back some other childhood memories. 'The Portuguese are a naturally melancholic people,' she says, 'but in 1974 the revolution was a mass movement out on the streets. Back then I was only eight years old, I made a right face, screamed and shouted, but my mum wouldn't let me go out. But in 2004 I was out on the streets – we all experienced something like the revolution all over again.'

While Ana danced in the streets the upmarket broadsheet *Publico* earnestly debated the significance of Euro 2004 for Portugal's national identity. Ana Santos declared, 'Thanks to Euro 2004 Portugal has managed to put itself in the centre of Europe, in the centre of the world, millions of people are watching closely what's happening here.' And Antonio Silva e Costa identified the specific place of football in this achievement: 'Football is the sole phenomenon capable of making all humanity celebrate the same festivity. It's a ritual, a religion, a communion. Does it have bad elements? Of course it has, because it is a mirror of society, but in this society there are things far worse than football.'

Warming to his theme, Antonio tossed aside carefully worded caution. 'Euro 2004 is perhaps the most important event this country has had since the Discoveries.' Vasco Da Gama's opening-up of the trade routes to India secured riches that turned the fifteenth-century Portuguese royal family from financial also-rans to the wealthiest in all of Europe, and provided this small country occupying the western edge of the Iberian peninsula with a half-decent empire. But according to Antonio all of this was only as important as three weeks and a bit of a European football championship in his country.

Sunder Katwala is the general secretary of the Fabian Society, an erudite think-tank impeccably loyal to the Labour Party. Fabians are fair-minded moderates – they're not going to be fooled into making wild claims about what football can achieve like Antonio and other hot-headed Latin types. Writing in the *Observer*, Sunder calmed down any grand expectations of what political impact a decent performance by England might effect: 'With a big game looming next Sunday we can hardly expect David Beckham to solve Europe's democratic deficit single-handedly.' Phew, that's a relief, though it meant we couldn't excuse Becks missing his penalty against the French because he was too busy thinking about how to sort out the EU rebate row, reforming the Common Agricultural Policy and securing our signing up to the Euro. Never mind, it must have been something else that distracted him. But Sunder is surely on to something when he goes on to suggest, 'Football's new European melting pot has hardly threatened to wipe out national and local identities. Is North London any less proud of Arsene Wenger's champions?' Well, if you're a Tottenham fan, 'proud' isn't quite the emotion we feel, but that's down to supporting a small club near Highbury rather than N17 being a Europhobic stronghold. From ownership to players, via coaching staff, shirt sponsors and fan base, all our clubs are Europeanized, if not globalized, through and through.

As for those who follow the national team, our away matches take us to an extraordinary range of countries in the course of a qualifying campaign or two, plus the odd friendly here and there. Slovakia, Liechtenstein, South Africa, Macedonia, Portugal, Austria, Poland and Azerbaijan. This is a hugely impressive roster of destinations visited in the space of eighteen months that must have anyone examining our passport stamps in ignorance of our habit scratching their head in puzzlement at what we're getting up to. Diplomats? Mercenaries? Oil prospectors? Add the 80,000 who made it out to Portugal for the European Championships and the scale and depth of this popular mix of football and travel begins to take shape.

The political class agonize over our falling out of love with Europe, but football represents a single currency we are all happy to exchange. Why should being in favour of Europe be reduced to a political point of view, the approval of remote institutions and swapping one currency for another? Football unites Europe more emphatically than any other single event. And then, for ninety minutes, divides us of course. A European Championship, a World Cup, these events feast themselves on some of the worst excesses of a nasty brand of nationalism. Yet for the most part they are festivals of a popular internationalism in which a decent chunk of England's support are full and eager participants.

It is this mixture of contradictions that throws commentators from left and right into a mutual tizzy. The writer Michael Henderson in *The Times* haughtily dismisses all this popular patriotism wrapped up in a football shirt:

When one sees the witless parade of faux-patriots clogging up the highways, trailing their flags of St George, this is not England they are celebrating. It is the empty-headed parish of Ingerland. It is not love of country. It is a form of exhibitionism, with the flag employed as a fashion symbol. So let us put away these flags, and tell the folk who wave them to grow up. Until they do I shall not be the only person who hopes for a resounding French victory against our boys on Sunday.

Well actually, Michael, apart from those who have no interest in matters on the pitch and just want the whole thing to be over so normal service can resume, your wish leaves you a lonely person indeed. But joining Henderson from across the political spectrum is Martin Smith, writing in the far-left newspaper *Socialist Worker*. Martin shares Henderson's petty-minded miserablism: 'Waving the St George flag is not about inclusion – it's all about exclusion. What are we supposed to celebrate? The Empire? Or the fact that we live in a society where the levels of inequality continue to grow? All you are left with is David Beckham and big profits for the breweries. Not much really.'

Martin Smith claims he knows better than all of us lined up behind our flags the real cause of Roonmania – it is 'a diversion from the real problems working people face'. Just because millions of us enjoy screaming and shouting for an England victory in the hope that some silverware might finally come our national way again, he seems to think all our critical faculties must have been clinically removed at the turnstiles. This is an extraordinarily one-dimensional understanding of a very popular experience. The fact that the same sneering point of view is aired by the cynics of both left and right makes it all the more bewildering.

Michael Henderson and Martin Smith are united in their suspicion of popular enjoyment founded on flags and football. From two very different political points of view they manage to conclude that this mix is worthless, and likely to cause an eruption of hatred or something worse. They dismiss entirely the potential for a flexible and friendly patriotism we can all be both proud of and part of. A pride without prejudice, hope emptied of hatred, and a commitment that disavows confrontation. Put these three elements together, wrap them in St George and what you have is a football nation that can enjoy itself but enjoys the company of strangers too. Not always, and not everybody, not yet. But for more of the time and involving more people than many would give credit for.

This is why what England expects of football in some corner of a foreign pitch does matter. Not because of the garish headlines and the multimillionaire superstars, but for us, the fans – and no transfer deal in history is ever going to buy up our loyalty. We're signed up for life, and love.

2

We're Not Going Home

I met up with Paul Mullinder and his mate Dave 'Simmo' Simpson in Vienna on the day of England's World Cup 2006 qualifier against Austria. It was lunchtime, and a get-together had been organized by England fans with the Austrian football fanzine *Ballesterer*. Nearly a hundred of us were packed into a disused shop in the city's Fifth District. The event had the feel of a warehouse party and there was a total absence of suspicion, antagonism or fear, just the shared intent to have some fun, and engage in what we all had in common, a love of good football. Not that England provided us with very much of that on this particular trip as we scrambled a 2–2 draw against a team both ourselves and the Austrians had expected us to comfortably and stylishly defeat.

Something like this party would never have been attempted a decade or so ago. The risks would have been too big. The police would have closed it down or the football authorities would have tried to instruct supporters not to join in. As for the fans themselves – both ours and theirs – suspicion of the others' motives would have meant not many would have bothered turning up.

Simmo and Paul have both been following England a lot longer than me. Paul started going in the early 1980s, and his first tournament was Euro 88 in West Germany. 'The numbers weren't massive then, just a few thousand even for a tournament. England away only really started getting huge with France 98.' The size of England's support meant the culture was very different. 'It was tight-knit in those days, you tended to stick with those you knew from your club. I was West Ham, and all the main faces from the domestic scene would travel.'

None of the paraphernalia of ticket allocation and distribution by the FA was in place either. 'We just phoned up the old FA headquarters in Lancaster Gate. If there were tickets available we snapped them up there and then. If not, we travelled anyway and took our chances on picking one up locally.' Paul has no doubt what it meant to follow England back then, saying, 'If you went in the 1980s you had to put yourself out to go, make an effort. We were treated appallingly by the FA, the government, the police and the media. Of course, we didn't take any notice. If you went you knew you were having a good time regardless of what everybody else said.'

The motivation back then, though, wasn't so different to those fans like myself who started going away after Euro 96. 'There was a couple of West Ham players in the squad,' explains Paul, 'Trevor Brooking and Alvin Martin, so that was part of the attraction, but there was also experiencing new countries, seeing the sights too.'

Paul had already been following West Ham for years when he started going to England games. 'You grew up very quickly. We all knew the risks and were willing to take them. Most of us had

grown up in traditional working-class areas – the East End for
me. We were streetwise, we could put up with the grief shov-
elled our way.' But Paul doesn't wear his experiences as
campaign medals to use against those who have joined in after
him. 'Who are the real fans? Us lot who go everywhere or somebody who just enjoys watching England at home games or on
the TV? Of course you don't have to have been going for as long
as me or travel to the other side of Europe to prove you're an
England fan.'

We all start somewhere on these travels with our football nation.
For me it was Moldova in September 1996. That summer I'd
been to Wembley for every one of England's Euro 96 games.
The press had confidently predicted blood-soaked streets as the
Scots, the Dutch and the Germans mixed with the English. Their
fiction couldn't have been further from our reality. 'Three
Lions' became our alternative national anthem and the stands
were full of St George's flags for the first time. Against Scotland
and Holland the team was good enough to have us dreaming of
some silverware. Stuart Pearce exorcized his penalty shoot-out
demons against Spain in the quarterfinals, while Gareth
Southgate acquired some new ones as he missed his penalty
against Germany in the semi-final. These were unforgettable
moments. Not glorious, but destined to be part of football's history, and I could say I was there. This was special, and I wanted
more of it.

The almost complete absence of crowd violence convinced
many of us that following England away was something we
wanted to try. Moldova is a faraway former Soviet republic. It
must be the only country that would want to merge with Romania
in order to give itself a leg up in the world. In all honesty it is not
a place I would have chosen for a holiday. But that is precisely

why trips to places like this are so special for a significant portion of England's support. Football takes us to places we otherwise wouldn't dream of visiting.

Craig Brewin was first attracted to follow England away by a March 1989 trip to see England play in Albania organized by the fanzine *When Saturday Comes*. The advert promised: 'If you're bored with run of the mill holidays and fancy the trip of a lifetime (nothing can upstage tales of a coach trip to Albania), write to us.' The organizers explained they would 'carry fifty readers to the heart of international socialism (and back for those that wish to return) not forgetting Albania vs England in an Italia 90 World Cup qualifier'.

Craig had been involved almost from the start with the Football Supporters' Association (the FSA – later to become the Football Supporters' Federation, or FSF). Together with another FSA activist he signed up for the trip. 'Only two or three on the coach had ever been to an England away match before. What attracted us was that Albania was such a difficult place to get to. This was before the fall of Communism and Albania was not usually open to travellers from the West.'

The culture clash wasn't just with Albania's unreconstructed Marxism–Leninism, but also with the England fans he found himself next to in the stands. 'Those of us who came on this trip looked like outsiders. We didn't help ourselves by setting ourselves up to be the good guys. We were going to show the rest of them how to behave. And worst of all we turned up for the match late, only just catching the national anthem, for which we didn't stand up.' The trip convinced Craig how wrong he and his fellow FSA activists and fanzine writers had been in what they had thought of England fans. 'Yes, there were some people out there I didn't like very much. But it's too simple to write off an entire fan culture as simply all bad guys. The tragedy is that this is still how too many describe England fans.'

Craig had enjoyed himself in Albania, he was going to be joining England on a lot more trips, and he was convinced the FSA needed to involve itself in improving the treatment of England's travelling support. 'Our power as a fans' campaign depended solely on what we could do ourselves, and so we had to be in and amongst these fans.' What the FSA offered was a positive view of football supporters that at least some in positions of power would recognize and respond to. The FSA became involved at Italia 90, when they organized the first Fans Embassy, an advice service for supporters run by supporters. The response from the fans was broadly supportive: they welcomed the effort, but the FA wasn't so keen. Craig explains, 'They really hated us. The FA was under pressure from the Thatcher government to support hardline law-and-order solutions to football's hooligan problem. The politicians and FA officials shared the same view – all fans were to be treated as potential criminals.' The FSA represented a different approach. Seeking to distinguish between the hardcore troublemakers and the rest, they were committed to helping the fans themselves change the culture around England's travelling supporters for the better.

During the late 1980s and early 1990s the FA tactic, supported by the government, was to try to limit the size of England's travelling support as much as possible in the mistaken belief that this would reduce the risk of trouble. In Italy for the first (and, so far, only) time since 1966, England got past the World Cup quarterfinal stages. In the semifinal we took West Germany first to extra time, and then those never-to-be-forgotten penalties – but the fans who actually saw the match in Turin were few in number compared to the tens of thousands who follow England to tournaments now.

Craig develops the point: 'We are such a huge football nation, yet why in Italy did we have such a small support? It was the.

same in Germany for Euro 88. We were hopelessly outnumbered by supporters of almost every country we played against. Hardly any of us wore England colours. Not many flags either.' What would happen if the support grew? Craig's view then, which remains the same now after nearly twenty years of following England, was that by opening up the opportunities to follow England abroad to the huge support that exists for the national team at home, peer pressure can emerge to marginalize and isolate the hooligans. 'We had to change what is acceptable behaviour. If the majority create a standard, then those that don't match it stand out.'

Rob Didd also went to Albania. He was already an experienced England away traveller, his first trip abroad to see the team play being to Madrid in February 1987. Rob reached Tirana the hard way: a flight to Belgrade, then an internal flight to close by the border with Albania. A group of fans hired a minibus to reach the checkpoint that would get them into Albania and were then marched fifty yards across no-man's-land. On the other side they were met by Albanian soldiers armed with sub-machine-guns. Rob recalls the restrictions: 'No beards, no porn, that was the regulations. One guy had his sideburns trimmed, another had his golf magazine confiscated because the cover star was a girl in a bikini.'

Albania was Rob's twenty-first England game, 'except I don't count it like that, because the previous November I missed Saudi Arabia away in Riyadh'. Rob is a sort of collector of England matches. By September 2004 he had attended 199 in total, with 179 games attended consecutively since 1989. 'That Saudi Arabia game broke my run after just twenty games. England were originally supposed to be playing Morocco but at three weeks' notice they cancelled this match and announced they were playing Saudi Arabia instead. There was no chance of getting the visa required to get into the country unless you had relatives out there, a job, or were in transit.' Since the following match, Greece away in February 1989, Rob hasn't missed a single England game.

As a collector of matches he had started domestically with Chelsea. 'Five hundred and seventy-five consecutive games from 1985 onwards for eleven years. And that's not counting every home reserves game, most away reserves games, and several FA Youth Cup campaigns. It started with my dad taking me, then, when I was fifteen, I started to go on my own, away as well as home. I would do two or three paper rounds in the morning, then another evening round to pay for it.' By 1986 Rob had been doing this week in, week out for two years and his grandad suggested he should give the Mexico World Cup a go. 'We had relatives in Canada and the USA so the idea was a sort of Grand Tour, but it would have meant missing my O levels and my mum wouldn't let me go.'

A few months later Rob had left school to train as an apprentice electrician and in October he was at his first England match, Northern Ireland at home. Apart from that Saudi Arabia game, nothing has managed to stop him from going ever since. 'The FA tried to ban us. The media was always saying we would be prevented from getting into the ground. But the hosts always let us in, no problem.' In the late '80s and early '90s this official discouragement in order to reduce the likelihood of trouble undoubtedly kept the numbers down but, Rob argues, it also had another effect. 'It turned us into rebels. There would be a few hundred of us, all packed into just a couple of bars, and we became targets – for the police, their hooligans, our media.' So the policy of containment had the opposite effect to the intention. 'It meant everybody who went had to be able to handle themselves. You didn't have much choice, there was nobody looking out for us. It was the opposite to a positive policy. It was so negative, it left us expecting the worst.'

The appeal of England away has become insatiable for Rob – once he even found himself the only England fan at a game. 'It was in Cagliari, a pre-1990 World Cup warm-up against a local side. They let the villagers in and I managed to sneak in too.' It is a commitment that has cost him – £17,000 in debt at one point – but left him with only one regret. 'I'm self-employed now so time off isn't a problem, but before I had to keep quiet about being an England fan. I couldn't admit to anyone I worked with that England was my passion, otherwise pretty soon everyone would notice how I was always off sick when the team were playing.'

At home he can now share his love of England with his partner Nicky whom he met on Mount Fuji in Japan during World Cup 2002. The pair of them had each fancied the appeal of climbing Japan's most famous mountain, and joined a group of England fans who carried off this feat for charity. Nicky had been following England off and on since the mid '90s but since meeting Rob, like him she hasn't missed a game. She's also organized Rob's mementoes of his travels. Tickets, programmes, team sheets, pennants and players' autographs are all neatly displayed throughout their home, leaving no visitor in any doubt about the scale of Rob's commitment. 'Following England, it's what I do, who I am.'

Moldova, Albania, Azerbaijan, Japan, South Africa, Finland, Sweden, and lots of other places too. But my ten years of travelling with England has taken me to only a fraction of the countries Rob has visited on the same mission. I share his passion, if not the depth and length of his commitment. After Euro 96 it became much easier to follow England away. The success of the tournament meant the fear of hooliganism was beginning to ebb. There was a growing realization that a huge audience existed for the national team, of which only a small proportion would be looking for trouble. At the same time cheap air travel and the Internet was making the organizing and financing of trips easier. The FA put in place a set-up of sorts to administer the distribution of tickets, and the police had the beginnings of a strategy to prevent those with a record of football violence from travelling.

Moldova in 1996 was as good a place as any for me and my partner Anne to start our travels. I found a travel agent who specialized in East European business trips and they managed to locate both connecting flights from Budapest to the Moldovan capital Kishinev, and a hotel in the city centre. This turned out to be a fourteen-storey monument to the Stalinist school of architecture, but it was clean, cheap and the food was plentiful. Over breakfast the tales of dogged endurance in reaching this destination were passed from table to table. A three-day minibus trip via Bucharest, including scoring a goal in Steua's deserted stadium, was one of the best I heard, though this was topped by the guy we met at the match who had told his wife he was popping out for a packet of fags, and a few hours later was standing in a Moldovan stadium waiting for England's World Cup 98 campaign to begin.

Kishinev had everything for the discerning football tourist, including a counterfeit McDonald's, though this was outshone for me by the match-day brawls. Not from the fans, mind – this was street Graeco-Roman wrestling. The prize for the winner was a live sheep, while the loser had to make do with a goat. We had seen a bit of post-Communist Europe we otherwise wouldn't have even imagined existed, with ninety minutes of international football thrown in.

Ingerland

It is too easy for those who write dismissively of England's fans to portray this mix of travel and football as a middle-class pastime hardly likely to be enjoyed by the mass of supporters. Patronizing and ill-informed, these kinds of accounts significantly underestimate the defining characteristic of an active England fan – all our away matches are overseas and most of us enjoy the travelling involved. In the wake of the widely reported trouble at Euro 2000 an editorial in *When Saturday Comes* pointed to the attitudes to all things foreign that help frame the outbreaks of abuse and violence. 'For too many of the fans who follow the national team, going abroad is about asserting England's superiority – not necessarily with violence, but with songs and aggressive behaviour that is meant to be (and is) intimidating to the locals.' The same article then went on to recognize the potential contribution that the coupling of travel with football can make to changing this mindset. 'It now seems there is a distinct travelling culture developing which has nothing to do with the mind-numbing nationalism of England's hooligan and sub-hooligan followers.'

Bill Lievens is a council caretaker looking after the block of flats where he lives, in Edmonton, North London. He remembers his first England away trip in 1977 as a 23-year-old to a World Cup qualifying match against Italy in Rome. 'We went in a van. Eleven of us, all West Ham, a crate of beer each and on the way we stopped off to see the Leaning Tower of Pisa. And in Rome we had a look round the Colosseum too.' Bill didn't appreciate the sights much on this trip; the excitement of just being there was enough. And dodging the bottles chucked at the England fans by the Italians during the game meant he wasn't as well disposed to having a look round the city afterwards as he might have been. But three years later, Bill was out in Italy again for the 1980 European Championships, this time staying on a camp site. 'One night the police raided the site, all our tents were pulled down and our kit scattered about for no obvious reason.' And things got worse: 'At the match with Belgium in Turin fighting broke out. We were tear-gassed, but it was a huge over-reaction, and when the riot police piled in there was panic.' After the match England manager Ron Greenwood laid into the fans: 'Bastards. I hope they put them in a big boat and drop them in the ocean halfway back.' FA chairman Sir Harold Thompson chipped in with his own description of England fans as 'sewer-rats'.

Bill Lievens felt betrayed. 'Yes, there were some England fans causing trouble, but the police totally over-reacted, and it was the majority who suffered. What did Greenwood say about this? Nothing. He never bothered to find out.' Bill had always respected Ron Greenwood as a manager. For twenty-eight years Bill followed West Ham, and he puts the bulk of the Hammers' finest footballing traditions down to Greenwood's management and coaching – but reading what he had to say about himself and his mates changed Bill's view of the manager. 'He didn't know what was going on in the stands and hadn't bothered to find out. He should have kept his mouth shut until he knew the full facts.'

Stuart Weir, a writer for *New Society*, did bother to uncover the story of what actually happened. He was at the match and reported, 'A few English lads joined in skirmishes. No more than two dozen, at most, were involved. First, squads of police waded into any English fan within reach, regardless of whether they were involved in the affray or not. Shortly afterwards, riot police lined up and fired tear-gas canisters into the great mass of English supporters who were nowhere near the original fracas.' This was one of the few reports that recounted Bill's, and others', side of the story.

But *New Society* was a magazine read by people working in the public services, social workers and teachers mainly. It was no match for the blazing headlines of the *Sun* ('Savage Riot in Turin'), the *Daily Mail* ('Hooligans shame England') or the *Mirror* ('British football – and Britain itself – has been disgraced'). Prime Minister Margaret Thatcher added her voice, calling it 'a very dark day for Britain', while Labour's former minister of sport Denis Howell described the events as 'a national disaster'. Of course, the disgrace, dark days and disaster belonged to England, not Britain, and had very little to do with the Scots, Welsh or Northern Irish, but for the moment we'll let that pass. Stuart Weir's words of sanity, read by a few thousand, were no match for this feeding frenzy of unreason, but that doesn't make the purpose behind his report any less valid. 'I want to show how removed our establishment – or opinion-formers, call them what you will – are from understanding, or even being willing to understand, the young working class. Even the men in the game instinctively adopt the same outraged attitude of moral superiority to the fans who keep football going.'

Bill is certainly one of those. After three decades following West Ham he eventually gave up on the Hammers when a hugely unpopular and very expensive bond scheme put a hiked-up price on his support for next-to-nothing in return. Even this didn't dull his enthusiasm for the game. He now follows non-league Dagenham and Redbridge, home and away, rarely missing a game. As for England, on that trip to Italy in 1980 he revisited Pisa and the Colosseum in Rome he'd first seen three years earlier and added Pompeii to his itinerary. 'These places were marvellous. I saw things I had never dreamed of seeing. I started wanting to find out more about them, how they were built, what the lives of the people who lived in those days was like. I've learned more about geography and history following England than I ever did at school.'

Bill doesn't set himself up as anything out of the ordinary:

'Wherever I go there's loads of fans doing the same thing. And don't get me wrong, I fancy a beer too, and not all of us are angels either. But the more you see of a place, the more you appreciate its history, beauty and people.'

Bill does, however, take his excursions further than most. Portugal 2004 was typical of what a tournament means for him. Not only all of England's matches but also the Roman temple at Evora, the cathedral at Braga, the port museums in Porto, Buccaco for the battleground where Wellington defeated the French, Alcobaca for the Cistercian monastery, Fatima for the religious icons and architecture, Portalegre for royal palaces, Tomar for another monastery, Elvas for the castle, and finally Batalha, another monastery. With three group games, plus a quarterfinal too, and all his travelling done by train or coach, Bill crisscrossed Portugal in search of his destinations. With the tournament over Bill was looking forward to Dagenham and Redbridge's away game against Carlisle United in the Nationwide Conference. Bill enjoys ticking off different grounds he has visited, 'so that game means both another ground and Hadrian's Wall is nearby too. That's going to be a good weekend.'

Despite Bill's humility his travel tales are quite extraordinary, and a touch too extreme for even those most committed to soaking up the local sights. Yet for thousands of other England fans overseas travel remains a huge part of the appeal and meaning of following England. This coexists uneasily with a cultural antipathy within 'Englishness' to all things foreign. For those overburdened by this baggage they would prefer all England games to be played at home. A trip abroad means putting up with the unfamiliar. The sole attraction of venturing overseas is to test their fighting prowess against some foreign opposition. For the rest of us the fact that England away means countries and places we've never visited before ignites our excitement and commitment. Understand the contrast between these differing attitudes to England's foreign adventures and the potential for what I-N-G-E-R-L-A-N-D might mean begins to reveal itself.

Katowice. Poland away, October 2004, and the four thousand travelling England fans have been held back in the ground after the game for almost two hours. There were no polite PA announcements to explain what's going on, but it is the kind of thing we're used to being forced to endure. 2004 was our second trip to Katowice – we'd been here in 1997 for a World Cup qualifier too. That time we'd hired a taxi to take us from where we were staying in Cracow, about sixty miles away, and back again after the match. Travelling alone or in a small group on a train or bus to the ground was ill-advised. Poland fans weren't known for being particularly friendly towards the English, and walking back to the station through Katowice, with or without a Polish police escort, was risky. Almost everybody who did ended up getting battered.

When we reached Katowice our taxi driver drove us round the streets around the stadium. He offered to drop us off if we fancied a drink, but the groups of Polish skinheads on every available street corner meant our thirst could wait. Don't get me wrong, Poland can be a wonderful place. Krakow in particular is beautiful: great food, with an amazing square in the centre of the city. But Katowice itself was the kind of place before, during and after the game where you took sensible precautions if you wanted to avoid getting hurt.

Fan cultures change, and this doesn't affect only our own, but others too. Robert Strupiechowski is a Wislaw Krakow fan. With the support of the British Council Robert came to London to meet England fans ahead of our October match. He was shocked by the bad experiences most of us had had with England in Poland but, he insisted, 'This was five years ago – our fans, our police, have changed. We are members of the EU, NATO now. It's not the same as back then.' Most weren't convinced, but on the night of the match Robert was proved spectacularly right. The Polish fans were like an England home crowd. They wore floppy hats, held huge cartons full of popcorn and treated us to one Mexican wave after another. England away fans are notorious for *never* joining in the Mexican wave. We're here for the football, not orchestrated jollification, but a Mexican wave is a hell of a lot more pleasurable to put up with than rocket flares.

Jacek Purski from the militant antiracist Polish fan group Never Again had warned me of another change to listen out for. 'The sound of the plastic horns, they are everywhere in Polish football. They are awful, manufactured passion, and the noise is terrible. We've produced stickers "No Horns, Just Real Fans".' Jacek was right, the horns produced a low hum, rising to what sounded like a swarm of giant bees whenever Poland had the ball. The Polish fans seemed more interested in making a racket than picking a fight with the English.

Some, though, were clearly untouched by these changes. There were less than thirty of them in each group, Polish and English, on opposing sides of the crowd barrier twenty-odd yards away from me. From the instant they entered the ground they were eyeing each other up. There was never any good nature in it. The swapping of insults would have turned to blows given half a chink in the fence. The two groups shared one thing though; a perverse interpretation of Polish history. The English group sang, 'If it wasn't for the English you'd be Krauts' – the Red Army and fifty years of Russian occupation had obviously passed them by – while the Polish group responded with Nazi salutes and shouts of *Sieg Heil*. After a while this rather unpleasant sideshow took a turn for the worse, with plastic seats flying through the air in increasing numbers. I'd seen enough of this in the past to expect that any moment the riot police in full body armour would wade in, lashing out as indiscriminately as they could get away with, their actions sure to do three things: spread panic in their considerable wake, fail to catch the guilty, and leave the innocent injured and disgruntled.

But tonight things were different. The police moved in slowly, pushing the offenders back, almost gently. They seemed to realize more aggression at this stage would simply worsen the situation. And the result was no one rushed to join in. The bad guys were stripped bare. If they wanted to ruin the night they would be doing it on their own, no longer backed up by the rage of those who had taken no part in any trouble yet ended up being mistreated and mishandled by overzealous policing. But the really clever bit was what we eventually realized was the reason for the long delay in letting us out. The pictures the video cameras had been recording of the seat-throwing earlier were now being used to identify and arrest those involved as we walked out in single file between two long lines of police.

'Back to the bad old days tonight then,' Paul Lamkin joked with me as we waited to be let out of the ground. Paul was in a good mood because he knew the trouble tonight hardly compared to what he had seen plenty of times before. Paul's England-fan career had started rather inauspiciously three decades before mine, at Wembley in 1967 when Scotland beat the then world champions England 3–2. But he wasn't put off and with his dad went to most of England's matches in the long-defunct Home International championship, at Cardiff, Glasgow and Belfast as well as Wembley over the next few years. Spain in 1982 was Paul's first World Cup, and throughout the rest of the 1980s he was an England regular.

Travel was different in those days, he recalls: 'Mainly ferries, trains and coaches instead of bargain flights. It was on the boats where the fighting would start, often down to club rivalries. West Ham versus Millwall, Liverpool versus Man United, that sort of thing.' But Paul avoided it, not bothering even to look. 'That's how most get caught up in it. They want to stick around to see what's going on.' Nevertheless, Paul's studious avoidance of trouble didn't do him much good. 'Everywhere we went, everybody we met, we were all called hooligans.' Back home Paul's mum would leap to his defence as neighbours and relatives started throwing the hooligan label at him when she explained her son followed England, but not many wanted to listen. 'Football wasn't so fashionable then. There wasn't the money around the game. It was a much more working-class culture, and the support that followed England was much smaller too.'

Paul was one of just a hundred who followed England to Greece in 1982 for a European Championship qualifier. Travelling in such a small crowd, Paul rapidly learned how to look after himself. 'In a bar or a town square you could sense very quickly what the mood was, and if you didn't like it you moved on. People who don't go won't believe it but it is so easy to keep away from the trouble.' With the number travelling to most qualifiers not amounting to more than just a few hundred fans, a lot knew each other, including those going for very different reasons, as Paul explains. 'I follow West Ham. All our mob knew us, and we knew them, but they made a point of keeping apart from us if they could. They were looking for somebody to fight, we weren't.' There were plenty more like Paul, except they were never noticed with the attention focused almost exclusively on the hooligans. 'We kept our heads down, looked out for bars where everybody was happy and jolly, rather than looking menacing. We avoided the city centre [and would] try to find a place where the local people were keen to speak English with us and chat about great players of the past.'

*

Mark Raven has the same approach to following England as Paul Lamkin. His first trip was Italia 90 as a 23-year-old. He has followed England home and away ever since, only missing two games in all that time. Some have been great performances, others not so good, but there's one match he will never forget, for all the wrong reasons.

Izmir. Turkey versus England in a qualifier for the 1994 World Cup. Inside the ground hostilities broke out early between the two sets of fans. The Turks were throwing rocks, half-bricks, sharpened coins, anything they could get their hands on, and with as much ferocity and velocity as they could muster. The police were doing nothing to stop this. Instead they hemmed the England fans together, making them an even easier target to hit.

Mark was trying to avoid the missiles but as he looked round to dodge the stuff flying through the air he felt a thud. He went numb and was covered in blood. After what seemed like ages he was finally evacuated from the stadium. Rushed to hospital, that night he lost all sight in his right eye, and never recovered it. After something like that, what possible reason could he have to want to keep going?

'Why should I have to stop?' he asks in return. 'I felt a sense of injustice, it was like Hillsborough or Heysel happening to me. I didn't want to let others take this away from me.' Mark admits he has had reason on occasions to question his continuing support. 'After the riot that stopped the 1995 match in Dublin I did feel let down by our fans, if you can call them that. Some of the people there I didn't want anything to do with, and you start to have doubts whether it really is worth going if you have to put up with all this lot.'

He never did stop going, though, and he has been around long enough now to see how much following England has changed. 'As the away support has got bigger there have remained those who will join in with the abuse, the racism, the violence, but there's also increasing numbers who don't.' Not quite self-policing, that isn't really the English way, rather a form of self-defence, leaving those who want to cause trouble exposed and isolated, without the camouflage of innocence a watching crowd provides. In the era when Mark started following England, as he learned to his cost, it wasn't so easy to avoid the consequences of trouble.

So, was it all worth it? 'Being there, at a match which everyone back home is talking about, and will talk about for years to come, knowing that I was at that game. Whatever the grief we were forced to put up with nobody can ever take the joy of that away from me.'

In the 1980s and early 1990s there were relatively few fans who shared this excited reality of being there when England played away. Three or four hundred for qualifying matches was typical, rising to perhaps several thousand for tournaments. At Euro 88 in West Germany it was estimated that, apart from the Soviet Union, England had the smallest travelling support. There were around 7,500, compared to 12,000 Irish, 20,000 Danes, 25,000 Italians and around 30,000 Dutch. And the numbers hardly rose for Italia 90 either. Even a semifinal showdown with West Germany was watched by only around 10,000 England fans in Turin. This is entirely different to today. Around 100,000 fans from England travelled to Portugal during Euro 2004 to see a match, or at least to be in the country when England were playing. Unlike Euro 88, England had the biggest travelling support by far, outstripping the Germans by 77,000 and the Dutch by a massive 94,000.

Estimating the chances of trouble isn't a numbers game. The sociologist John Williams pointed out in his report about Italia 90 that the actions of a small group of fans could have an enormous impact. 'One hundred young Englishmen could, quite literally, become the centre of attention of the world's media, simply by parading drunkenly up the streets of Cagliari singing the national anthem. If you had been involved, the next day you could read about yourself on the front page of the English tabloids, which had been specially flown in to Sardinia for the occasion. This was fifteen minutes or more of instant fame. Its attractions proved compulsive.' The tendency on the part of the football and policing authorities, however, was simply to define trouble in terms of limiting the numbers, and to deter, sometimes with brute force, as many as possible of those who wanted to follow their football nation abroad.

Anne-Marie Mockridge was one of the few women who travelled in these earlier days. A Manchester City fan since the age of six, by the time she was twelve years old she was standing on City's Kippax terrace on her own. 'It was the early 1970s, there was a group of us girls, all hardcore City. We were young, we didn't notice the trouble, or at least we didn't care about it. I was brought up to be a tough little cookie.' Anne-Marie is five-foot-nothing. 'I may be small, but that doesn't mean people can take advantage. I can give as good as I get.'

It was in the 1980s she first went to an England game, joining a group from her local pub who travelled down to Wembley for most home matches. Anne-Marie was working as a stock-control clerk; money was tight, there were clothes, make-up, records and fags to pay for. It was sometimes a struggle to pay for her football too, but somehow she always managed. Then she became pregnant. 'Football had to take a lower priority. I was a single mum, a kid to bring up on my own, I had no choice but to take a bit of a break from football.' In 1989 she met Stephen, her husband-to-be, and she remembers, 'First thing he said was that he followed England and he had no intention of stopping.'

Anne-Marie admits she was worried. She loved her football

just as much as Stephen did but, with a young child, it wasn't so easy for her to travel. Stephen duly headed off to the Italia 90 qualifiers and left her behind. By the time England had completed the qualifying campaign, Anne-Marie had a new commitment that made it even more difficult to travel to the World Cup. The group stages and second-round matches of Italia 90 clashed with her exams to become a special-needs teacher. 'Four years' hard graft. I couldn't give all this up. Stephen left for Italy without me. Then he gave me the biggest surprise of my life. All the girls were having a party to celebrate the final exam and Stephen turns up completely unannounced. He'd come back to whisk me off to Naples for the quarterfinal against Cameroon. I rush home, pack, and the next morning I'm at the World Cup finals.'

What sticks in her mind was the mood of the fans, 'There was this chant "Let's all have a disco". It's what we all sang at every game. We made our stay out there one big party. There were friends I made on that trip I still travel with to see England now.' After Italy, Anne-Marie and Stephen planned right from the outset that they would go together to Euro 92 in Sweden. Scandinavia can be a bit pricey so they decided to economize on accommodation by hiring a car and sleeping in it. 'It was our passion wagon,' says Anne-Marie, 'our blanket a twenty-foot England Ashton-under-Lyne flag.'

In Malmö Anne-Marie was caught up in a riot that turned a beer festival into a battleground. 'I was gutted. The Swedes had been fantastic to us, everybody mixing. But I was treated just the same as those who wrecked all this. I was embarrassed, ashamed. How could our fans do this? The perfect hosts and this is how some of ours reward them for it.' Back home Anne-Marie found herself having to justify herself as an England fan to workmates. 'I had to explain what it meant to me. The friends I made, the travelling, the places we saw. Most of all that pride I felt to be English, and not being told I was a bigot, a racist, a xenophobe.'

These were the good times others didn't hear about and Anne-Marie started to make it her business that they did. 'The FA weren't listening to us. I don't like being walked over and I wasn't going to stand for this any more.' After the success of Euro 96 in England the FA did start to change and Anne-Marie was invited to join a consultative group they set up to hear the fans' views. 'I don't mind making a nuisance of myself,' she says. 'We work bloody hard for the money that pays for our England trips and if what's needed to get our point across is a gobby cow then I'll be her.'

Peter John-Baptiste's loyalty to the England cause might surprise some who should know better. 'I remember my first day in France for the 1998 World Cup. These two English lads were asking me what my next game was. "England versus Romania," I kept telling them, but they weren't having it. Surely, I must be a Jamaica fan? After all, I'm black.'

Peter's first footballing hero was Kevin Keegan: 'His name was on my pencil case at school. He was the best of his day, an inspirational player, glamorous too.' Ever since, Peter has had a soft spot for Liverpool, but for a team to follow he prefers Wealdstone FC of the Ryman Premier League. Their ground is a ten-minute walk from where he grew up and still lives. This is where in his early teens Peter first went to watch football and learned the songs, the bad language, the lot. When he was fifteen he went to his first England game, the 3–1 home victory over the reigning world champions Argentina in 1980. By the mid-1980s he was a regular for most of England's games at Wembley.

In 1990 Peter went to Italy for the World Cup. 'It was everything I had hoped for, and a bit more. I can remember my first TV

World Cup. 1978, Argentina and the endless streams of ticker tape. But this time I was there, and there was nowhere else on earth I'd rather be.'

Peter is now closely involved with fan-friendly activities that today are a feature of most England away trips. 'In Vienna two of us met up with a bunch of Austrians at the lunch-time fans' party when Austria played England. There was fifteen of them and just the pair of us. All together we went out for a beer and a meal up near the stadium before the match. This sort of thing couldn't have happened when I first started going. It was only fear, ours and theirs, which stopped us. We had all accepted too readily that football meant trouble.'

Peter explains the impact of the initiatives he takes part in: 'The school visit we did in Lisbon during Euro 2004 was one of the best days of the tournament for me. The kids were great, all incredibly friendly and what we were doing was appreciated. I just thought what it would have been like for me as a football-mad teenager if a bunch of Italian or Argentine fans had come to my school. I know it would have been something I would have never forgotten. I had a sense it was the same for them.' Portugal for Peter was one mad dash from game to game. Not content with England's three group matches and a quarterfinal, he managed to squeeze in an astonishing total of fifteen games. As he did so, he visited every single tournament stadium apart from two.

Peter admits his love of football comes close sometimes to being an addiction. He has followed England for more than twenty years, not missing a single home game since 1990 and not many away either. When he was in Rotterdam for the 1993 defeat by Holland that effectively ended England's hopes of qualifying for the next year's World Cup in the USA, he reckons he was one of only two or three black faces in the England end of the ground. In the tournaments in Japan and Portugal, and at England's home matches of the last few years, there are now hundreds more. Almost all are new to following England, and few share the vivid aggression towards other countries' teams that some of our fans seem to think qualifies you as an authentic supporter. 'All that matters is that they share the passion,' says Peter. 'But if we're demanding hatred to be a "real fan", since when has that been obligatory?'

Since Euro 2000 outbreaks of violence when England play away have been pushed to the margins. They are still very nasty for those involved, and enough to make the occasional front-page splash. But they do not dominate an entire fan culture as they once did in the 1980s and after. This is thanks to a dogged determination to cling on to all that could be good about I-N-G-E-R-L-A-N-D in the face of everything that is thrown at us: a resolve that first emerged amongst some of those fans who stuck it out through the trouble-strewn 1970s and '80s. The pleasure in experiencing new places and countries mixed up with a passion for football has always been there amongst our support. Except precious few watching us or writing about us ever bothered to take the trouble to notice. England fans today are constructing a new tradition. And like all traditions, it is being built on foundations that already exist. We are not talking about something imported from else-where. Angels with painted faces? No, thank you. Instead we are witnessing something deep-rooted, largely spontaneous and bottom-up. Whether those who join in started going in 2006 or 1966 hardly matters. England fans are made, not born. We all have to start sometime and with a combination of loyalty, exploration and passion not many of us will go far wrong.

Rossio Square, Lisbon, 2004. England have been knocked out by Portugal and after the match a group of our fans are drunkenly singing, 'We're the best-behaved fans in the world.' Irony is scarcely possible after extra time, penalties and a few lagers inside us. Perhaps there was just a hint of it as this chant of defiance was thrown back at all those who would doubt us. But it will do for starters.

3

In Front of the Children

Barbara Gill and her 13-year-old son Peter are both regulars at England's home games. Peter was first taken by his mother to football when he was hardly out of his pram: 'I was at Welling United as a baby in her arms, and when I became a bit too tired in the second half they let Mum put me in the executive lounge for a sleep.' Peter is no teenage glory-hunter: unlike most of his school-mates he has forsaken the more popular likes of Manchester United, Liverpool or Chelsea to follow his local non-league side. 'I get teased at school but I'm proud to support Welling, even if me and my mum are the only ones in our road who ever go to see them play.'

Barbara has brought up three sons. It is they who made football so important to her life, as her husband has work commitments making it difficult for him to take time off to go to a match. Of the three boys Peter is the youngest and now the keenest to go. 'We'd always wanted to watch England together but we never knew how to get tickets. Then a friend of ours took us to Wembley for

England versus Germany in 2000 and we've been to every match we could get to since.' For Peter these trips with his mum are very special: 'There's nothing else quite like the atmosphere at an England match. The anthem, the flags, everybody together, you just know this is a very special occasion.'

After five years of home matches Peter is now thinking of the future. 'When I'm older I'd like to go to away games. One day I want to share in that commitment going away with England represents.' For now, while Peter might miss the odd day of school for England games at Old Trafford or St James' Park while Wembley is being rebuilt, Mum won't countenance anything more than that. But Barbara knows how following England together has benefited their relationship. 'We're close, we share a laugh,' she says. 'We have had experiences together the rest of the family have missed out on.'

For Peter it is particularly special that his mum spares the time to take him. 'Most kids my age wouldn't be seen dead with their mum, but I'm more than happy to spend this time at football with mine.'

None of this is likely to impress Colin Johnson, author of *St George in My Heart: Confessions of an England Fan*. In his book Johnson regrets the likes of Barbara and Peter turning out for England. 'Families and females are now the main group of people attending the games and we have to listen to their expert opinions on a game they have only been interested in for five minutes. It sickens me to see people like this at games.'

A false opposition is set up – 'real' fans versus 'new' fans. Of course, families and females are nowhere near the majority at any England game, home, away or at a tournament. As the game has evolved, though, particularly since Italia 90, different constituencies have been attracted to following football. Undoubtedly, sometimes this broadening of appeal has been driven by commercial ambition rather than any commitment to the good of the game.

However, the wholesale blame often heaped upon new fans for being themselves responsible for rising ticket prices, sponsors' logos that ruin a classic strip, overzealous stewarding and moving grounds from their ancient location makes no sense at all. Barbara and Peter follow their local side, and travel up and down the country in the cause of England. They might not shout expletive-congested abuse, dress up in designer-label gear or drink themselves stupid, but does that make them any less legitimate in the fan-credibility stakes? Only for those for whom childhood is something best forgotten and women best stuck at home with dinner on the table ready for when their man gets back from the match.

Andrew Mott would certainly have those clinging to the myths of real fandom choking into their beer. Andrew is an import/export trader. He commutes to London from the Hertfordshire commuter-belt town of Bishop's Stortford and he takes his stepdaughter Rebecca to England games. Yet his football history is as steeped in tradition as those who savour what they think it should mean to be a fan.

His first game was when he was just eight years old, a 1964 match where Liverpool beat Leeds 2–1. Andrew didn't grow up in a household immersed in football but when his dad saw his young son's enthusiasm for the game he took him to the occasional match and, finally in 1971, an England game at Wembley, against Switzerland in a European Championship qualifier.

Andrew had the passion but his childhood opportunities to follow football were intermittent. His dad was a policeman and the job meant the family moved around the Home Counties: St Albans, Ware, Hertford, never quite close enough to a ground for Andrew to become a regular, and matters took a turn for the disastrous when he moved up to secondary school only to find the former grammar school had banned the kids from playing football in favour of the sport Andrew hated, rugby.

With adulthood, new opportunities came along, though not straightaway – Andrew never found a bunch of mates to go to football with. He was often working away from home, and so the social side that gets so many fans into the habit of going never came together for him. It was Rebecca who changed all this. From the age of three it was obvious she shared her stepdad's love of the game, which for so long had remained unfulfilled.

'Indoctrination? I'm not sure if I would quite use that word, but it wasn't far off.' This is how Andrew's wife Meryl describes what went on. She says all this with some affection, though her disinterest in the game her husband and daughter so adore remains implacable. Andrew did try to get Meryl involved, but she made it clear from the start that while she was happy to see the pair of them sharing football together she had absolutely no intention of joining in. Especially when Andrew and Rebecca would transform their living room into a practice pitch, with Andrew standing in front of the curtains as a makeshift indoor goal, and Rebecca sending him the wrong way with her carefully struck shots.

Andrew follows Bishop's Stortford FC, while Rebecca prefers Manchester United. 'I'll be honest,' she admits, 'the good looks of Beckham was what first appealed to me, but I can appreciate his skills too, and the rest of the team as well.'

It was Euro 96 that brought Andrew and Rebecca together on the sofa watching England on the TV. 'After the crushing disappointment of the semifinal we talked about the match,' remembers Andrew. 'Rebecca was only nine years old but she clearly understood what losing a game in the worst of circumstances meant.'

Three years later, June 1999, and they finally made it to Wembley to see England play in the Euro 2000 qualifier against Sweden. 'I wanted to wait until she would be old enough to really appreciate it. I was a bit on edge when we were on the Tube. We were packed in and there was a big squash at Wembley Park station when we got off.' But Andrew needn't have worried; Rebecca loved it and, as soon as the match was over, she asked Andrew when they could go again.

Over the next few years they took in as many home games as they could manage. As Euro 2004 approached, Andrew began to think it might be feasible for the two of them to go to Portugal for their first England away game. Andrew asked Meryl what she thought. Despite Meryl's total disinterest in football she knew how much this trip would mean to Andrew and Rebecca, and immediately agreed to Andrew's plan. 'I chose England versus France,' says Andrew. It was the opening group game, and on a Sunday, so ideal in terms of timing – we were able to make a long weekend of our trip. I kept the whole plan a secret from Rebecca, though. It would be a big surprise, but also I was really worried we wouldn't be able to get tickets.'

Andrew was lucky. England's match with France was to be played in Lisbon's Estadio da Luz, the biggest stadium of the tournament, which meant a correspondingly large allocation of tickets for members of englandfans, which Andrew and Rebecca had joined. Eventually the confirmation that his application for two tickets had been successful arrived. Andrew had their tickets, and Rebecca could be told of her big surprise. Her first away match: Lisbon, England versus France.

'I was excited,' she recalls. 'There were England fans everywhere we went in Lisbon. But I was quite calm too, I wanted to be able to take it all in. It was nothing like what I'd seen on TV. The fans didn't intimidate me. I just felt part of something. In the stands when we scored we all hugged each other. And when Beckham missed that penalty we all swore together too.'

For Andrew as a stepdad the England games the pair of them

have been to have acquired a particular significance. 'It is what Rebecca and I do together. These are experiences that we share. Football, more than almost anything else, is what the pair of us have in common.'

John Williams, director of the Sir Norman Chester Centre for Football Research, reports in his study *Football and Families*: 'Football, arguably, offers a shared passion on a more equal footing than almost any other mutually shared leisure activity. Authority relations never completely disappear at the match but children and parents do also noticeably share a common identity as fans, and often talk together on that more or less level basis.' In an era of generation gaps, family break-ups and the increasing atomization of the way we live, football has a remarkably enduring capacity to bring parents and kids together. Of course, exclusions can emerge too. Football remains a predominantly male culture; Mum can feel left out, daughters discriminated against, but increasingly the game is a shared experience, with these former exclusions eroding, or at least becoming negotiable.

For the Pheasant family the common experience of football is its special appeal to Mum and Dad (Debbie and Andy) and teenage son Matt. Andy, like his son, became a fan in his teens. His uncle took him to his first Leeds game when he was fifteen, and when he was eighteen he made his first trip to Wembley for England's Home International match against Northern Ireland in 1980. The national team was doing poorly, having failed to qualify for two World Cups in succession. Andy wasn't put off, though, and after this match he attended every single England home game for the next twenty years.

Newly engaged Debbie started to join Andy at the matches from the late 1980s onwards. 'I had always been interested in football but until Andy took me I'd never been to a match, so it was nice to have something we could share.' But there was a side of going to football Debbie didn't like: 'I was taken aback by the segregation, the police were really threatening, and the language was awful. But none of this stopped me enjoying myself.' They went together to all of England's Euro 96 games. 'For the first time the atmosphere really was superb – the ugly side of going was pushed to the margins. The singing was nonstop, the 4–1 beating of Holland one of the best games I've ever seen.'

After Euro 96 Matt started asking if he could go too. Debbie was pregnant so Andy took him to his first game. Matt admits, 'I was only five years old. I can't remember very much. Just being happy, contented that I was there with my dad.' Debbie confesses she was concerned, and relieved when her young son was back home safe and sound.

For France 98 Debbie and Andy were determined to make their first away trip. Joining them was Andy's dad, who had taken him to his first league games. Matt was too young to travel abroad. Things changed, though, four years later for the next World Cup in Japan. Matt was now going regularly to Leeds home and away. His two younger sisters, Isobel and Eloise, were looked after by their grandparents, though this did mean the trip to Japan could only be for ten days. Matt, Debbie and Andy had been at Old Trafford to see England secure qualification in heart-stopping circumstances against Greece and this had made all three of them determined to travel to the Far East.

Debbie is certain the trip was about more than just football. 'It's sometimes difficult for a family to spend real quality time together, but we certainly did that in Japan. We shared this trip into the unknown and I don't think any of us will ever forget that.' Andy and Debbie had always enjoyed travelling and this was their opportunity for them to experience this with their young son.

Andy compares Matt's first World Cup with his own memories:

'I remember World Cup 1970. I collected the stickers, and listened attentively to the David Coleman commentaries. Japan for Matt was completely different, he was actually there.'

As the 2002 World Cup approached, lots of TV production companies were scrabbling around with the same idea to sell to BBC or ITV; a fan's-eye view of the tournament. This was yet another indicator of the huge changes in how England fans are perceived and represented. A decade ago we were hardly ever seen on TV, and certainly not in anything approaching favourable coverage. Our voices were not heard, never mind listened to. As someone who has spoken up for fans, my name and number appears in a lot of journalists' contact books. With researchers rifling around for the angle that might secure them their production contract I was being called constantly for ideas.

One of these outfits sounded more switched on than most, and they liked the idea in particular of following a family on their way to Japan. I had met Andy and we'd chatted about his plan to take his family to Japan. I thought it might make a good story so, with his permission, I passed on Andy's number to them. When Debbie heard the drop-dead-gorgeous Sean Bean was to be involved she was immediately sold on the idea, although sadly for her she never got to meet the screen hunk. She had to settle for drooling over his South Yorkshire drawled voiceover as he introduced their segment of the final film: 'The Pheasant family from Surrey are setting off to Japan with son Matt.'

Andy admits, 'We'd never done anything like this before, and we were a bit worried how we would be portrayed.' Andy didn't need to be concerned. Debbie took charge of the filming with the camcorder they had been given, and as Beckham stood up to take his decisive penalty against Argentina Andy filled the screen in praying position, moments later throwing his hands heavenwards as if offering celestial thanks.

'It was a great shot,' Debbie proudly boasts, before admitting the reason why: 'I was too nervous to watch the penalty, so consoled myself with filming Andy and Matt's reactions instead.' Matt was suitably starstruck, gazing wide-eyed into the camera lens before joining in with yet another chorus of 'Ingerland – Ingerland – Ingerland!'

The programme, *Breakfast with Beckham,* was broadcast over Christmas 2002. Andy was thankful for how faithful it was to the experience of the wide selection of fans. 'We were both impressed and relieved about how we were portrayed. I couldn't believe how many people saw the programme. Even at Euro 2004 I was stopped in the toilets at one game by a bloke who remembered seeing me on the show.'

This kind of imaginative and positive projection of what an England away trip can mean to mums, dads, sons and daughters could undoubtedly help to encourage other families to join the Pheasants when they next follow England abroad.

John King, author of *The Football Factory*, denounced the 2002 World Cup. 'It shows that passion has become a commodity, something to be controlled and channelled towards a profit, the off-field carnival sanitized, passion crushed and bottled and sold off to the highest bidder.' The fear often expressed by writers like King is that the efforts to make football more appealing to families are the excuse for the sanitization he is so fearful of. Yet this is a criticism most families who follow England would endorse. A big part of the attraction of football to these parents and kids is the edginess; the gritty realism of victory and defeat, the unpredictability of outcome compared to a pre-packaged holiday treat. And many of these families have also done their time up and down the motorways of England following their club, whether non-league or Premiership. They are part and parcel of the pyramid of

commitment on which fandom is founded, and to pretend otherwise is rather insulting.

Nicky Quinlan took her daughter India to her first England
game in October 2000, the dire defeat by Germany that marked
both the closure of the old Wembley and the end of Kevin
Keegan's term as underachieving England manager. 'I grew up in
Stoke and met my husband Gary in 1996. I knew he was a big
Stoke City fan and that football was bound to become a major part
of our relationship.' India, just two years old, went with them to
Wembley. 'We were right by the barrier dividing the German fans
from the English. Everyone around us wanted us to move. It was
obvious why, they were looking for trouble. We refused to budge –
why should we help them with their hooliganism?'

For the return match in Munich the following September Gary
agreed to stay at home and look after India while Nicky travelled.
'This was my first game on my own,' she says. 'It was quite a sacrifice of Gary's not to go but looking after India had to be shared
out, so we couldn't always go together. I went with a group, a lot
of men leaving their wives at home, which left me looking a bit
odd.'

With 2002 World Cup qualification secured, Gary made it perfectly clear this was one trip he would not be missing. Nicky was
similarly keen to go, and if she went that meant India was going
too. 'India doesn't remember very much. She was only three years
old but she loves to look at our photo albums from the trip, it
helps with her memories, and she's acquired a liking for noodles
too, especially eaten with chopsticks.' Did other fans resent India
being there? 'Quite the opposite. All the blokes wanted to have
their picture taken with her, and the wives and girlfriends were
saying to the men that next time their kids would be coming with
them too.'

India, like her mum and dad, is Stoke City through and through.

'She didn't have much choice,' Nicky recalls. 'I was out of hospital on a Sunday and six days later she was at her first home match.' In 2003 Nicky and Gary split up, but even this wasn't going to stop the three of them following England. 'We had already planned to go to England's May match in South Africa. We knew India would be hugely disappointed if we didn't go, so we went; separated, but together as England fans.'

The following year Nicky took India to Euro 2004. 'Two years older, she was able to take a lot more in. The noise and the excitement meant much more to her. Some fans are a bit much. They stand up for the entire game, which makes it difficult for a five-year-old to see, but most at least make the effort not to block her view.' Like so many other parents Nicky values the experiences football has enabled her to share with her child. 'I'm a single parent now, and a working mum. I'm stuck in an office all day long and hardly see India during the week, so football has become when we spend the most time together.' The varied cultures, places they visit, different foods they sample, all add to the richness of the experience, pored over back home via their photo albums.

Nicky encourages India to use football as part of her education too. For instance, 'For Euro 2004 India would write up the games, the things she saw. It helped her with reading, writing and drawing, although her school didn't seem very interested which was a shame.' Nicky has also come up with a unique way to encourage India to appreciate how important goal-scoring is: 'One Smartie if the other team scores, five when England score.'

But what about some of the less attractive aspects of England away? 'India would join in with the "Ten German Bombers" song without really knowing what it was all about. After all, it sounds a bit like a nursery rhyme, even if it is sung by grown men. Then afterwards we would chat about what it meant: looking backwards, belittling a very real sacrifice and using it for other means today.

India came to her own conclusion, kids can, and she doesn't sing it any more.'

Writing in the *Guardian*, political commentator Martin Jacques noted the enduring importance of the family. 'The central site of intimacy is the family. Expressed in the relationship between partners, and between parents and children. Intimacy is a function of time and permanence. It rests on mutuality and unconditionality. It is rooted in trust.' Jacques compared the intimacy, understanding and trust of family relations to the privatization of emotions. Communications technology has taken the place of friendship, and corporate logos substituted for symbols of local and national belonging: 'The decline of settled community and the rise of the media-society has desensitized us as human beings. We have become less intimate with the most fundamental emotions, without which we cannot understand the meaning of life: there are no peaks without troughs. Life becomes shopping.'

Football itself is, of course, ruthlessly marketed but whatever the efforts of the sponsors they cannot fully exploit for their own ends the emotional investment of us as fans. Families are a key target market as new consumers of all the assorted trappings of the game. Replica kits, scarves and hats, a flag to wave, a computer game to play in the car on the way home from the match; kids and their parents will queue up to buy the lot. Yet at the same time as this huge process of commercialization is under way, football remains a site of intimate family relations, a place where the traditions of fandom are passed from generation to generation. A process largely unspoiled by all this marketing of our sport.

The Potter family certainly know all about the worth of tradition in football. They live on a farm perched on the edge of the Peak District. It is so windy here that the St George Cross flag they tie to their flagpole each year has to be replaced every twelve months after being ripped to shreds by the gale-force gusts which whip through the valley. Down the hill from where they live is Ashbourne, and gathered around their farmhouse kitchen table Ian, Carole, son Jack, and daughters Lydia and Harriet recount for me the historical place of their locality in football's history. 'Ashbourne's Shrovetide football was first recorded in 1682, though it certainly dates back before then,' Ian explains. 'There is a goal at each end of the town. All windows are boarded up as the Uppers battle it out with the Downers. A thousand or more are on each side. It's basically a mass free-for-all every Shrove Tuesday. Over three centuries after it first took place and despite constant attempts to suppress it the match is still played.' Ian is proud of living in such close proximity to the origins of football, a pride reinforced by being one of the founders of the 'Ashbourne Rams', dedicated supporters of Derby County.

Carole helped organize the group with Ian and she remembers how it began: 'It was 1998 when it started up and it's still going today. We would run coaches to games, home and away. Eventually the whole operation more or less took over our lives. Every week a coach to book and fill, it became a bit much really.'

Ian had grown up in York, a schoolboy fan of York City. 'I went for nearly ten years. Every match or thereabouts from when I was eight years old. Then a kid pulled a knife on me at Hillsborough and that was it for me.' Twenty years later and Ian was settled in Derbyshire. He had married Carole, a successful businesswoman, and was busy establishing a good career for himself as a livestock auctioneer when his teenage daughter Harriet started bothering Ian to take her to a football match. 'We had to settle for a Derby County reserves game. It was Derby's final season at the old Baseball Ground and it was impossible to get tickets to the first-team matches.' What sort of game they went to hardly mattered – most important to Ian was what Harriet's youthful enthusiasm meant for the pair of them. 'After twenty years of absence it was a way for me, and now the family too, to come back to football.' Like Ian, Carole had followed football as a teenager in the 1970s. Growing up locally, Derby County has always been her team, and like her husband she abandoned her side when the match-day fighting took over and became impossible to avoid. After Ian and Harriet started going, the rest of the family very soon followed suit, plus Carole's dad Alf.

After two very intense years of the Potter family supporting their local side, Ian became enthusiastic about following the national team too. 'I wanted to go to Euro 2000, though I had no idea how to go about getting tickets. Eventually I was put in touch with the FA-run supporters' club, the England Members Club.' Ian went to a fans' meeting with the FA in Leeds and heard from fans who were there that, while officially all of England's tournament tickets had been sold out, there were almost certain to be spares for anyone who bothered to make it over to Belgium and Holland. It seemed a risky venture, going to their first tournament and travelling ticketless, but as Ian met other fans he became more and more convinced it would be worthwhile travelling. Only Ian and Carole travelled to the tournament. They got into every England game they tried for, had a fantastic time and when they returned home were determined the next time they went the whole family would travel.

Times columnist Mick Hume has written how efforts to change the base of England's support often hide behind a 'family-friendly' agenda: 'The new etiquette is often justified as an exercise in making football a "family game again", something it never was in the first place. As usual, however, women and children are just being used as human shields, behind which the authorities can pursue their agenda of sanitizing the game.'

Hume, just like John King, Colin Johnson and other defenders of a so-called 'reality' of fandom, is in fact seeking to preserve one particular type of fan experience and prioritizing it at the expense of others. He treats family fans as mindless dupes, allies even, of this policing of our passion. It is an unfair allegation, and forgetful of how most of us became fans in the first place – thanks to a parent, elder brother or sister, or other relative taking us. For Ian Potter the fact that what he calls 'my lot' are his family, rather than a bunch of mates from Derby County, is a vital part of his experience of following England. Does that make him any less a fan, or a part of the fan community?

Gary Kitching played semi-professional football for Worksop Town, Bridlington Town and Spalding United until his late twenties. He gave up playing regularly when his eldest daughter, Grace, was born. He didn't finish entirely, though, continuing with Sunday league football, before becoming first player-manager of his local team, Maltby Town, and then chairman. Gary is devoted to his football, and his 8-year-old son Will is much the same. He has already graduated from Maltby Juniors and Wickersley Youth FC and is now training at Rotherham United's football academy.

England is what connects the football experience of this father and son. In his twenties Gary was desperate to follow England regularly, but newly married to wife Leanne, with a plumbing apprenticeship to qualify for and, within a few years, his own business to establish, England trips, home or away, were few and far between.

Gary is an emotional character. He knows precisely what his relationship with Will means to him: 'I was an only child – Will is the younger brother I never had.' At just four and a half years old Will joined Gary on the trip that began the pair of them on their England travels. In February 2002 father and son joined a flight the

FA had organized for family fans going to Amsterdam to see England play Holland. 'The two of us looked around the city centre,' says Gary. 'I wanted to get a taste of the atmosphere, but as soon as the Sky TV camera crew spotted Will they were all over him.' Back home, friends, neighbours and relatives couldn't believe it. Will and Gary on the TV – nothing like this had happened to the pair of them before. 'We're just a normal family. We know we're not celebrities or anything like that. When we appeared on the TV it was a bit of a shock.'

At the game Gary had to cope with the emotional turmoil of a young lad experiencing his first England game. 'Holland score first and Will promptly bursts into tears. I tried to console him but he wasn't having it: "Get off me, you promised we'd win," he was saying.' A packet of sweets helped calm Will's disappointment. This wasn't quite the sort of match experience Gary remembers from his first England game as a 17-year-old. Fortunately Darius Vassell scored a belter to equalize and Will's tears were brushed away, forgotten in all the excitement of this first trip away with his dad.

When the trip was over Gary was surprised to get a call from the FA's head of public relations. He had seen him and Will on Sky and wanted to feature the pair of them on the FA website. Gary was happy to oblige, as the article was to be used to encourage other families to have a go at following England abroad.

A few months later, Gary and Will were heading off to Japan for the World Cup. 'It was a present to myself for my fortieth birthday,' Gary explains. 'I had always wanted to go to a big tournament, but now I had a travelling companion too, my own son.' Gary admits, 'I'm not a square, but I was never one for away trips as an excuse for boozing and one-night stands, so Will is my ideal mate to go with.' They spent nearly four weeks in Japan, establishing a friendship based on football that far exceeds simply being father and son. But Gary never forgot just how young Will was, and the responsibilities this imposed on him: 'It was a big adventure for Will but there were times when he missed his mum too. At our first game, against Sweden, it took a five-minute call to Leanne just to stop Will crying. Everyone around us was turning away embarrassed as Will sobbed his heart out.'

After the game Gary and Will were once again on Sky, but this time it didn't cheer Leanne up, quite the opposite. 'It left me down in the dumps for days. Will had never been apart from me so long before. I was scared something awful would happen to him.' Yet her mood changed for the better after the Argentina game. Not only had England won but a picture of the happy faces of her husband and son were gazing out at her from every newspaper she picked up. 'Everybody would be ringing me up, "Have you seen the paper today?" I couldn't believe it was my husband and son in the papers.'

Gary couldn't believe it either and wanted to put all this publicity to some sort of good use. 'I thought the pair of us might be able to help with the initiatives for a positive England. I didn't want Will to grow up having to watch his football surrounded by hooliganism. I'd seen enough of that in the 1980s to know what harm it can do.' Phoning up their local radio station with reports on their away trips, joining goodwill visits to schools in South Africa the day before England played in Durban, and collecting shirts to give away to an orphanage fans adopted in Azerbaijan are just some of the positive things Gary and Will have done towards this goal.

After the World Cup Leanne joined Gary and Will for the away match in Bratislava. As the match started Will was in his usual position, perched on Gary's shoulders, with for the first time at an England game his mum at his dad's side. All of a sudden the Slovakia riot police started aggressively pushing back the England fans in the section alongside the home supporters. Gary thought it best to stand still. Surely with a kid in his arms and his wife by his side they would realize he was looking for anything but trouble. But next, as Gary remembers, 'Five of our idiots decided to storm the fence between us and the Slovak fans.' The police promptly went crazy, lashing out in all directions. Kids, wives and stationary husbands were all targets of their uncontrolled ferocity. Within seconds Will was passed over the heads of fans in a time-honoured fashion straight out of the 1930s terraces. He ended up in a neighbouring pen. Leanne was pulled out too, shaking with fear, and hysterical at the thought that she might have lost contact with her son. Gary scrambled over the fence. He gathered his family together and kept them as far away as possible from any remaining risk of trouble.

None of this was enough to put Gary and Will off. 'We love watching England. We mix with good people and, if we get in a bad situation like in Bratislava, we get out, fast. We have a great time and I want to ensure that my lad, and thousands more like him, are able to be a part of that.'

Leanne had a different view. How could she let her small boy be put through something like this? But then Gary took the trouble to introduce her to the supporters they travel with, men and women who cared passionately about each other's welfare and safety. They look out for not just themselves, but their fellow fans too. Not in an aggressive, territorial sense, but with a collective care Leanne felt comforted by. With good planning and sensible precautions Leanne understood Gary and Will would always be secure with these supporters on their side.

Gary is bringing up Will in a football environment that retains some very rough, and often unpleasant, edges, but none of this puts him off. 'Why should it? I've never seen England lift any silverware, and nothing is going to stop me and Will being there when they finally do.' This is their dream, although one particular England match is sure to stick in Gary's memory as a bit special, even after the World Cup has been won again. For each home game the FA organizes a lucky draw to choose a boy or a girl as the team mascot and lead, hand-in-hand with David Beckham, the team out on to the pitch. 'It's all I've ever wanted,' says Gary. 'Will to lead that team out. Not just for him, but for our whole family. It would be such an honour.'

When the call came through from the FA Gary could hardly speak. And on the night of the game Will, usually so confident and self-contained at matches, was incredibly nervous. The FA staff who work with the mascot and other children who will carry the two teams' flags around the pitch ahead of kickoff are quite used to the kids' nerves getting the better of them. They set to work with Gary, calming Will down in order to prepare him for what was certainly a huge occasion. The opposition might only be lowly Liechtenstein, but the game was a sell-out and a vital stage towards Euro 2004 in Portugal. Gary had brought a football with him and, as the time approached when Will would join the England players in the tunnel, he took him off to the quietest space he could find, a luxurious executive box, for a calming kick-about.

Then it was time to meet Becks, who greeted Will with, 'Wotcha, Will. How's it all going?' His nerves disappeared in an instant. He was chatting amiably with quite possibly the most famous footballer in the world as if he was a playground mate. Becks commented on Will's personalized stitching on his boots, just like his own. Quick as a flash, Will tries to score a deal: 'Our neighbour Mark Rhodes did my boots for me. It only cost six pounds, he'd do yours no problem.' Beckham cracked up, laughing his head off. Not only was Will now completely relaxed, but the England captain headed out of the tunnel with a huge grin on his face.

Gary, meanwhile, had tears of joy rolling down his cheeks while he tried to hold the camcorder steady to record this once-in-a-lifetime moment. The whole family were there: Leanne, daughters Grace and Frances, and Gary's mum and dad. As the national anthem began Will was concentrating hard as he carried out his dad's most important instruction: 'Don't forget to sing as loud as you can. Let the whole country see what this means to you.'

Leanne admits to a more than occasional argument with Gary about leaving the rest of the family at home while he and Will head abroad for England away matches. Her fears for her own safety had stopped Leanne going after Bratislava, but with Euro 2004 in Portugal and Gary reporting no repeat of the kind of incidents she had witnessed in Slovakia, she was now determined all of them should make it out to the tournament. 'It was my fortieth birthday in June 2004 and there was no way I was spending it stuck at home.'

Gary describes the family holiday Euro 2004 turned into: 'We were on a camp site. We had St George Cross flags all over our pitch. The Kitching family "Camp England" is what we christened it.' The Spanish, Czech, French and Swedish fans on the same site would all come over to marvel at this entire family of England fans: mum, dad, son and daughters. Gary explains what this meant to him, 'For me, that was the best part of Portugal. All the fans from different countries getting on so well with each other.'

And Leanne agrees: 'After Bratislava I'd vowed I would never go again but this was so different. I was so pleased I'd come out and brought the girls too.' Determined not to be left out, Grace returned home to join Bramley Sunnyside Girls FC as a goalkeeper, though she's not sure yet if she's ready to stop her younger brother's curling free kicks.

The Kitching family 'Camp England' was used by *The Times* to portray all that was best about England in Portugal. The weekend after the defeat by Portugal and a dodgy Swiss ref, journalist David Sharrock wrote: 'Gary Kitching was busy disassembling his extraordinary personal tribute to the team he loves – an entire camp site emblazoned with the England emblem. As he sat under an England pagoda, his son William dejectedly kicked an England football.' Gary provided a picture of national gloom but it was Will who provided the headline: 'Beckham used to be my hero, but not now.'

Childish ingratitude? Not really, it was the same all over the country, the golden-boy reputation damaged goods after two match-losing penalty misses. Five months later it looks like Will has forgiven Becks for his inaccuracy with just a goalie to beat. The photos of David and Will leading the team out are still pinned up in his bedroom, with pride of place given to Beckham's soiled socks, spirited out of a laundry basket at the Vaduz stadium after the Liechtenstein away game for Will by one of Gary's enterprising, and thoughtful, mates.

Ben Pearson doesn't have much of a choice about being accompanied by his mum and dad, John and Carolyn, to England games. Ben suffers from cerebral palsy. He is confined to a wheelchair, the whole of the right side of his body is paralysed, his bones are brittle and the curvature of his spine is affected. John and Carolyn are an essential part of the operation to get Ben safely into and away from the stadium. Ben started going during Euro 96 and went away for the first time to Munich in September 2001 for the 5–1 thrashing of Germany. Going to England games at Wembley was the first rude awakening for the three of them to how difficult this could be. Carolyn details what Ben was forced to endure: 'We had to queue up in the royal tunnel to race to get a decent position. Every other fan in the stadium had a numbered seat – why couldn't we?' Luckily Carolyn can be a pushy individual and after the ninety-minute wait in the tunnel she was so fired up with anger she had all the incentive she needed to elbow Ben into the best position possible. Not very nice, but it was the only way they were going to get a decent spot.

But where the wheelchair supporters were put was low down, beside the touchline. Even though Carolyn had pushed and shoved to get Ben a front-row position, the sightlines were very poor and the indignity they felt had been heaped upon them by the whole shoddy episode spoiled a lot of Ben's enjoyment of the match. 'No toilet access,' he explains. 'I couldn't get to the bar or food outlets either – do they think I don't fancy a beer and a burger like the rest of the fans?'

Euro 2004 was the first away tournament trip for the three of them, something Ben had long dreamed of, with all the prospects of a great family holiday. The location seemed ideal – brand-new stadiums would surely mean decent access. But Ben was to be bitterly disappointed: 'The Estadio da Luz was a massive let-down for me. I was stuck on an inner concourse behind row after row of fans. OK, if they had all sat down I could have seen, but that's hardly realistic, is it?' Ben shows me his photos of the England–France match. Every one is of the backs of the fans standing in front of him. 'They kept offering to sit down. They were really apologetic, and almost as upset as I was. But when they sat down they couldn't do anything about the rows in front of them, so what was the point?'

Ben's anger isn't directed at the fans but at the stadium management and the football authorities. 'Munich in 2001, my first England away game, I was stuck behind an advertising hoarding. I could barely see the heads of our players, never mind the goals they were scoring.' There's scarcely been a game since where things have been much better. John, Carolyn and Ben insist they aren't special. They don't want to be treated as such, but just like any family they want a decent view of the match, what they have paid their money for. Is that really too much to expect from modern stadiums that pride themselves on their family-friendly design?

For many families, football fandom is something parents pass down from one generation to another in the hope that their sons and daughters will eventually do the same in turn. Howard and Fred Thompson have done this, but sort of in reverse. Father and son, both Wolves fans, it is Howard who takes his 73-year-old dad to England games.

In the beginning it was the other way round. Nine-year-old Howard was taken to his first Wolves match on New Year's Day 1974 by his dad. Howard was too small to see over the wall at the front of Molineux, so Fred brought in a beer crate for him to stand on, then retreated to the back of the stand to have a drink with his mates. Fred had been a Wolves fan back in the 1950s, the glorious era of Wolves and England captain Billy Wright. England games had never been something he could get to, though. He lived out in the Worcestershire countryside, a good distance from public transport and with a time-consuming job as a self-employed lorry driver. It just never seemed possible to go to Wembley, let alone abroad for an international match overseas.

Fred's enthusiasm, which had started to dip as the Wolves glory days under Billy Wright's captaincy disappeared further and further into the past, was revived. With Howard enjoying his first match so much, Fred, wife Beryl and their young son were soon going to Molineux regularly. This was something he could be grateful to Howard for. Twenty years after his first match it was Howard's turn to repay his dad for introducing him to football and taking him to so many matches as first a child and then a teenager. By the late 1980s Howard had left home to become a civil servant. He lived first in Nottingham before moving to London. Trips to Molineux with Fred, and lunch or supper with Beryl too, was a way of keeping the family in touch both with one another and something they had all shared through Howard's childhood and adolescence. Unlike his dad, Howard had travelled abroad, and after one holiday in America he returned home determined to persuade his dad to join him at the USA 94 World Cup.

Fred, even though England had failed to qualify, didn't need asking twice. Together they crisscrossed the country, following Brazil to Los Angeles, San Francisco, Boston, New York and Washington. Howard sums up what that trip meant for the pair of them. 'It was the longest period we'd ever spent together, just the two of us. We packed everything we could into those three weeks.' On their return they decided, having enjoyed themselves so much, they would begin to follow England away, and since 1997 they've only missed two games. On their travels Howard has found at thirty-nine he has more in common with his father than he had previously realized. 'It has made us really close. There's no one else I'd rather watch Wolves or England with.'

It is football that has injected this emotional closeness into their lives. They share the same likes. Under-21 games played on the night before the full international are always a must on any trip. However hard these extra matches are to get to, seeing the players of tomorrow develop is a thrill they savour together.

Fred, without Howard to encourage and accompany him, may not have ended up travelling much further afield than his own father who, like many of his generation, never ventured very far from home, and not once abroad. He left his county, Worcestershire, where Fred still lives in a secluded country hamlet, just three times in his life. Following England has so far taken Fred to four continents, and there's no sign of him stopping either.

Howard took Fred to England versus Wales at Old Trafford in

In Front of the Children

October 2004. For most families, of course, it was Dad, and increasingly Mum, taking their kids, rather than a son taking his father. Amongst the parents and children filling so much of the stands for this and every England home game, traditional expectations of childhood and adulthood were being defied. Match-day passions disrupt and discomfort. The kids were singing their hearts out, leading their parents on, sometimes unsure of the meaning of the words, but at full volume nevertheless. They were as knowledgeable as their parents about our line-up, and the Welsh one too. Though not yet immersed in the history of the encounter – Dad will soon enough show off by filling his kids in on that – they were acutely well informed of who's who on the pitch nowadays.

At how many other public occasions do adults and children participate as near equals? These kids aren't here just to make up the numbers. They are the next generation of fans. Many are continuing a family tradition that stretches back generations, while others are helping to initiate a new family tradition that maybe one day in the future they will pass on to their children too. The basis of these kids' commitment to England isn't a replica shirt or a poster pinned on a bedroom wall, though they all have plenty of both. Rather it is the experience they share, home and away, parents and children, as fans.

Children seen but not heard? Not when Becks curled his shot into the top corner of the Welsh net. The adult baggage of grown-up responsibility? Tossed aside with the realization that a victory against our wannabe home-nation rivals was assured.

England's family fans are scrupulously well behaved, bordering on the saintly. Yet, like most English families, they are mainly godless. The established national religion, the Church of England, that once codified relations between husband and wife, parents and children, is today followed by the faithful few not the many. The modern church is a place for baptisms, weddings and funerals, but not much more. Spiritual capital and emotional investment has been marketized, turned into just another economic transaction, to be bought and sold over the counter. For these families of fans it is their faith in football that provides confirmation of the principles of loyalty and commitment. For some, this is a faith they were born into and for others something they have made up for themselves along the way. The crowd, the terraces and stands, the songs, the chants, the crush and clash of bodies is their baptism. This is what they share with thousands, tens of thousands of others, in the stadiums, and on the planes, trains and buses as they travel the world in the common cause of I-N-G-E-R-L-A-N-D. And when they are ready they are confirmed – no longer just a spectator, they share in the communion of fandom. They have earned their place in the power and the glory of the match. For ever and ever, our team.

4

Lie Back and Think of England

Eileen Rigby is hopping mad. The day before we met she had made the round trip all the way from Bolton to Chelsea to see her beloved Wanderers take on the capital's Premiership table-toppers. She had travelled to the match on a coach full of supporters, all of whom had been prevented from entering Stamford Bridge. Through no fault of their own they had turned up after kickoff and their sorry tale of motorway tailbacks and the unearthly hour they had begun their journey cut no ice with the stewards and police at the stadium. Jaidi's equalizer, which had secured a hard-won draw for Bolton, went unseen by one of the team's longest-standing fans.

Twenty-four hours later and Eileen was still fuming: 'We left at six-thirty in the morning, got back at midnight and didn't see a minute's worth of football. What did the police think I'd do, riot?' Hardly likely – Eileen is in her mid-sixties. She was first taken to Bolton's previous ground, Burnden Park, in the 1950s by her dad. 'My mum didn't go, but my dad had followed Wanderers on their glorious 1920s FA cup runs. He saw the side lift the trophy in 1923, 1926 and 1929. When we were growing up he took me and my sister. The three of us would go for a Saturday afternoon stroll then get to the ground early so we could stand as close as we could get to the touchline. Otherwise I would never have seen a thing.' And her dad gave Eileen a piece of advice she's never forgotten about how to watch the game: 'Always follow the ball.'

By the late '50s Eileen was going regularly. 'I went with a bunch of teenagers. Mostly lads, but two or three girls too. For five years I hardly missed a match.' Years later Eileen was joined by Helen, her eldest daughter. 'I remember Helen coming home from college one day. She'd been studying sociology and announced that what we were doing qualified as "role reversal". Mother taking daughter to football rather than father taking son.' Eric, Eileen's husband, has never shared his wife's enthusiasm for the game. 'He's not very keen at all. We've been married forty-two years, but he's never shown any interest in football. He puts up with me though. He knew I was crazy about football when we first met so he knew what he was letting himself in for.'

It was at Euro 96 that Eileen started going to England games. She travelled down to Wembley with Helen's ex-husband Alan, but when she decided to go on away trips as well she knew for most of these it would mean going overseas on her own. Husband Eric sometimes accompanies her, but only if England play somewhere nice and even then he hardly ever bothers with the actual match. 'He's not interested so I leave him in a bar and arrange to meet him when the game is over,' Eileen adds.

Over the fifty years Eileen has been a football fan she has noticed a steady growth in the number of other women fans. 'There are such large numbers who now come. I would never have believed that could happen when I first started going.' Germaine Greer, one of the pioneers of twentieth-century feminism and author of the classic *The Female Eunuch*, isn't convinced the presence of Eileen and these other women fans is of any great significance to the sport. In the *Daily Telegraph* as Euro 2004 began, Greer wrote: 'A wise woman remains silent until the game is over. Chances are that her presence will simply be ignored. A discreet woman can use the opportunity to enjoy the beauty of the players rather than the play.'

Eileen denies ever availing herself of such a chance. She prefers to remember her dad's advice – 'follow the ball' – and never mind the legs, backside, torso and face of the man hoofing, passing or heading the spherical object of her female gaze. Though like any fan, male or female, Eileen has heroes who shaped her introduction to the sport. Nat Lofthouse, the Bolton and England centre forward of the 1950s, went to Eileen's school. She remembers: 'He would come visiting sometimes. All the lessons would stop and we'd mob him in the playground.' Just over fifty years after Nat was dubbed the 'Lion of Vienna' following a brutally physical encounter on the pitch with Austria in that city, Eileen saw England play there in September 2004. At the fans' party with the Austrian fanzine *Ballesterer* Eileen presented a signed photo of Nat lifting the FA Cup after Bolton's 1958 victory to the editor and his team of writers. 'It was nerve-wracking standing up in front of all those fans. But I was proud too. Wearing my England shirt, representing my country, my club, and in a way my girlhood hero.'

Club and country, Eileen is a highly committed fan. She has a healthy attitude to putting her commitment in some sort of perspective too: 'If football isn't about bringing people together then what's it for? It has the power to do good and so it should.' She is encouraging these values early in grandsons Thomas and Robert, who are already Bolton regulars. 'They sit with me and people around me who have been following Bolton for twenty years or more.' Granddaughter Bethan, just six years old, has already made

93

it to her first England match. 'She loved it,' Eileen proudly admits, with more than a hint that the female side of the family's footballing tradition is already being busily secured.

Eileen, like many women fans, was first taken to a match by her dad, and now she is continuing that process with Bethan. But some women find their own way to football. Tanya Parish grew up in Torquay in the late 1970s. 'I really wanted to see Torquay United play but even though this was a lower-division club it was blighted by that era's hooliganism. Away fans would frequently come down for the match, stay for the weekend, fight in the town and smash up bars.'

Having been prevented from fulfilling her dream in her teenage years Tanya's adolescent interest in football waned. University followed, and a move to London. Italia 90 reignited Tanya's interest, and she persuaded a boyfriend to take her to Wembley for an England match. 'He'd not been before either – football was new for both of us. I didn't want to go on my own so it was good to have someone to accompany me. What struck me was all these people, with one common interest, their football. And everybody watched every move on the pitch. They talked through every kick of the ball. It was like one huge conversation involving seventy thousand people.'

Tanya was an instant convert. She decided there and then to go to England games as often as she could, and whenever Torquay played in London or the Home Counties she would go to their matches too. Euro 96 was when her commitment became really serious. 'Now I felt what a stadium full of people was really like. And all those blokes chanting "Seaman! Seaman!" without thinking what that sounded like to us women. I'll never forget that, it still makes me laugh.'

Four years later and Tanya made it to her first England away match, in Paris, with her younger sister Yvonne, by now also a Torquay United regular. 'I wasn't sure whether going away was for me. I was worried about travelling on my own so it was great that Yvonne could come too.' Tanya noticed that, compared to Wembley, there were far fewer women among England's away following. Nevertheless, she returned home determined this would be the first of many more trips. 'I'd proved to myself, with my sister's help, that I could do it and now I wanted more.'

Japan was her first tournament, joined again by Yvonne, and since then Tanya has become a regular, going wherever England play. After the 2002 World Cup she has mostly travelled on her own. 'There is a sense of the unknown, risk even. But nothing different to any situation where you're a lone woman. I'm careful at a game, conscious of when I'm not in control of the space or the situation I find myself in. The police certainly don't discriminate. If they're treating us badly, it makes no difference I'm a woman, I receive just the same rough handling.'

Tanya has shared in the trials, tribulations and more than occasional joy of her fellow England fans. How does she feel when the mood of a shared community, all together, changes? As soon as a pretty girl wanders by, up goes the chant, 'Get your tits out for the lads'. She cheerfully admits, 'It just confirms the generally low opinion I have of most men. That sort of thing doesn't particularly bother me. It says more about their lack of imagination and insecurity than it does about me being there.'

Journalist Julie Burchill is convinced in her own narrow mind what the outcome for a great mass of male England supporters rubbing shoulders with one another will be. In her book *Burchill on Beckham* she describes the experience as men bringing out the worst in each other: 'Intent on playing out some sort of *danse macabre* amid the ruins of brute masculinity, determined to take as many as they can down with them.' Tanya isn't so easily convinced, saying, 'Following England remains a mainly masculine culture but that can vary from match to match. What determines the mood is the extent to which as fans we all feel our safety is at risk. When an outside threat becomes apparent the automatic response of some men is to retreat into the certainties of their masculinity.'

The presence of women fans challenges this reaction. Tanya is cautious about the pace of change but is nevertheless convinced something is beginning to happen thanks to the increasing, and often unnoticed, numbers of women who follow England home and away. 'Our presence dampens down the aggression. If women are around most men will behave differently.'

In an influential essay on the legacy of Prime Minister Margaret Thatcher, social commentator Helen Wilkinson describes twenty-first-century young women as increasingly assertive in pushing back the barriers of exclusion. They are 'Women who welcome the breaking down of gender stereotypes and who want the opportunity to develop their masculine as well as their feminine attributes.'

Football is undoubtedly part of this process. Alison Hale is a care-management team leader in Morley Health Centre on the outskirts of Leeds. Her small office is full of fellow fans. Paul follows Doncaster Rovers, Louise is a Liverpool supporter, while Alison's team is Sheffield Wednesday. Above her computer is pinned a picture of Sven-Goran Eriksson, a great manager in her view, though husband Les disagrees. 'He reckons Sven is a time-waster, an underachiever. He wanted him sacked after Euro 2004. We've argued about that plenty of times.'

Alison follows England with Les, though she first started going to football long before she met him. 'I was six years old. My dad would take me with my elder brother to see Barnsley at Oakwell. Joan and Carol, my cousins, would go too – sometimes my mum joined us as well.' Like many girls who were first taken by their parents, Alison lost interest in football as a teenager. 'There was schoolwork to do, and obviously lads to see too.' After leaving school and starting work in a local Littlewoods store, football became an even more distant childhood memory.

In 1980 Alison met Les. 'He took me to Hillsborough to watch Sheffield Wednesday. My dad went mad. Barnsley fans don't have much time for Wednesday.' The following year Alison and Les were married. 'Dad still wasn't too happy with the pair of us. He couldn't understand how people from Barnsley – Les was local too – could follow another town's club.'

Football dominated their married life. Les was playing three times a week, plus five-a-sides and turning out for his pub side on a Sunday. With two young children to bring up, Clare and Andrew, Alison was stuck at home for most of the 1980s – going to see Wednesday play was one of the pleasures she had to give up. Alison had left school at sixteen with no qualifications, so as the kids grew up and she became determined to go back to work she wasn't sure of her career prospects. Alison had always fancied nursing but without having passed the necessary O levels she thought she would have no chance, so when she saw a post as an unqualified auxiliary nurse advertised at her local job centre she snapped it up. In employment again, earning some extra money, and with their two kids now old enough to accompany them, very soon Alison and Les were organizing their weekends once again around going to see Sheffield Wednesday. For five years the four of them didn't miss a match, while during the week Alison used every spare moment to study to qualify as a Registered General Nurse. The trouble was, once she qualified, the promotion meant extra responsibilities and weekend shift work. Football once again lost its priority status in her life.

Parental responsibilities can be tough. With the children in their teens Les had started following England, home and away. Alison joined him too, going to all the World Cup 2002 qualifiers. But Alison had to miss out on going to Japan in 2002 as the finals clashed with Andrew's GCSE exams. She felt she had to be at home to support her son. Alison recognizes football has been a big part of their relationship with Les – it has brought them together. 'But it has its downsides too,' she admits, 'it's also kept us apart. However, when it came to travelling to Japan Alison was certain in her mind that Les should go: 'I insisted, he would be out there for the both of us. There was no point in us both missing out.'

Alison rather revels in the fact that in their private moments together Les admits following England is not the same without her there. On these trips they travel in a mainly male group. This sometimes has its disadvantages: 'There was ten of us in this villa in Portugal for Euro 2004. I was the only woman so they seemed to think I was there just to do the fry-ups every morning for them. I soon put them right on that.' Once she'd convinced all these men they were doing their own cooking she found herself acting as their counsellor. 'They were confiding in me how much they'd like it if their girlfriends or wives would travel with them like I do with Les. They were going home and sort of holding me up as a role model – "Alison enjoys it, I'm sure you would too dear".'

Football is a hugely emotional experience for Alison. Her late dad, who had first taken her to Oakwell, is celebrated at the Barnsley ground with a brick in the stadium wall the family paid for. On it is inscribed: WALT CLAY – A TRUE RED. The atmosphere Alison experienced as a child continues to thrill her today. 'I'm a watcher. For that moment when we score our fans will be the happiest people in the world. I love to see how they all react, look round at all those faces; beaming, smiling, cheering and shouting.'

Alison confounds the reason chick-lit author Jenny Colgan gives, writing in the *Independent*, for why women would choose to watch a match: 'Female football fans – hey, let's not kid ourselves here: female boyfriend fans – are investing in record numbers of football-related garments in the hopes of diverting the male gaze from its beer-pizza-telly axis.' Alison goes to a match to enjoy the game, not to provide a distraction for Les or any other bloke who might register his fancy. 'When Les was in Japan I was stuck at work crammed into our manager's office watching the Argentina game on the TV. Of course I missed Les. It was the longest we'd ever been apart, but I missed being at such a big match just as much.'

Alison loves her football, but she doesn't believe this attachment is the same as it is for the men in her life. 'Les and Andrew both play for the same pub side in the York League – there was one match when they were both sent off. All hell let loose between them at teatime when they each tried to explain away their foul to the other. I was just a bystander for that one.' This is the intimacy of the playing side, which Alison has no experience of. It is part of the equation of fandom that still only a few women share with male fans. This doesn't limit their involvement, it just makes it different.

Juliet Mayne has always been fascinated by football. But her dad wasn't interested, and there was no elder brother to take her either, so her childhood interest of the late 1970s and early 1980s remained just a memory long into adulthood. 'There was nobody at home even to talk football with. It was just an occasional TV thing. Liverpool always winning some cup or other.'

By the time Juliet went to secondary school she had learned enough about the game to understand she needed a team to support. Living in Lewisham, Millwall would have been the obvious local favourite, 'But I had heard enough about their racist reputation to make it impossible for me as a young black woman to give them my devotion.' Instead she adopted Crystal Palace and has followed them ever since, at first from an armchair then, since meeting partner Dave, as a regular at Selhurst Park. 'When I met Dave he was already a fan – Leicester City is his team – and he knew how keen I was finally to go to a match. He took me. We went to see Leicester, and straight away I felt safe. It was as if I belonged at a place like this, and it helped that this was a ground where black faces, particularly Asian, aren't uncommon.'

In her twenties, this first flush of live football action left Juliet desperate to take everything in. 'The floodlights, the sending-offs, the mug of tea at half-time, poring over the programme, I was hooked on the lot.' Juliet admits to an unusual bit of fortune that she and Dave share: 'It's lucky we support Leicester and Palace. Match tickets are much easier to get hold of for this pair than for the Premiership big boys.' The pair take in the games of each other's club. ' It is a good match we're looking for. That's something we have in common. Of course we want to see our own side win most of all, but appreciating the skill factor is important to both of us too.'

After going to Crystal Palace and Leicester City matches came their first England game. 'We'd seen an advert for a match at Wembley for a World Cup 98 qualifier. We were both worried about the racism I might have to put up with, but having enjoyed the league games so much we decided to give it a go.' The experience wasn't completely positive. 'At England home games the crowd are mainly really accommodating, mostly welcoming. But it isn't always like that. At Wembley you can't always choose who sits around you. A bit of bad luck and, at some games, instead of lots of friendly fans, we ended up next to a bunch I just didn't want to be anywhere near.'

Time has improved things. 'I feel much more comfortable now. People are less likely to go out of their way to block your view and refuse to budge, or give you abuse and fight. But it does still go on; no one can pretend it doesn't.' After their first few Wembley matches Juliet and Dave decided to join the England Members Club and apply for World Cup tickets. 'I'd always travelled. The Caribbean, Spain, Portugal, bits of France, so the whole idea of going to another country to see England play really appealed to me.'

Their first game, though, England's opening World Cup match in Marseilles, was quite a shock. 'It was great on the train down there, but once we arrived in the city we could feel the tension immediately. Neither of us felt safe. One moment we were having a drink in a bar with a bunch of really pleasant fans, made to feel welcome. Then in the next instant the place explodes. Glasses are flying, windows smashed, the place besieged by local Arab youth looking for the English to fight. We managed to get out. We escaped to our hotel and locked ourselves in our room. It was awful, horrible.' Match day, and after an easy England win, they decided to venture out again, this time to a restaurant for a celebratory meal. 'It was a lovely place, we were eating outside on the pavement. Then the police come crashing down the street. We're tear-gassed, forced inside. The waiters pulled the shutters down to protect all their customers from what was going on outside. They wouldn't allow us out until eventually it quietened down enough for us to retreat to the security of our hotel for the second night running, this time between lines of riot police.'

None of this managed to put Juliet off. 'The travelling, the journey getting there, is a big part of the thrill for me too. There's lots of laughs on the way so the unfortunate bits you tend to blank out once you get home. Any danger is certainly not part of the appeal!' Football has helped shape her relationship with Dave, as she says, 'It is certainly a big part of it but it's not everything. I'd say I quite like football, but Dave really loves it. We respect each other's differing level of commitment and cope with it. We both adore travelling though, so that equals things out a bit.'

During Euro 2004, columnist Mary Kenny commented in the *Guardian* on the growing influence of an inclusive Englishness associated with football: 'It is one of the few experiences of real community in a world tyrannized by individual egotism.' Juliet's own experience confirms this: 'I now feel relaxed as an England fan, confident in my place. Some might still think women fans are only there to ogle at the players' legs. Well, if that's what rocks your boat, so what? There's plenty of men there seduced by the glamour of it, they just don't admit to it.'

There remains one part of being a fan Juliet has still not fallen for. 'Trivia. I just can't get into all those facts and figures, who scored what, when, where. That is definitely a bloke's thing.'

Writing in the *Daily Telegraph* celebrity chef and self-anointed domestic goddess Nigella Lawson confessed during Euro 2004 she had discovered the joy of talking football.

> I think I am turning into a man. I blame the football. Much of my grocery order was taken up with an appraisal of Ledley King, whom I rate very highly, as does my grocer. What I've found out is that being a man is much less high-pressure than being a woman. Now that I'm a man, I have endless conversations in which nothing personal is said, and very relaxing it is. Female exchanges are drainingly personal. Worse, they are based on the free flow of insecurities.

The certainties of England's central-defence partnership have an appeal against which the calorific impact of the Atkins diet, or whether your bum looks big in this or that, clearly can't compete. Nigella was having a Hornbyesque conversational moment. Nick Hornby's classic account of life as a fan, *Fever Pitch*, contains this brilliant account of what talking football means for men: 'The first and easiest friends I made at college were football fans; a studious examination of a newspaper back page during the lunch hour of the first day in a new job usually provokes some kind of response. And yes, I am aware of the downside of this wonderful facility that men have: they become repressed, they fail in their relationships with women, their conversation is trivial and boorish, they find themselves unable to express their emotional needs.' What Nigella and tens of thousands of women probably quite unlike her have discovered is that, today, talking football is no longer a 'men only' preserve.

For almost as long as we've been together, my partner Anne has tussled with what Nigella went through in 2004 and what Nick Hornby has made a career out of writing about; the inclusion that football provides, and the exclusion it can provoke. Anne has written a book about it, *One of the Lads*, in which she summed up neatly the position many women fans find themselves in: 'We have not yet reached a stage where women fans are developing their own footballing counterculture. The result is that women, unlike men, rarely find the same kinds of bonding processes through football that men do so easily.'

When I first met Anne I was already a Spurs season-ticket-holder, though I wasn't one of those fans who had grown up with football. The bonding process, most often founded on a family connection to the club you choose to follow, hadn't been a big part of my entry into fandom either. As a child I grew up in the north Surrey commuter belt. Ours was a lower-middle-class family and in the late '60s football wasn't something that particularly shaped our family life. The local flower show was what my dad was more concerned about on the day of the 1966 World Cup final. It rained and nobody came – I wonder why?

By 1970 I was busily nagging my parents to fill their tanks up with as much Esso petrol as their car would take so I could complete my World Cup Coin Collection. These are the tools with which masculinity is shaped, 'swapsies' injecting boys with that curious fascination for trivia and obsession. The occasional match added to my growing interest in football. Crystal Palace were the nearest league side so it was their games I mostly saw, though sometimes Chelsea too. Fandom wasn't that important to me. I don't have the inherited link with a club from an early age that others can boast. Instead I just became bookishly obsessed with the records of all and sundry sports.

On the pitch I was worse than useless. A bewildering lack of eye and foot co-ordination coupled with a rather too ample teenage tummy ruled out any place in the school first eleven. Notwithstanding my near-total lack of footballing prowess it was the compulsive consumption of the facts, figures and history of the game that gave me a head start for my future fandom compared to Anne. She hadn't had the benefit of those early-years preparation. When knowledge of the game is reduced down to trivia, it is nearly impossible for women who become fans when they're adults to catch up with all this 'boys' own' education.

It wasn't until I moved to Tottenham in my mid-twenties that football became anything like as significant to me as it is now. My late teens and twenty-something years were dominated by left-wing politics. Rocking against racism, banning the bomb, digging deep for the miners. I did the lot and still have the badges to prove it. The revolution always seemed just around the corner. If I could just finish reading another volume of Marx or Gramsci, grapple with the implications of designer-socialism, and flog a few more copies of *Marxism Today*, then Britain would be set fair on its road to socialism. Not much time was left for football, apart from a cursory glance at the back pages now and then. But not for too long. Overdosing on feminist texts had left me deriding all the blokiness of football. How could these stadiums full of men possibly have any redeeming features?

Thankfully the fan activism of the early 1990s put me right. Rogan Taylor had helped found the FSA. After Italia 90 he wrote a piece in the magazine that I was busy selling to fellow earnest idealists, *Marxism Today*, about the changes in England fan culture. 'A new wave of post-fanzine football fan is emerging. They combine a genuine enthusiasm for the game with a raised critical awareness of its past mismanagement and recognize the new role they might play in its future.' Rogan's account made a lot of sense. My latent enthusiasm for the game was further reignited by reading the early issues of the fanzine *When Saturday Comes* and by the steady flow of books recounting fans' experiences I would collect on weekly trips to the Sportspages bookshop on Charing Cross Road. There was something stirring in football which had a passion and meaningfulness that, it was slowly dawning on me, most of politics, of whatever complexion, sorely lacked.

By the time Anne came along I was gradually dumping all the meetings, conferences, resolution writing and endless pointless rows that take up far too much time of any self-respecting political activist. Not completely though – we first met at a seminar which set out on the hopeless task of defining postmodernism. A somewhat untypical evening's entertainment but the sort of thing serious-minded types would get up to in 1990s Stoke Newington.

Anne knew politicking was something we shared, so she could put up with that, but as football relentlessly took its place this was a new relationship challenge. Still, I was sort of certain that if she liked me then surely she would like going to football with me too. I hadn't jettisoned all those feminist principles – our relationship would always be founded on sharing. I had Spurs to share with her, what could be fairer than that? Fortunately, or otherwise I guess we wouldn't still be together, Anne had some affection for an afternoon spent watching an under-performing club that last won the league over forty years ago, if not quite as much as me. There was something about the raised hopes, so swiftly dashed, which White Hart Lane provided week after week, that became faintly irresistible for me, and more or (to be honest) less the same for Anne.

When England became my additional obsession, Anne's introduction to the perverse joy of the collective misery that Spurs so regularly provides for its fans came in handy – it meant my powers of persuasion required less flexing than otherwise might have been required. This would be different, I told her. England means trips to Europe, whereas we realized early on Spurs would be unlikely to provide much in the way of European competition. Plus the team at least have a half-chance of glory.

Together we have shared in the excitement of our first England away trip, our first World Cup, the 5–1 stuffing of Germany in Munich and post-match sushi in Sapporo. But I have to admit all of this has become mixed up with me imposing my priorities on Anne, confusing togetherness with the smothering of difference. Many women do of course share their partners' fandom, but they must also have the space to define it for themselves; not be measured by masculine standards of commitment and emotional investment but by their own. Wading through all that 'if you know your history' isn't for Anne. Her undying devotion to Paul Scholes is good enough for her and she doesn't need the match statistics to back her choice of all-time favourite England player.

Anne likes her home comforts abroad. On away trips she demands her fair share of sightseeing, leaving me to read through the match reports on a bench amongst the ruins of Sintra castle in Portugal while she studies the view. And if I can't find another conversation piece apart from who should be starting up front for England, I might be looking forward to some stony-faced silences over the breakfast table. But funnily enough I wouldn't have it any other way. Her rounded enjoyment of a four-week trip to a tournament, or a few days in a foreign city for an away match, helps keep the dark side of obsession at bay. When all that matters in life is the game, the football nation loses too much of its humanity for my liking.

Julie Nerney puts her fandom down firmly to her father. The ritual of Saturdays spent together as father and small child at Villa Park are still fresh some thirty years later. 'The bus journey to the ground and the interminably long walk. Through the turnstile then buy a programme. I would stop to check my pocket in case I'd forgotten my pen to mark off the team selection and then we would walk up the steps to enter the stand. The whole magical picture of the stadium would unfold before my eyes, and always, whatever the weather, the green of the grass would be so bright and rich it would take my breath away.'

Her dad passed away in 1987 but the memories are still with Julie: 'Me and my dad, together, for a whole Saturday.' For a while after his death she felt it wouldn't be the same without him, so she gave up going. 'But then I realized it was about more than being a place we went together. It was somewhere he had taken me to show what loyalty and passion meant, about believing in something, and if I stopped going I would be in danger of losing the meaning of those qualities in my life.'

Julie never followed England with her dad: her first England match was Poland away in 1989, two years after his death. 'Katowice was intimidating,' she says. 'The ground was in a terrible state. There was a constant threat of violence. And there were hardly any other women amongst England's support either.' Despite all this Julie didn't feel out of place. 'I had been to enough Villa games that nobody, English or Polish, was going to make me feel uncomfortable about being there.'

A year later she made it out to the group stages for England's Italia 90 campaign. 'I didn't have the money, or the time off work, to stay any longer but I knew that this was where I belonged.' Julie has the credentials of following her club side, home and away, for more than thirty years, and England likewise for fifteen years, but she still finds she has to prove herself to others. 'When men I work with find out I follow England, they are always surprised how long I've been doing it, the number of games I've been to. It can be a bit of a posture, asserting yourself as a woman fan, but once I've got that out the way we can all relax and talk football.' Julie doesn't have much time for those who criticize women who have joined in more recently. 'I joined in around Italia 90. If others join in after Euro 2004 who am I to question that? All that matters is that they are there for the right reasons, to see some football and support the team.'

Having missed England's march through the knockout stages to the semifinal in Italy, Julie was determined now to follow England as much as she could. Work sometimes thwarted her commitment but she hardly missed a qualifier in the Euro 92 and USA 94 campaigns, travelling on her own. It was those early years at Villa Park with her dad that equipped her with the resilience to be a solo woman on these trips and to share in the energetic appeal that being a fan meant to her most of all.

In 1998 she managed to persuade her boyfriend Pieter, who preferred rugby to football, to join her at the World Cup. 'He'd never been to a football match before. I had to explain all the rules to him, which got in the way. I wanted to concentrate on the match.' But there was a pride too. Taking someone along who was new to the game. Introducing them to it, just like her dad had done with her. 'Best of all, it was great when we scored to have some-one to celebrate with.' But Pieter's liking for the game proved short-lived and he refused to join Julie at Euro 2000. 'I'd gone on my own before so it was no big deal doing it that way again.'

After marrying in 2001 they are no longer together. Julie now recognizes how seriously their inability to share football affected their relationship. 'There was a lot we shared but after France 98, never football. So sometimes I wouldn't go, which meant I was losing some of my freedom. Football is a huge part of my life and this wasn't getting the recognition from my husband it deserved.' Julie is fairly certain in her mind much of this was to do with gender. 'Football is still a male pursuit. If you're a woman who follows a team and your boyfriend, or husband, isn't a fan then problems are almost bound to arise.' She doesn't blame the football on its own for the break-up – 'it was my choice in the end' – but it certainly played a part.

Now Julie travels with her new partner James. A Southampton fan since his teens, James still cannot match Julie for her length of commitment to the England cause. She has been to far more England games than James, but never mind, Julie jokes, she still treats him as an equal. 'I know now that without James the trips wouldn't be as much fun. It wouldn't be the end of the world – football is too important to me not to go just because James can't, but there would be something missing.' Football is what Julie describes as their 'unspoken bond'. It is what has brought the pair of them together, and while bigger emotions than even England winning a trophy could inspire have kept them together, it has given them shared experiences they are never likely to forget. Julie admits being with James has helped make following England away more sociable: 'It's easier to get on with people being a couple, but if other men think I'm just along for the ride he soon puts them right – he knows his place!'

Jenny Walker dates her fandom back to the immediate post-war years: 'I was living with my mother and grandmother in Croydon.

On Saturdays I was left alone as Mum was out at work and there was no school to go to, and I became hooked on the radio commentaries.' In this all-female household Jenny invented her own way to be a fan. 'I cut up some cardboard boxes and made a league table with tabs for each team, so every Sunday I could check the results and move the teams' positions around.'

Televised football didn't arrive for Jenny until two decades later. 'It wasn't until the 1966 World Cup I finally saw a football match on TV. We had one with a tiny nine-inch screen and six of us all crowded round it for the finals.' She was now married and following the fortunes of her local club Crystal Palace on the back pages. Jenny's husband wouldn't let her go to a match. 'He absolutely refused, and I didn't think it was worth causing a fuss.'

In the early 1970s her husband had to work abroad. 'I saw him off at Heathrow, rushed home, phoned a few friends and together we went to Selhurst Park. They all knew how much this meant to me after all these years of my husband's opposition.' Instantly she knew this was where she belonged every Saturday, but Jenny was in for a shock when her husband returned to Britain a couple of years later. 'He had the bloody cheek to say he would join me on the terraces, to look after me, I suppose. I told him I didn't care what he did. There was no way he could stop me going, not ever again.' The time apart had changed everything and within a few years the pair had parted. Jenny became a Palace regular, standing first on the Holmesdale End, always there early to get a good view. Then she moved to the opposite end when the new stand was built, which is where her seat has been ever since.

Her commitment to following England came long after her first Crystal Palace match. 'It was Euro 96, everybody at work was talking about the tournament and I decided to go. It must have taken six hours on the phone trying to book tickets, but I'm pretty bloody-minded when I set my heart on something so I wasn't put off by that.' And she wasn't intimidated by the crowds either: 'Oh, no. I might be on my own but surrounded by everybody singing, bouncing up and down on the escalator, wearing their colours, I love all that.

England in 1996 made Jenny feel at home. For the next four years she didn't miss a single home match. By now she was retired and had time on her hands, and there was no husband standing in her way either. She decided she would like to go away with England too. 'I was a bit wary. I had never done anything quite like it before. England were playing in Amsterdam, February 2002. I didn't get to know anybody on that trip, but I didn't mind that too much. I was new to all this, and I'd had enough of a good time to convince myself I wanted to do it again.'

The following year Jenny followed England to South Africa. 'My son was convinced this was the last he would ever see of me. I soon put him right. I'm quite capable of looking after myself, thank you very much.' During 2004 Jenny made it to ten away games. She travelled to Portugal for the European Championships, and saw matches in Sweden, Austria, Poland, Azerbaijan and Spain. 'There's people I meet on one trip and then see a couple of months later on the next one. We have plenty to talk about and catch up on. That makes a difference compared to when I first started going. I fit in now, and never feel under threat or made to feel unwelcome. Quite the opposite, I'm amongst friends.'

There is one rather curious impediment to Jenny's travelling though. 'Most weekday games are on Wednesday nights, and I teach ballroom dancing on a Thursday night. I quite often have to rush back from the other side of Europe to get back in time for the class.' I am fairly certain that while the number of women fans is on the increase, ballroom-dance teachers remain few in number amongst our travelling support.

Jenny is an experienced club fan, and this certainly helps her with knowing what to expect, the things you have to put up with. Now in her late sixties, she spent most of her working life studying balance sheets in the offices of various insurance companies. It is a background that probably gave Jenny her well-organized manner. Standing up to her husband's obstinate opposition to her going to football provided Jenny with the realization of what her independence meant to her. As for the ballroom dancing, Jenny is convinced even this adds something to her fandom. 'It gives me great spatial awareness. I never bump into anybody when we're all coming out of a stadium in one tightly packed fast-moving crowd.' All this contributes to her self-confidence in what remains a very male environment. 'I can understand people standing up at games. I do it myself. But somebody standing on top of a seat and completely blocking my view I won't put up with. I'll tell them that, however big they might be. The same goes for those who block the aisles when they pile in late. At my age I need a handrail to get down steps safely. I have to tell them to get out of my way.'

Back home at the ballroom dancing, Jenny's students think she's crazy, finding it hard to square their instructor with the image of England fans they have. 'They're always saying, fondly I'm sure, that they now know an England fan who's old enough to know better.'

Growing up in Marlow, rugby union was much more popular than football amongst Camilla Castree's family and friends. Football doesn't feature very much in her memories of childhood or adolescence. Then in 1993 Ian Wright entered Camilla's life. 'Ours was never a football household but I sort of became interested that season when Wrighty was scoring all those goals that helped Arsenal win both the League and FA Cup. The finals were on the TV and I just found myself watching them and enjoying myself.'

Back then Camilla was working for British Airways and cheap flights were one of her perks. England were playing Brazil in a pre-World Cup tournament in Washington. With the offer of cut-price tickets on Concorde she found it easy enough to convince her mum and dad to join her on the trip. 'The match was a completely new experience for me, I'd never felt such intensity, and this was only a friendly.'

Back home the fateful World Cup 94 qualifying campaign continued, and after enjoying Washington Camilla decided she would go to Rotterdam for the crucial group match against Holland. This time she would be on her own. 'I only saw one other woman on that trip, and she was with a bloke. But all the guys around me were really sweet. They kept checking I was OK, that I could see. Then in an instant they would change from these gentlemen into animals as soon as the rocket flares started landing amongst us. They were ripping up the plastic seats and throwing them back at where the fireworks had come from.' This was an extreme expression of masculinity, though Camilla felt as a woman she was part of this culture too: 'It was strange, but I felt protected, and that made me feel as if belonged too. The riot police certainly treated me just the same as the guys. They seemed to think I was about to attack them too. That made me angry but also aware of how this kind of offensive policing made the men around me feel. I'd never been in a situation quite like it before.'

A few days after returning from Rotterdam, at the office where Camilla worked everybody was talking about both the match and the widely reported crowd trouble. 'I was the only one who'd actually been there. It was quite scary really the way people reacted to me when I told them.' The negative reaction from workmates wasn't enough to put her off. 'Two years later, and after a lot more games at both Highbury and with England at Wembley, I went to Dublin for the friendly in 1995. I travel on my own and I felt I knew what I was letting myself in for by now but I never expected the match would have to be abandoned because of rioting in the stands. I'm not particularly political, so all that anti-IRA stuff and the far-right groups that stirred it up that night wasn't something I was aware of.'

It was a rude awakening for Camilla. 'I remember a couple of blokes standing to my right after the match had had to be abandoned. They were congratulating themselves for what they'd accomplished. It was pretty obvious it was all pre-planned. I'd just been looking forward to a football match. I knew there might be some trouble but nothing like this. My night was ruined, the trip wasted – I wasn't happy.'

After the game was stopped Camilla was glad to make it safely back to where she was staying. 'There were all these fans, theirs and ours, with badly bloodied faces, really nasty wounds. I didn't hang about. At my hotel the Irish were really good. They reassured the English fans recovering in their bar. They didn't blame us, let alone hate us.' Their comforting words didn't stop Camilla from being ashamed. 'I'd never thought football could have such an impact on what it means to be English. The next morning I didn't even want to hail a taxi. What would my accent tell the driver about me after a night like that?' So why did she keep going? 'Hooligans – the name sounds a bit glamorous, but they're just bullies. If we give in to bullies we've got nothing left.'

Camilla has another football experience apart from following Arsenal and England as a fan, which seems to reveal there is something worthwhile in comparing and contrasting the differing experiences of male and female supporters. For eight seasons she worked as a crowd steward at Highbury. 'The women stewards are more effective. We don't intimidate. We ask fans politely to abide by any regulations, and they tend to be too embarrassed to give us any serious grief. We get a few comments, of course, but not as much as you might expect.' As a fan Camilla also recognizes the difference the presence of women can make as part of the crowd. 'We break up this great mass of maleness. Instead of this huge group of men all together there's pockets of women. It does make a difference, however subtle.'

Since Bulgaria away in 1999 Camilla has travelled with the same group of mates to England matches. 'There's more women in our group now than when I first started, which makes it easier to join in the conversations. That is definitely more difficult for a woman on her own with all these blokes. Although the ones who know me know I'm there for the football. This also stops any resentment from other women, as I'm single and a lot of the guys who have wives and girlfriends still travel without them.'

After going to the 2002 World Cup Camilla took a year off football, travelling the world instead. 'I didn't miss it as much as I thought I would. There is no great compulsion inside of me that I simply must go at the cost of everything else that interests me. I'm not obsessive about football. I go when I do because I want to, not to keep up appearances.'

So there is something different in the attachment to the game for many women. 'I'd say I was more rounded in what I feel I get, and sometimes don't get, out of football. I'm less likely just to get swept along, going just because that's what is expected of me, behaving in a certain way because that's what everybody else does. In a sense it is easier for a woman to be a fan. We are less anonymous, not as much part of the crowd, because there's fewer of us. Our experience is more individualized.'

Following England for Camilla, like most fans, is wrapped up with expressing a popular patriotism. 'It's not just the football, there's a real feeling of national pride in an England crowd. Not a lot of people can define what being English means, but maybe it's just about taking part in something that makes you feel good about your nationality. All these fans of different clubs, bitter rivals too, united behind England – where else would you get so many people putting those differences aside?'

George Orwell was one of those who tried to come up with a definition of Englishness: 'Solid breakfasts and gloomy Sundays, smoky towns and winding roads, green fields and red pillar boxes.' But compiling these neat lists of what we have in common is an increasingly out-of-date task. I prefer the contradictions of Englishness that Miranda Sawyer, writing in the *Observer*, catalogued: 'Other countries can't decide whether we're a nation of football hooligans or homosexuals, of princesses or slags. Because we are all and none of these things.' Miranda defies the inclination to offer a pre-packaged summary of Englishness, preferring something less structured.

> It's you. It's me. It's all of us. Clichés to a man, woman and child; yet individuals one and all. We may all fit nicely into politicians' neat-speak (are you a Mondeo Man or a Pebble-dash Person?), we may boil down to self-help stereotypes (me Martian, you Venusian), we may find it convenient to dismiss each other with an airy 'you know the type', but we are all more complex, more tricky and wayward and human than any classification could ever reveal.

This understanding of what it means to be English has something in common with Camilla's enjoyment of just being a part of an England crowd, while contributing something herself to what that crowd means, both to itself and to others.

None of the women fans I spoke to described their fandom as symbolic of feminism. Nor did I expect them to. Fans, male and female, are too often categorized by outside observers under the influence of their own political ideas. They want to impose their models of explaining human behaviour on this group of assorted individuals going by the name of I-N-G-E-R-L-A-N-D. At the same time it would be foolhardy to think we can divorce football from the society in which it is played and supported.

Ros Coward in her book *Sacred Cows* details the processes that are shaping the experience of women at the start of the new century. Male networking survives, but increasingly in the face of a growing self-esteem of women in public life. Men remain obsessively interested both in each other and themselves, but today are forced to compromise with their girlfriends, partners and wives, who have better expectations than ever before. Some men may maintain a hostility to women, but they do so now in the knowledge and experience of how powerful a few women have become. And sex no longer takes place in an environment of female financial dependence on male partners. Coward concludes: 'This is not a society in which feminism's old descriptions work any longer. It doesn't have simple gender lines. It has many different occasions, practices, lifestyles and styles in which gender is a significant division but not one which consistently ascribes discrimination to one side of that division.'

Women remain a minority following England. This doesn't mean they are an insignificant presence nor that all of those who go are victims of discrimination. If it was as bad as that then why are the numbers of female England fans growing? Their presence is changing what it means to be I-N-G-E-R-L-A-N-D, helping to soften its roughest edges but not necessarily in order to dull the brightness of commitment and loyalty that makes us fans not spectators.

I'm always a little uneasy about joining in that chant, 'England till I die. I know I am, I'm sure I am, I'm England till I die.' It reminds me of the old *Monty Python* 'I'm a lumberjack and I'm

OK' sketch – it states the bleeding obvious. We're hardly going to swap being English for French, never mind German, are we? But then the *Python* sketch collapses into a heap of hilarity as the lumberjacks reveal a preference for cross-dressing – all that pumped-up masculinity wasn't as secure as we first thought. The 'England till I die' chant lacks the sublime surrealism that Cleese and company came up with to subvert certainty; instead it is numbingly definitive, imagining Englishness as something we are born into, unchanging, not an identity we can make up as we go along.

Simply by being there, and making their presence felt in a culture of a rare masculine intensity, women fans are part of the making of I-N-G-E-R-L-A-N-D. A national identity not pre-packaged, historically determined, or in our blood, thank you very much. Instead, a do-it-yourself nationality founded on the freedom and independence that staking your place, as women fans are invariably required to do more than any man will ever have to, demands. Of course, this isn't the cause which fires up Alison, Eileen, Tanya and all the other women who follow England. They are there, every bit as much as the men, for the football. But if their presence helps change the I-N-G-E-R-L-A-N-D we thought we knew for the better, then who but the most embittered male chauvinist – or national chauvinist, for that matter – is going to complain?

5

Red, White and Black All Over

England versus Turkey, a Euro 2004 qualifier at the Stadium of Light, Sunderland. The atmosphere has a raw, undiluted intensity, our crowd the loudest in a long time, the fans' commitment unquestionable. They roar as every pass reaches every player it is intended for. They cheer each move forward across the halfway line towards the Turkish goal. These are supporters determined that our team gives no quarter in their contest with the Turks.

Turkey have never scored a goal against England, let alone scrambled a victory. It's not so long ago we were able to rack up cricket scores against this lot: 8–0 twice, in 1984 and 1987, 5–0 in 1985, 4–0 in 1992. But after qualification for Euro 96 Turkey have become a fast-improving side. They did better than us at Euro 2000, making it through to the second round. Then at World Cup 2002 they reached the semifinal and finished third.

Turkish fans have a fearsome reputation. An away leg in Turkey for our club sides is full of trepidation for the supporters. The 'Welcome to Hell' banners at Istanbul airport became a grisly reality for the two Leeds lads murdered by machete-wielding Turkish thugs on the eve of their match with Galatasaray a few years ago.

England had just returned from a frankly undistinguished away victory over tiny Liechtenstein. Turkey were top of the group and playing as well as they had during their highly impressive campaign in the 2002 World Cup. The night was sizing up as a marker in the changing European football order.

Add to this the particular circumstances. Asylum-seeker hysteria had been raging in the tabloids for months. The scare stories of benefit scroungers, health tourists and the swamping of communities mounted up, accompanied by a barely disguised editorialized combination of ignorance and hatred. Turks, they're just another bunch of immigrants, aren't they? After the Twin Towers came crashing down in an orgy of international terrorism the West's 'war on terror' has become hopelessly confused with a demonizing of most things Muslim in the popular mind. Turkey is engaged in its own political struggle of definition: European or Asian? Secular or Islamic?

But never mind all that. Tonight, they'll do as surrogate Iraqis and their al-Qaeda pals. 'Attack! Attack! Attack Iraq!' replaces the jolly humming of *The Great Escape* theme for a sizeable proportion of the crowd. The local conditions aren't too favourable either. Sunderland is the only city in England where the British National Party will contest every single council seat in the forthcoming local elections. The area is 98 per cent white, lacking the multicultural environment other cities now boast, proudly or otherwise.

I'm at the game with Pritpal, 'Pritt' to his mates. This was the second England game we'd travelled to together. His first game had been the friendly against Australia in February. 'My friend Smit had come with me to that match. There was a moment of uncertainty before we set off. We didn't know what to expect, but then we just thought, fuck it, what's stopping us? Let's go.' Before the Australia match there was an encounter that almost made them think again, as Pritpal explains: 'We were wearing our St George Cross T-shirts on the way to the game and the platform where we were waiting for the tube was full of young Bangladeshis. There was thirty or forty of them, all looking at us and we knew exactly what they were thinking, "Who are these Indians with their St George Crosses?" I can sympathize with that anxiety, that doubt, but I also had an absolute pride in what I was doing, the flag I was wearing, the team I was supporting. If I take that shirt off for someone else, black or white, then I'm allowing them to dictate who I am.'

Pritpal is thirty years old. He lives in London having grown up in Leicester. 'In the 1980s Leicester was a scary place for an Asian kid to be a football fan. I was restricted to watching games on TV. We all thought the Leicester City ground, Filbert Street, was too unsafe for us to go to. We'd heard stories of racial abuse and vicious attacks by the Leicester City hooligans, the "Baby Squad". It was our folklore; probably untrue, but it sounded real enough so why take the risk? The graffiti we saw in our own neighbourhood always linked football with a violent racist hatred, and that was enough to confirm our worst fears of football crowds.'

It was different at the local park or in the school playground. 'We all played football. There was nothing else to do and at that age, thankfully, everyone was colour-blind. Race just wasn't an issue. If you wanted to play you got a game.' By the time of the 1986 Mexico World Cup all of Pritpal's family were England fans. 'Mum even came out of the kitchen to watch the TV. In those days that was a big event in an Asian household!'

There was a real sense of enjoyment and participation, but a contradiction still complicated what football meant to Pritpal. 'We watched football on the TV. We learned to love the game without actually going. It meant we could become supporters without all the negatives we still associated with the game. But they hadn't gone away. At school the bullying, the racial abuse, was all mixed up with football. Those who picked on us because we were Asian always claimed to be hooligans. They probably weren't, just kidology, but it worked. We were convinced we wouldn't be welcome at any football ground and that no decent people actually went.'

In the early 1990s Pritpal left home to study medicine at Birmingham University. 'I'd lost interest in playing while studying for my A levels, and at university the sports-club culture was so suffocatingly middle-class, joining one of the university teams didn't appeal to me. Then a friend offered to take me to Villa Park to see a match. I don't mind admitting that I was petrified. I was convinced that there would be trouble. I was astounded by just how little there was, and certainly none of it was directed at me. The authenticity of the experience was overwhelming. If this was what being a fan was really like I was determined that I would become a part of it.'

Far more England fans will cheer the team on from in front of a TV than ever make it to a home match, never mind travel across Europe, or further afield to a tournament or a qualifier. Nevertheless 'being there' remains crucial to the essence of fandom. This is where the black and Asian absence is noticeable, not just at England games, but league matches too. I live in Haringey, one of the most multiracial boroughs in the country. The latest census in 2001 recorded 87 per cent of the English population as white – in Haringey this falls to 65 per cent. On a match day as I cycle up the High Road past Seven Sisters Tube station and through the hustle and bustle of Bruce Grove towards White

Hart Lane, the streets are a clash of Caribbean, African, Indian, Chinese, Turkish and Kurdish, and East European faces and voices.

Yet White Hart Lane is defiantly *White* Hart Lane. When the crowd sing 'C'mon you Lilywhites' it is a chorus of Anglo-Saxon voices, even if the team is made up mostly of second and third-generation immigrants, with team-mates from South Korea, Egypt, Morocco and elsewhere. If I wanted to celebrate my whiteness there are few places more exclusively white than a football stadium's stands. But if we include in our definition of fans all those cheering on their side in front of the TV, the picture is totally different. I rarely watch a Spurs home match in a local pub – with a season ticket I don't need to – but sometimes if there's an away game I can't make I'll pop down the pub at the end of our road.

The punters there are all Spurs. They're out of their seats, shouting, cursing, cheering when we win. Their knowledge of the team is comprehensive, they know their match and player statistics, are able to quote games and performances I've long forgotten. And they're practically all black. While the crowd at the ground is virtually all white, the Spurs fan base, outside of the stadium, is as representative of its locality as you might wish for. To a lesser or greater extent, depending on locality and the success or failure of the team, the same is true of most clubs, and increasingly England's support too.

After graduating in 1998 Pritpal spent a big chunk of his first pay cheque on an Aston Villa season ticket, and he has renewed it every year since. But England initially was a different matter. 'During Euro 96 I quickly realized just how strong this anti-England thing was amongst the Asian lads I watched the games with. They all wanted England to lose.' He puts this antagonism down to two principal reasons: 'Firstly, it's a reaction to the racism we had to put up with in our adolescent and teenage years – you don't forget that in a hurry. And secondly, we're not exactly turned on by all the pumped-up English patriotism. In fact we tend to resent it. Instead we prefer a more reassured appreciation of the quality of the football, the movement of the ball, passing, formations.'

The way supporting England is often expressed actively repels him: 'Why should we have to hate just about anyone we play? We've grown up with the consequences of that sort of hatred. If it's the Turks this week just because England have a match against them, will it be back to us after that?' Add all this together and it is hardly surprising there was little support for England amongst Pritpal's mates. Ten years on he senses a polarization unfolding. 'There is both a growing acceptance that it's OK to support England and an intensification of resistance to it, from both blacks and whites.'

The home game against Turkey exposed the seriousness of these contradictions. 'I knew I could be mistaken for a Turk. I felt much more at risk than at the Australia friendly a few months previously. The tension was there from the moment I arrived at the ground. People making eye contact, sizing me up, thinking, "What's he doing here?" It made me feel uncomfortable, but if I'd not been going to football for so long and sort of knew what was going on I would have been terrified.' Pritpal was glad he was wearing his St George Cross T-shirt. 'It was both a badge of pride, and it was my protection too. The hatred for Turkey that night wasn't just about the football, it was racial as well. If I'd not been wearing that shirt I could have very easily been a victim of it.'

Pritt is also certain the problem of racism can often be misunderstood by well-meaning white observers. 'Protective measures are something any Asian is used to taking. There is nothing unusual about that. It doesn't justify what we have to put up with, and no one is happy about it either. But simply by being there, at this or any other match, we actively challenge the racism that says we don't belong. The racists absolutely don't want me there supporting England, so if I let them stop me going they've won, haven't they?'

Pritpal wasn't the only one wary of the atmosphere that night. 'Stand up if you hate —' whoever the other lot are is something you hear at just about every club ground, week in week out. I've never been to a Spurs match without being asked by the entire Paxton and Park Lane ends to 'Stand up if you hate Arsenal'. Not very nice, but part and parcel of that confusing collision of the embittered and the banter that makes us fans rather than spectators. That much I can just about put up with. At the Stadium of Light 'Stand up if you hate Turkey' was chanted with a real venom: a racialized hatred for an entire country, their culture, and everything associated with it. In some parts of the ground the chanting very soon became racially abusive – 'I'd rather be a Paki than a Turk' – and where Gary Kitching was sitting one group of fans even turned on England's black players. 'How do I explain to my six-year-old why his hero is being called a "black bastard"?'

The explanation of all this isn't helped by simply seeking to expel all emotions in the cause of civility. In *The Times* Simon Barnes pointed to the mix that made the atmosphere at the Stadium of Light both repulsive and attractive: 'The night of England's match against Turkey was out of control: dark, hysterical, disturbing. It was also powerful, thrilling, inspiring and splendid because passion is not a simple matter. Passion inspires people to love, self-sacrifice, courage. It also inspires people to hatred and murder. Football is full of good things, and full of horrible things. A bit like life, really – and passion is at the heart of most of the good and the bad.'

Would those chants of 'I'd rather be a Paki than a Turk' have been sung if there had been a more obvious black England presence in the stands? Does the fact there are no England players from an Asian background mean that while many feel they can get away with 'Paki', trying it on with the equally offensive 'coon', or 'nigger' or something else from the vile vocabulary of racism is almost unheard of? Piara Powar, director of the antiracist Kick it Out campaign, is certain that a more significant Asian representation in the stands would make a difference. Commenting in the *Guardian* after the Turkey match, he summed up the potential impact very sharply: 'To put it crudely, you're less likely to shout "I'd rather be a Paki than a Turk" if there's a Paki sitting next to you.'

Jos Johnson has always watched and played football. He has lived in Leicester since he was seven years old, and his first footballing memory was watching the 1968 European Cup final when Manchester United thrashed Benfica at Wembley 4–1. Like plenty of kids all over the country, he woke up the next morning a true Red.

And it started him off playing too. In the street at first, mostly with other black kids, playing disorganized games with makeshift goals. But as a child Jos never went to see Man United play at Old Trafford, or make it to Filbert Street to watch Leicester City either. His parents had split up, so his mum's priority was to earn the money to keep their household together. There was no spare time or cash to take Jos to any matches.

Jos can first remember watching England on TV in 1973. 'It was that decisive World Cup qualifier against Poland. Peter Shilton was in goal, a Leicester City player, so that helped convince me I should support England. By the end of the game I really, really wanted them to win.' But this was still unusual amongst most black kids in the 1970s. 'Hardly anybody else I knew was interested in England, never mind supported them.' Instead, Brazil was the favoured team. 'They were a predominantly black team – their style of play was laid-back yet hugely skilful. After World Cup 1970 our heroes were Pelé, Jairzinho, Rivelino, never Charlton, Moore or Banks. Even the colours Brazil wore, yellow and green, reminded us of our own Jamaican flag.'

Jos doesn't mind admitting his support for England has never been unconditional. 'In the 1970s England were an all-white team. It wasn't until 1978 that Viv Anderson became the first black England player. But Brazil were hardly ever on the TV, so the memories faded. We all got to know, and to idolize, the England players. A fair few of them were either current or ex-Leicester City players: Shilton, Alan Clarke, Keith Weller, and this helped our interest in and support for the national team to develop too.'

By now Jos was playing schools football on a regular basis. Every Saturday morning would begin with a game, while the day ended with watching *Match of the Day*. On a Sunday he managed to get out of going to the local Pentecostal church with his mum by signing up to a Sunday league side. Through the 1970s more and more black players broke into club football. 'Viv Anderson being picked for England was hugely important. For the first time I felt there really was a place for black people in football. But we expressed our participation by playing, rather than going to matches as fans.'

For Jos, where England fits in remains uncertain. 'This is my home. Once we accept this, and others do too, then we can move on. There's plenty who still feel they are outcasts, unwelcome, and that's not right. But those of us that don't shouldn't be uncomfortable with our feelings of belonging either.' Jos is very clear what makes him still feel unsure about supporting England: 'When I went to my first England match, a friendly with Serbia

Montenegro at the Leicester Walkers Stadium in 2003, there was all this "No Surrender" and "Attack Iraq" stuff. What the hell has that got to do with football? I was shocked, angry.' But it wasn't enough to make Jos feel he didn't belong there. 'I was wearing my England shirt when I popped down the off-licence for some cans a few days after the game. I could see these lads giving me a double take. They couldn't believe I'd been to the game. It was great, we were chatting about the match and all that.'

A couple of months later I met up with Jos at the England match against Croatia at Portman Road, Ipswich. 'I felt more comfortable. I sort of knew what to expect, the good and the bad, and I was determined I wouldn't let anyone ruin the occasion for me. I was proud to be part of it too, so different to just watching the game on TV.'

At the Croatia game the FA produced car-window stickers, 'England Against Racism', which were placed on every single seat. It was this sort of effort that helped make Jos feel welcome. Sitting with Jos I felt pleased, and a little bit amazed. I never thought I'd see such a thing: 'England' and 'against racism' in the same sentence, complete with the three lions. A few rows in front of where we were sitting there was one fan desperately trying to rip up the sticker. He was getting more and more angry – plastic doesn't tear very easily. For once he didn't feel like he belonged. What must have made it even worse was the sight of all these kids picking up any of the stickers that had been left behind ready to plaster them over their bedroom windows that night.

After the match, a few fans complained to the FA about the stickers. They didn't like the message on them. If they felt threatened because their racist opinions were no longer defining what it means to be an England fan, then good. Their disgruntlement is a price worth paying.

*

Every weekend the park football pitches I jog past in south Tottenham are full of black players. Replica club shirts, and England ones too, are now worn in their tens of thousands by black and Asian kids. The one very particular place where black participation is almost completely absent is in the stands and on the terraces.

Is this continuing absence because of racism? Quite possibly, but a focus simply on blaming supporters for this is completely wrong – the patterns of exclusion are more complex than that. Most fans welcome the effective elimination of the racist abuse, monkey-chanting and throwing bananas at black players that once plagued our game. Of course we will always find exceptions, and to a large extent it is the rarity of the abuse that forces the attention on it, but I will never forget a freezing-cold October 2000 night in Helsinki, scene of a vital World Cup qualifier following defeat at home to Germany and the instant resignation of Kevin Keegan. Emile Heskey and Andy Cole put in one of the worst performances up front for England most of us had ever seen. We wanted them off. Almost anybody else, surely, would do better. Everyone around me was shouting, 'Get those two bastards off, get them off.' A midweek away England crowd is as hardcore as you can get, but not once was it about them being '*black* bastards' and that's the only distinction required. The colour of the shirt matters, not the colour of the skin underneath.

Four years later, another freezing-cold night, this time in Baku, Azerbaijan, and a badge seller is working his way down to where I'm sitting. One of the badges catches my eye: 'Asylum Seekers Out' was engraved in tiny letters encircling the St George Cross. To pretend this is a badge everybody who follows England would be proud to wear would be as wrong as pretending none would. Attitudes have changed, certainly enough to suggest that more black football fans might understand most crowds will welcome their presence. But it's not happening, and any increase in the numbers of black and Asian fans at England games remains painfully slow.

Black fans are mainly second or third generation. Their parents were much less interested in the game than they are. The natural inclination amongst new fans is to be drawn towards the biggest, most successful, clubs: Liverpool, Manchester United, Arsenal and, most recently, Chelsea. To get a ticket to one of these games is very hard, as a huge proportion are pre-sold to season-ticket holders and members of various club schemes. The remainder will be sold out within a matter of hours when they go on general sale four weeks or more before kickoff. The result is watching football becomes something you become used to doing at home, or down the pub. Actually going to matches doesn't feature strongly in your fandom.

England tickets are just as difficult to get hold of. Most home matches will sell out anything up to three months before a game takes place, snapped up by those with the knowledge of on-sale dates. Or, better still, membership of englandfans, the official supporters' club which awards priority booking to those who belong. Tickets are pricey, but not much more than a night out clubbing, with drinks, a taxi home and the latest designer labels to purchase. However, if this is how you and your friends are already spending any spare cash, there's not much left over for football. All of these factors, not simply the fear and expectation of a racist reception, add up to exclusion and absence. Of course, plenty of lower-division clubs have row after row of empty seats and vacant terraces, and the same sometimes goes for the Under 21 and more junior England sides. But without an imaginative promotion of their appeal, many black fans new to football will pass them off as not worth the bother or the expense, second-rate alternatives to the real thing.

*

Ian Maynard will never pass off Reading FC as anything but first rate. He was born in Reading and his dad first took him as an eight-year-old to see his home-town club. 'Football was always a big part of his life. He came to Britain from the West Indies in 1955. He never had the time to play himself but I can remember he was always watching it on TV. He didn't go much either at first, but once I was old enough he started to take me at least two or three times a season. It was a big treat for both of us.'

Ian's dad worked as a telephone engineer, and back in the West Indies cricket had been his first love. Over here football was a relatively new sport to follow for him and most of his generation. For Ian it was different; he grew up loving football. By the time he was old enough to start going on his own in the early '70s he was also aware of the racism that was obvious in most football crowds. 'This was when *Love thy Neighbour* was on the TV. Every other sentence in that so-called family comedy had either "coon" or "nigger" in it. It was the same at football but at that age you just tried to ignore what was being said by those around you on the terraces and got on with enjoying the game.' By the mid '70s Ian was going to most of Reading's home games and half of the away ones too. England featured later: 'I first went in the mid-1990s, nearly twenty years after my first Reading games. I'd already learned that you had to be able to look after yourself in the old Division Three with Reading, but England games just seemed too much of an effort. It was the hooliganism I read about, almost always mixed up with racism too, that put me off going. But gradually this resentment built up. I'm a football fan, why am I allowing these people to stop me watching England, my team? And when I was there for the Euro 96 quarterfinal against Spain, with the whole stadium singing, I immediately felt part of it. No one was ever going to stop me going again.'

After Euro 96 the St George Cross came to symbolize supporting England. The days of waving the Union Jack were over, almost overnight. There was an intensification of English emotionalism, always tied up with nationalism. 'I was a part of this,' says Ian. 'There are good bits and there are bad bits, but for me the positives always outnumber the negatives. Take the flag: a minority, often the far right, have been allowed to dictate what it means. But the flag itself doesn't have opinions, so why do we let them get away with it?'

Ian is now a regular at England's home games and has been on a few away trips too. 'Of course black fans are in the minority, it sometimes seems like people expect us to make up the same numbers as on the pitch, but that's not realistic. Ten per cent, that's roughly the black population in England, so that is the kind of figure you might expect, though we're still an awful way short of even that. But give it time, take into account generational change, family pressures, the commitment to study, our deep love of other sports, cricket in particular. OK, some of this sounds like stereotypes, but they're based on cultural realities too.'

Ian is uncertain whether just concentrating on antiracism is enough of a response to the absence of black fans. 'I certainly want racism taken seriously, but I also want a culture in football that welcomes all new fans, and most black fans will inevitably be new. That's all I'm seeking, inclusion. Surely sharing a common experience is what being a fan is all about, so none of us should be precious about it, keeping it to ourselves.'

In Sunderland just before the Turkey game, me, Pritpal and some other friends had an early-evening meal with a group of young Turkey supporters. We'd met up with them earlier in the day, and in the traditional way of fan friendship had swapped badges, scarves, shirts, that sort of thing. With kickoff approaching we left the restaurant and made our way together to the match.

All of a sudden our Turkish friends were being jostled. 'What the fuck are you doing wearing our flag? That's our flag, not yours,' queried one of the blokes pushing the Turks wearing the scarves we'd given them. He was incredibly angry, sore that his picture of mutual hatred was being chipped away at. Of course the Turkish fans wanted their team to win, and we made it perfectly obvious we wanted England to win too. But they adore our players; many support an English premiership club and are envious of the rich footballing tradition England boasts. So if some of them are happy and willing to adopt England as their second-favourite team, the same way the world over favours Brazil against just about anyone else, what's the problem? In fact, it's something we should be rather proud of. We walked a bit faster, leaving our critics grumbling behind us, desperately clinging to the wreckage of a pure national identity they'd rather not see change.

A popular Englishness based around the St George Cross flag is a relatively new phenomenon. It has emerged in the era when black players are no longer a rarity in the England line-up. Since Viv Anderson's 1978 debut it would be inconceivable for there not to be a reasonable number of black players in any England squad. When Kieron Dyer came on for Paul Scholes in the forty-ninth minute against Denmark at World Cup 2002, the majority of the England players on the pitch were black.

It was hardly commented upon. The symbolism of Englishness can be amended to racist ends – there *are* those who wear and fly the St George Cross as a sign of white racial pride. Yet it is undeniable that most, including the increasing number of black England fans, don't. The St George Cross has become a sign of a newish England, with a make-up we're increasingly at ease with. The Union Jack simply seeks to smother the differences between the Scots, Welsh, Northern Irish and the English, while St George offers the unfulfilled potential for England's national liberation.

Ingerland

Guardian columnist Gary Younge is usually unconvinced how far such a process will be allowed to go by more conservative, defensive national impulses, yet he also recognizes the process offers more inclusive opportunities which could yet write a very different story of Englishness. 'The Scots and the Welsh still think of themselves as primarily white nations where black people happen to live. This would not happen in England. The English no longer have that self-image; the apparently seamless link between Englishness and whiteness has long since been broken. Even though nobody would question that England is, and most likely always will be, predominantly white, it remains that it is almost impossible to imagine it without black and Asian people as part of it.'

Sateesh Khanna is very much part of this England. His dad came over from India in 1953, invited like tens of thousands of others by the British government to help cover the increasing shortfall in the manual workforce, and his mum followed a few years later. The family moved to Harrow when he was a small child and Sateesh has lived there ever since. At his secondary school Sateesh never joined in with playing football; the family pressure was to do well in education, anything else was treated as a distraction.

Sateesh is certain this prioritization was central to Asian family life for his generation. It meant a split between his very Indian home life and the white English culture of his schooldays. His mates at school would often spend their Saturday afternoons watching the local non-league team, Wealdstone. 'I used to go shopping with my mum close to where the Wealdstone ground was, right in the centre of Harrow. It was an awesome sight to me as an Asian kid who'd never seen anything like it before.' He desperately wanted to go but his parents wouldn't let him; they had read stories of 'Paki-bashing' before and after football matches, and weren't willing to take the risk. 'But then there was a charity match at the ground, organized by the local Round Table, with Radio One DJ Ed "Stewpot" Stewart playing. This was respectable enough for them to let me go, so off I went.' Home safe and sound, Dad was happy enough to let Sateesh go again.

But in the mid 1970s another adolescent interest took over – punk. 'I was into the lot,' admits Sateesh. 'The Sex Pistols, Stranglers, Damned, Buzzcocks. It was like two different worlds. Eighty thousand in Hackney's Victoria Park at this huge Rock against Racism carnival, and none of the intimidation, abuse, or violence that any young Asian in those days had to endure at football. Wealdstone was OK, but all the big London clubs had a sizeable racist element amongst their support which you tried to avoid on their match days.' He still kept an eye out for the Wealdstone scores, but the appeal of a music scene that allied itself so strongly with the antiracist message while retaining the rebellious anti-Establishment politics that had inspired it was too tempting. 'I was spending all my spare cash, and time, following the bands. This was do-it-yourself music. I even bought myself a drum kit and dreamed of cutting a record. There was no money or weekends left for the football.'

A successful Wealdstone FA Cup run dragged him back, but now he'd seen something of punk's potential to unite black and white, he had something to measure his football experience against. 'When we played Barnet we had to put up with the "Wealdstone – you're just a bunch of Pakis" chants. Offensive, and pathetic really. We've a handful of Asian fans, but in non-league more than the other clubs, so they used this to wind us up. It wasn't exactly threatening, but why should we have to put up with it?'

By the mid-1980s Sateesh was following Wealdstone home and away, and the mates he travelled with started to invite him along to

England games. 'I'd never thought about going before. I'd had enough of the racism which I'd put up with at school, when I stuck out as the only Asian. I didn't want that all over again. I wasn't confident anybody would back me up if I was threatened. I had all these anxieties but after the first game, while those fears didn't disappear, I'd had enough of a good time to convince me to go again.'

Sateesh watched the Mexico 86 and Italia 90 World Cups at home on the TV, as he didn't have the money to travel. But when his Wealdstone friends suggested combining their summer holidays with a trip to Euro 92 in Sweden, he mustered the money together to join them. 'We read all the stuff in the papers about the threat of trouble. We never thought that we would be affected by it but when you find yourself being called an "English hooligan" by all and sundry it sort of knocks you back. There's a sort of fan who follows England who, if provoked, lashes straight back. I'm not like that – they need to lighten up, concentrate on having a good time.'

Twelve years later Euro 2004 showed just how much football had changed. 'We went by minibus to Lisbon, and when we got off the bus the first thing we saw was this big group of Asian lads, all wearing England shirts. I'd never seen anything like it before, just the odd one like me. This was different. They were so at ease with supporting England, wonderful. I was surprised, pleased too.'

Sateesh is convinced that when trouble erupts it is down to a combination of factors. Racism is just part of the mix. More important is the tribal inclination to defend our ground and exclude those we're not comfortable with. The researchers Les Back, Tim Crabbe and John Solomos, in their book *The Changing Face of Football*, confirm this connection between a tribal defensiveness and trouble: 'Those England supporters who are typically characterized as seeking an involvement in football-related violence and associated racist or xenophobic behaviour can be better under-stood in terms of their refusal to back down in the face of aggression.' Each twist in the tale turns the screw of conflict, punch followed by counter-punch.

Sateesh is clear what this means for him as a fan: 'Whether it's Wealdstone or England there's always a part of our own support I'm uncomfortable being with, but you just do your best to keep as far away from them as possible.' He is careful neither to understate nor overstate his experience. 'As an Asian following England I've never once been racially abused. But I don't get any pleasure out of the hate-filled abuse we sometimes hurl at others in our own cause either. It's not what football for me is about.'

The writer Yasmin Alibhai-Brown is one amongst many who uses the symbol of the football hooligan to summon up all our worst fears of the nationalist impulse. In the pamphlet *Reclaiming Britishness*, published by the well-respected Foreign Policy Centre, she wrote: 'For far too long it has not been possible for English people either to air their sense of dislocation or their her-itage in any positive way. Thoughtful English people fear that in doing so, they might be seen as neo-Powellites or football hooli-gans wearing Union Jack underpants and murderous tattoos.' Never mind the fact that a thoughtful observer might have at least noticed the substitution of the St George Cross for the Union Jack on our Y-fronts, but we'll let that pass. What this kind of lazy stereotyping fails to account for is the internationalism of our fan culture, the cosmopolitanism of our sport, the Europeanization of football's institutions. And there is a total failure to understand what motivates Sateesh, Jos, Pritpal and an increasing number of others to follow England. If we are to explain why many more black and Asian fans don't join them, we certainly need to ask those who have.

Ingerland

Like Sateesh, Sudhir Rawal grew up and still lives in Harrow. He is a Chelsea fan, a Stamford Bridge regular, though he takes in as many games as he can of his local team, Wealdstone, too. 'Me and my brother were football mad by the time we were teenagers. I suppose it was the first sign of the clash with our parents' culture.' He never had a problem supporting England either, 'not at football. The identification with the team was immediate, but when it comes to cricket I always support India.' This is another sign of the complexity behind the easy assumptions that leave us labelling rather than understanding. Sudhir continues, 'Take "Asian" – it might only be shorthand but to me it's meaningless. I've hardly anything in common with a Bangladeshi or a Pakistani, never mind the rest of the continent. It's like calling the English "European", and we know how most of you would resent that.'

Throughout the '70s and '80s Sudhir would go to two or three England games a year, then he went to France 98, Euro 2000 and Euro 2004 in Portugal. 'Now I take my kids – Akhil went to the Spain friendly at Villa Park in 2001, he absolutely loved it. My youngest, Nikhil, has been signed up by Arsenal's youth development centre. My generation, and my children's even more so, are immersed in football. Our parents' generation wasn't, not at all. We're ten years behind the Afro-Caribbean community. For them sport was a massive outlet in a way it wasn't for us, but that is now changing.'

Education was one factor that kept many Asians of Sudhir's generation away from football, and parental pressure to play cricket was another. Both are now declining as outright alternatives to football; rather they now coexist and complement. And for the 2006 World Cup in Germany Sudhir is already planning to take his two sons to their first tournament, something his father would never have imagined doing.

Quite what following England, wearing the shirt and flying the flag means to each and every fan will vary, though it is inconceivable that for the vast majority of the tens of thousands who travel to a major tournament popular patriotism won't feature highly amongst our emotions. England in this sense isn't just another, but bigger, club side. Local loyalties and identification are of course important to club fans too, but with England our fandom is inextricably connected to the kind of national identity we are comfortable with.

If the team represents the nation on the pitch it certainly challenges a racial definition of Englishness. Only a tiny (and disappearing) minority would demand Jermaine Defoe, Rio Ferdinand or Shaun Wright-Phillips should be dropped because the colour of their faces doesn't fit. And not many more would resent an increasing presence of black and Asian fans in the stands either. These are important advances to counter any revival of a popular racism in football, or anywhere else for that matter.

Harpreet Grewal first started following Liverpool in the late 1970s. Like plenty of kids in this era, she was drawn to the team's phenomenal domestic and European success. They played attractive football, won things and were hardly ever off the TV. And when her first job was on Merseyside, without a second thought she went to Anfield as often as she could get a ticket. She felt she belonged. But her first experience at an England game was different: 'It was England versus Romania at France 98. I didn't exactly feel threatened but it was obvious all these guys were looking at me and thinking I must be mad. A lone Asian woman amongst them all. Then Michael Owen scored and everybody went crazy. In the crush I ended up six rows from where I'd been sitting, but it was bizarre, we were just all so happy that any threat seemed to disappear.'

Harpreet is an England regular. She travels to home matches, away matches, and all the tournaments. She has no doubt that she is an England fan but she's wary of some of the associations too. 'I always wear the colours of the team, a white top if we're playing in white, that sort of thing. But I don't wear the England shirt. I want to be able to walk away, say I'm not part of it if there's trouble. I've been in scary situations and I like the fact that people won't necessarily know where I'm from. I lost count the number of times at Euro 2004 I was mistaken for Portuguese. It just gives me another option if things turn nasty. If I was a hundred per cent certain there wouldn't be trouble I wouldn't worry about it, but I'm not that sure, not yet.' Harpreet's Englishness is measured by her own experiences too. 'I can't get into all that anti-Scottish stuff, it's not something I grew up with, it was never instilled in me. I don't share it, why should I?'

In Japan and then Portugal, Harpreet has noticed a change that is not just about an increasing number of fans being more aware of, interested in and sensitive to the countries and cultures they are visiting. 'A very welcome side effect is that it also makes me feel more welcome. There is more of a mixed group travelling, especially to the tournaments. That can only be a good thing. It wasn't an instant change as the media sometimes tries to make out, but gradually over the past ten years or so something has been happening.'

Harpreet is still unconvinced we will see in the next few years much increase in the number of black and Asian fans at England's away matches. 'You have to be really passionate about football to go to a game. That passion is growing amongst Asians but travelling away takes a huge commitment, not just time and money, but taking the risk of the unfamiliar. There aren't many who will make that effort, but if the numbers going to home matches grows then we will see more going away too. Especially if their experience at a home match is positive, and what they read about those who do go abroad is positive.'

For club or country, the away support is always hardcore. Some 2500 made the October 2004 trip to see England play in Azerbaijan, but how many of these hadn't travelled abroad to watch England play before? Most had been to countless England away matches, often in similarly far-flung parts of Europe, and over a good few years. For them this would be one of the travelling highlights of the campaign.

The make-up of this part of our support won't change overnight. But even in terms of support at home matches, the generational process means change is gradual. If family pressures and domestic priorities meant parents had little interest in taking their kids to a game, then second-generation black and Asian fans are in many instances pioneers of a new fandom.

Kofi Ohene-Djan is in his early thirties, and has been following Spurs for more than twenty years. 'It was their 1981 FA Cup final victory that started me off supporting them. Garth Crooks, Glenn Hoddle and Steve Archibald, they were my early heroes.' A keen sportsman at school, Kofi ran the 100m, 200m, and 400m, reaching the English Schools finals. 'Doing all this sport meant I didn't have the time to go and see Spurs. My first match wasn't until I was sixteen.'

Kofi is an England fan too, and dismisses those who don't welcome his support. 'They have to realize that the game is changing. England is every much my team as it is theirs. Simply me being at a game, supporting the team, proves that change, and might alter some of their opinions too of what it means to be English.' He recognizes that wearing the same shirt helps how he is received by other England fans. 'I'm wearing an England shirt, we're all in this together and that sort of thing takes over. I know it's not perfect – racist attitudes persist – but at least they shut up when I'm around, so that's some sort of step forward.'

Ingerland

At the Croatia friendly I'd gone to with Jos Johnson, Kofi appeared on a 'Kick racism out of football' poster being given away with the 'England Against Racism' stickers. 'This bloke came up to me in the toilets. He was saying, "Is that you in the picture?" I wasn't sure what he was getting at, I hoped he was saying something positive. And thankfully I was right. He just slapped me on the back. "Good on you, mate, great to see you here".'

Football's young superstars of today, black and white, have the potential to appeal to second- and third-generation young black and Asian fans, which would have been unthinkable for their parents and grandparents. And this poses a challenge for how Englishness is defined by both ourselves and other nationalities. Kofi recounts encounters with Croatian, Brazilian, German and Portuguese fans on his travels following England. 'They don't get it. They think, "African", how can I be an England fan? Not in an aggressive way, it's more they're just curious.' This, of course, is precisely the reality of what England has become, and while some don't like it, plenty do.

Ben Carrington, co-editor of the book *Race, Sport and British Society*, has a neat way of distinguishing between satisfaction and dissatisfaction with a black and white England.

It is not that all English fans are fascist or racist, and neither that it is just a fringe on the edges of good spectatorship. The problem is that most English fans tend not to be aware of race as an issue, with a small element being actively, and politically, racist and perhaps a similar small number who could be described as actively antiracist. This means that the vast majority tend to see themselves as not being racist, and would certainly deny the charge. Yet it is this 'non-racist' majority who will often engage in certain banal forms of racism, and under certain circumstances, join in more overt expressions of racial and xenophobic abuse and violence.

Billy Grant has followed his local side Brentford since 1979, and England, home and away, since 1988. 'I started going to Griffin Park just after the 1978 World Cup. It was crazy, we copied the Argentines, ticker-tape welcomes at every home game. I loved it, but looking round the terraces there was only one other black face.'

Billy remembers the racism, the far-right presence, the intimidation and physical violence, and having to stand up for his right to be there week after week. 'Through the sixties, seventies, eighties we were constantly looking out for black icons. When my parents came over from Jamaica in the fifties they had never imagined the racism they would have to face. A few iconic figures in TV, boxing, athletics would give us some sort of hope of a better future for ourselves. This was when the *Black and White Minstrel Show* was on prime-time TV – entertainers got laughs blacking up and putting on so-called funny accents, so seeing a black newsreader, boxer or runner did make a difference to us.'

In 1988 Billy went to his first England match at Wembley, and a few months later followed the team to Germany for Euro 88. He arrived at Frankfurt station, found it full of England fans looking for an excuse to cause trouble, and promptly caught the first train to the student town of Heidelburg, where he'd heard the atmosphere was much calmer. 'It's been the same ever since. I find the place where the people go to get as far as possible away from the risk of trouble and then make it my home for as long as I'm out there.'

He did the same at Italia 90 and had a really good laugh, but after the tournament England played the Republic of Ireland away in a Euro 92 qualifier. 'It was horrible. *Sieg-Heil*ing everywhere. It stopped me going for four years after that. Why should I have to put up with a crowd like that?'

Ingerland

As Euro 96 approached Billy took in a few home friendlies; his mates at work were going so he thought he'd give it a go again. 'There was a nice vibe. I could tell things were getting better.' After that Billy found a bigger and bigger group of mates wanting to go to games, up to sixteen for some. 'Some hadn't been before, but because I was going they just fancied coming along. They wanted a taste of what an England game would be like – they loved it and came back for more.'

When Jamaica qualified for the 1998 World Cup in France, Billy used his England experience to organize a coach to Jamaica's game with Croatia in Lens. 'Fifty of us, music blaring out the speakers, rum punch, the whole Caribbean experience and, most important of all, a coach full of happy people. Feeling like this was a crucial breakthrough for me. It made me realize the distance that still existed between being black, and being an England fan. On our coach that difference disappeared. We were all fans, and we all wanted a good time. Some of us black, some not, it scarcely mattered. And it wasn't just us. Lens was packed solid with people all feeling exactly the same.'

Billy recognizes that much progress has been made: 'No doubt about it. People are more aware of what multiculturalism means, the dos and don'ts which are expected of them. And most are comfortable with that. Twenty years ago how many white England fans had even met, talked to, made friends with a black fan?' Billy believes England's association with trouble remains the principal deterrent to increasing black and Asian support for the team. 'If this link with hooliganism continues to diminish, and is promoted by the media, it will have a big impact. Add the declining influence of our parents' generation, who weren't as interested in football, and the pace of change will accelerate.'

But Billy is searching for an irreversible momentum, and he is unconvinced we can be certain this will happen unless aided by an encouraging push. 'A sticker here, a poster there, it's not enough. Just compare the resources put in to these campaigns with the hundreds of millions spent on policing. Doesn't anyone see the link between the two?' He is less concerned by the organized hooligans – they are already the subject of increasingly successful surveillance, bans and prosecutions. Rather he wants something done about the much larger numbers who, given the wrong circumstances, will sing, 'I'd rather be a Paki than a Turk', something scarcely more civilized than the Spanish monkey-chanting we were so ready, and right, to condemn when England played Spain in November 2004. 'It has to be a hard-line message of zero tolerance. I'm more bothered about those who such a stand would attract than those whom it will upset. Once it is declared that racism is just completely unacceptable, and proper punishments handed out, we'll start to tackle the violence it is connected to as well.'

Following the widespread racist abuse of England players at that Spain match, Patrick Collins in the *Mail on Sunday* was one of the observers who recognized that the united response by fans, players, FA, media and others was an important moment. 'What happened in the Bernabeu Stadium was wicked beyond words, yet I believe the reaction to those events may represent the most encouraging phenomenon that English sport has known in years. It was the passionate unanimity that an insult to Ashley Cole, Shaun Wright-Phillips and Jermaine Defoe was an insult to all of us. The human dignity of talented sportsmen had been trampled on and the country wasn't having it.'

England fan Peter John-Baptiste was at the match and has a common-sense answer to those who would offer excuses for the Spanish racism, passing it off as part and parcel of supporting the team, ours or theirs. 'I find it strange that any England fan would object to fellow supporters not being amused by members of our team being abused purely for the colour of their skin.'

Peter's argument is a territorial antiracism, in defence of our own players rather than necessarily anybody else's. But if that territorialism begins to make the abusing of others a more distant possibility, then why shouldn't we be thankful? It symbolizes both how far we have come, and where we might end up too. We have reached a stage, at the very least, where we can confidently expect that the vast majority of fans won't put up with any racial abuse of our players. Just a few years previously we could not have been nearly so confident that such a reaction would be forthcoming.

Forty years ago, when England won the World Cup, Bobby Moore would never have had to address his team having to endure this kind of attack. Yet when David Beckham came off the pitch at the end of another match, Slovakia away in October 2002, where racial abuse had occurred, he grabbed the BBC's microphone. 'Emile and Ashley should never have to put up with that, it's disgusting.' It was a remarkable instant of recognition by the most famous, and white, player of his generation that this wasn't 'their' problem, it was ours.

The reaction to the Spanish racism was another vital stage in what hopefully is an accelerating pace of change in attitudes. Patrick Collins and other writers were right to recognize and applaud the depth and breadth of the anger at the Spaniards' racism. Those black players are wearing the same shirt as us, but for most of us they're not the same colour. When increasing numbers are willing to stand up and loudly protest at these insults we will never have to face ourselves, it matters. The transition, of course, isn't complete. From Bobby to Becks is roughly the space of one generation. The same few years from black and Asian mums and dads with little interest in the game, to sons and daughters with a growing affection for it.

Now the waiting game has to come to an end. Those insults we resent when chucked at our players by their lot can no longer come with the home territory either. The St George Cross with Handsworth, Southall and Brixton across its crossbar has to become as likely to be hung from the England end abroad as Bexhill, Chippenham and Stourbridge. Pritpal, Jos, Sudhir, Billy, Harpreet and the rest should be there as England fans, rather than singled out for special attention, affectionate or otherwise, because they are black and Asian. Prejudice persists in England – nobody in their right minds would deny that. To use this to claim football can't be any better is pathetic. The mantle of the national game brings with it responsibilities. The measure of the shift is amongst the young black and Asian fans who wear the England shirt, cheer the team on, and fly the flag. Will I-N-G-E-R-L-A-N-D welcome that change, and encourage more and more of the same until exclusion starts to ebb away? When this happens we really will begin to replace the old-fashioned cold comfort that England offered those whom we treated as strangers to both our nation and our sport, with the warmth of a new-fashioned English humanity.

6

The Blame Game

It is not often a journalist apologizes for a story he has written. Even rarer for that apology to be given in front of a room packed full of those who feel they have been victims of the writer's misrepresentation. But this is what Oliver Holt, chief sports writer on the *Daily Mirror*, had the courage to do as Euro 2004 approached. Invited to meet a group of England fans keen that they receive some decent coverage during the championships, Oliver admitted, 'I was as guilty as anyone covering what happened in Bratislava. The assumption I made was that it was England fans that started the trouble.'

Two years earlier Oliver had been out in Japan covering England's World Cup 2002 campaign. When it came to a sorry close in Shizuoka, like almost every other English football journalist out there, he didn't just comment in his report on whether Ronaldinho's free kick was fluke or flair, but also remarked on the England fans' performance off the pitch. 'The England fans did not wreck the train, abuse the ticket inspector, or belittle Japanese travellers. They talked and joked and drank like normal human beings. Seeing an England shirt on a station platform or the street is starting to inspire pride again here, not shame or dread.'

How different to the way the *Daily Mirror* had described the fans in an editorial during Euro 88: 'We apologize, fully and without reservation, for the fact these vandals, these scum, these children of the six-pack culture, shattered the peace of the good people of Stuttgart. They are coarse and hideous louts. It would be wrong to compare them with animals because no animal is like them.' The turnabout in the coverage was dramatic.

Barely three months after World Cup 2002 ended everything seemed to be moving backwards once more. 'Business as normal' was how Oliver described the events at England's away match with Slovakia. And, thinking back to the positive words he'd used to describe the fans in Japan, he expressed regret for his optimism: 'Those are fond memories now. But that's all they are. Relics of naivety and a foolish, ignorant innocence.' The press ridiculed FA spokesman Paul Newman for blaming the trouble caused by our fans on the provocation of racial abuse aimed at our players from large sections of the Slovakian supporters. Oliver expressed his disbelief sharper than most:

Don't try and tell me, like the FA did for a while, that England fans weren't to blame when they tried to attack the Slovak fans inside the Slovan Stadium. Don't insult me with this ludicrous idea they only tried to tear down a dividing fence in the stand because they were so enraged by the monkey chants of the Slovaks. This type of England fan enraged by racist chants? Do me a favour. They've got the patent on racist chants. Why do you think it is that a black England fan on a trip abroad is a rarer sight than a unicorn? Do you think, maybe, it's because they feel they might not be welcome? Do you think, maybe, it's because they may suffer the same treatment from their fellow England fans that Emile Heskey and Ashley Cole got in that stadium on Saturday night?

After all the positive words written about us in Japan, this was certainly 'business as normal' in terms of the words used to describe, or more accurately demonize, the entire England support. We'd waited nearly twenty years to read the kind of words even our most embittered critics wrote about us in Japan – journalists like Jeff Powell in the *Daily Mail* who reported: 'From the vile, brawling, drunken and shaming rabble of so many football championships, they appear to have been transformed into human beings who love the game for its own sake and seek only to share in that delight, with all whom they come into contact.' After Bratislava, how long would we have to wait before Jeff and others wrote another piece like this?

England fan Peter John-Baptiste wasn't willing to wait. He'd been in Bratislava. He had heard the racist abuse from a large section of the Slovakian fans and witnessed how most England fans had tried to get out of the way of the flailing police batons, while some idiots couldn't resist stirring it up with punches thrown and missiles chucked. Oliver's account was partial and unfair. But most of all it failed to represent Peter's own experience as a black fan following England away. Peter wrote to Oliver hoping, he suspected forlornly, that he might listen to his side of the story:

> Please read this, Mr Holt. It is very important. Firstly, I have to say that I am black. I read your column in the *Mirror* and I felt I had to respond. I always find you very honest and thought-provoking. I don't always agree with you but that is why I read your column. You make me think.

Ingerland

I read your piece about England supporters and it left me feeling angry, dismayed and slightly betrayed by a lot of what was written.

I will never defend racist, violent or prejudiced English (or any other nation for that matter) football supporters but there seemed to be a sweeping generalization about what English fans are like in your article.

I went to Bratislava on the Thursday before the game. I was in the bars in Bratislava till 3–4 a.m. Thursday and Friday and never once felt in danger from Slovakians or English people. My colour was no barrier. Perhaps I was lucky but I seem to get lucky a lot as this is definitely the norm.

The ground at Bratislava had many dangers and problems that I'm not sure you're aware of. No checks on tickets by stewards, just riot police pushing you along and randomly tapping people with batons for no reason. It was dark and scary.

The monkey-chanting provoked one dickhead England fan to start pushing the fence and hitting a riot cop with it. Instead of arresting that one man the police laid into anyone and everyone in their way, which forced the England fans back. A few idiots weren't having this so they started rocking the fence. This caused a second and even worse police baton charge. They hit innocent men, women and children.

I had a great four days in Bratislava. I am not prejudiced against Slovakians due to the hurtful actions of a minority just like I am not prejudiced against white English people due to the actions of a minority. I know what it is like to be distrusted because of how you look or where you are from so I know better than to do that. Because of the minority of idiots and inaccurate journalism I don't think I'll ever make many black or Asian friends through following England. Very sad.

The Blame Game

Please reply if you get the time.

Journalists, photographers and camera crews all have a job to do, deadlines to meet, editors to please, papers to sell and ratings to boost. But they also have a duty sometimes to listen to us, to peer behind the stock of stereotypes, to seek out both sides to the latest episode of violent disorder, and just occasionally to run some feel-good alongside the customary diet of bad news and scare stories. There are plenty of journalists who, given the opportunity and the information, will do all this. Peter John-Baptiste was lucky that when he wrote to Oliver Holt he found one. Oliver responded almost immediately to Peter's letter:

Thanks for your letter. It made very interesting reading. There's not a lot I can say, really. I can't really contradict you. And as you say, you can't just have been lucky for ten or fifteen years. I'm sorry if I misrepresented the situation but I have heard a lot of reports coming in recently from friends and colleagues sitting in crowds at English league games where racism has been on the increase.

I accept all your points unreservedly. I just feel that we've still got a long way to go in our game but, once again, your personal experiences suggest maybe that is not the case. Love to have a drink some time. Maybe in Liechtenstein or dodging bullets in Skopje . . .

England fans abroad are an easy and obvious target for media criticism. Too many European Championships, World Cups and away trips have been scarred by serious outbreaks of public disorder, racist abuse and offensive behaviour. We have become used to reading the dread with which our arrival is awaited by the host country. Our excursions are almost always described as an 'invasion', invariably accompanied by banner headlines about the threat we pose. After our departure we are treated to page after page of gory photos, depicting the mayhem and rampage left in our wake.

At Euro 88 the *Daily Mail* described England fans as 'Vicious, lewd and boorish in their booze, our riffraff abroad remain the recognized champions of thuggery'. During Italia 90 the *Sun* reported on our growing reputation as the most unwelcome guests at everybody else's World Cup party: 'How many times must we suffer this vile, foul-mouthed and drunken mob, who laughingly call themselves supporters, destroy and defile our country's name abroad?' After more trouble at Euro 92 the *Guardian* reflected on the possible causes: 'With misplaced nostalgia for the days of the empire, these young men are suspicious of foreigners to the point of xenophobia' And France 98 marked for Claudia Fitzherbert in the *Daily Telegraph* the exhaustion of any patience with the excuse that most fans are not troublemakers: 'I don't care that it's just a minority who provoke the violence time and again. The point is that the violence happens time and time again, and is therefore part of English football culture.' When disorder broke out again two years later at Euro 2000 Hugo Young in the *Guardian* speculated on just how serious the problem had become and the reasons why, according to him, not a single England fan seemed capable of good behaviour: 'English football has become a threat to England, a curse on football, a menace to the citizens of every country where it's played.'

Tabloid, mid-market or broadsheet. Liberal, right-leaning or voice of the people. It hardly mattered; the tone of the coverage was virtually the same, the damning of all England fans just about universal.

Those who neither caused nor were victims of trouble scarcely merited a column inch. Too often the media accounts of England fan behaviour or, more likely, misbehaviour, allow no space for differentiation. In Japan they finally recognized the contrast between those who follow England looking for trouble and those that don't. Then in Bratislava they promptly forgot that there might be a difference. Their opinion of us was fundamentally flawed. Many of those the media praised for the way they behaved in Japan travelled out to Bratislava too. It was just that the journalists who wrote their accounts of the trouble rarely noticed us or gave us a mention.

If this is ever going to change we can't simply blame the media, but Oliver Holt believes the coverage of England fans is affected by the overall mood of how a tournament is covered. 'The *Mirror* was hammered during Euro 96 for that ACHTUNG SURRENDER headline, and that kind of thing has been toned down ever since. This definitely makes a difference. After Euro 2000 there has been no serious crowd trouble involving England. That's what really changes the way the fans are covered. I was amazed, and heartened, by all those England fans out in Japan at World Cup 2002. Suddenly we could celebrate England fans for all the things we used to praise the Scots and Irish fans for.' One particular memory has stayed with Oliver ever since Japan. 'I was on a train back to Tokyo from Shizuoka after the defeat to Brazil in the quarterfinal. England fans were conga-ing up and down the entire length of the bullet train, and we'd lost! This was something I thought I would never see.'

So why did Holt go back to castigating the entire support after the Bratislava game? 'We knew the really nasty element hadn't been there in Japan, and at the Slovakia game they seemed to have reappeared.' The caution in recognizing the shift is understandable, but becomes inexcusable when time after time the same sweeping statements about all England fans being xenophobes, racists and hooligans are made. This condemns those of us who are none of these things to an increasingly vicious circle. If the impression is created that the only way to follow England is to be thuggish, is it any wonder that many are scared off, while some are attracted for all the wrong reasons.

In the *Sun* Paul Hooper and Steve Warr described the impact of England's support at Euro 88 on their front page: 'Britain's soccer army of shame invaded another German city last night – and threatened to start World War Three.' Twelve years later at Euro 2000 the opinion of David Thomas in the *Daily Mail* had scarcely changed. If anything it had worsened: 'For every malevolent maniac who sets out to cause trouble there are a hundred hangers-on who haven't the wit to organize a riot, but are happy to join in one.'

Those intervening years were pockmarked by violent outbreaks of disorder at every tournament England qualified for, except Euro 96 at home, plus a fair few away trips. As rampage followed riotous assembly with numbing predictability, it became almost impossible for fans offering any kind of hopeful alternative to be heard above the clamour of rightful condemnation.

So why did Oliver bother to reply when Peter John-Baptiste contacted him? 'I realized that I needed to listen, to cover the other side of the story, and that much of what I had written about this particular episode in Bratislava was deeply unfair.'

When England played Portugal in a pre-Euro 2004 friendly, on past form it would have been the ideal time for a *Daily Mirror* column stuffed full of dire and depressing predictions of the human tragedy our fans were about to inflict upon the Portuguese. Oliver Holt began his article recounting the forecasts he was used to making for England abroad: 'I drove from Lisbon down to the Algarve yesterday, fighting the thought that this was the route that might allow the hooligan hordes to march on England's European Championship dream this summer.' So far, so familiar, but the rest of the article was full of carefully worded optimism based on what he had found out about changes in our supporters from Peter. 'Let's not forget the contributions of England fans. The vast majority aren't hooligans. They are people who love travelling to watch England. And more and more, there are signs they are so sick of being lumped in with the lunatic fringe, they have decided to do something about it.'

Oliver had joined the group of England fans who had met up with Faro's Portuguese 'Ultras' on the eve of the match for a peaceful, engaging and friendly party I had helped organize. It was the first time a tabloid had given us any kind of coverage. Finally, in the section of the press most likely to be read by the bulk of England fans, somebody was taking notice. Oliver, of course, expressed some reservations; it was far too soon to claim that everything bad about I-N-G-E-R-L-A-N-D had been eliminated: 'Perhaps what happened in Faro is evidence of another step towards extinguishing hooliganism. At least when I drive back north to Lisbon tomorrow, the journey will be filled with more hope and less foreboding.'

After all the trouble that had been created by others, but in our name, we could live with Oliver's caution. At least he was offering the possibility of a different outcome. He explains why he felt able to give us the kind of write-up that in the past had been so rare. 'I thought it was important to give credit where it was due. To acknowledge the really positive things the fans were getting up to. But I can only write about what I see. If I spot a bunch of England fans behaving like twats I'll write about, and criticize, that too.'

This is fair, all we would ask for. Trouble will always receive the editorialized condemnation it deserves. But if the bulk of our fans are neither involved nor victims, this needs reporting as well. And if around the corner another lot of fans are getting up to something in vigorous and fun-filled opposition to the trouble, this also deserves to be compared and contrasted with the more depressing scenes elsewhere.

*

With fights breaking out two nights running in Albufeira during the first week of Euro 2004, the pre-tournament assertions of inevitable trouble seemed to be ringing true. Ahead of our first game against France, John Sadler in the *Sun* had tossed up the chances of expulsion against the odds on elimination: 'I'm not sure what or who is likelier to get us eliminated first – the drunken, antisocial behaviour of fans or the indecisive muddled thinking of the man preparing and selecting the team.'

Once the trouble actually started the papers paraded their principles in strident editorials. In the *Sun*: 'What's happening in Portugal can't be blamed on soccer. We are paying for decades of liberal hogwash, when self-discipline vanished.' While in the *Guardian* Richard Williams was ready to bring the team home showered in the national disgrace that Albufeira was seemingly in danger of covering us all in.

The question must be asked: what has to happen before England's footballers are sent home. Sooner or later, perhaps within the next 24 hours something could happen to make a withdrawal unavoidable. The sort of event – Heysel, Hillsborough, James Bulger, Soham – that forces the English to take a hard look at themselves, and to do something about what they discover. Conventional methods of deterrence can no longer be relied upon to protect ordinary citizens from this English disease. Repugnant as it may be to those who cling to traditional British attitudes, the idea of fairness to individuals must take second place to effective action on behalf of a wider majority. What this situation requires is someone prepared to look at the broader picture and to act on the belief that although this week's disgraceful scenes are not football's fault, it is with football, and a gesture of supreme self-sacrifice, that corrective action must begin.

The Blame Game

The kind of instant political punditry offered in different formulations for their dissimilar readerships by the *Sun* and the *Guardian* were swiftly overtaken by events. Albufeira became the exception rather than the rule, as the carnivalesque took over. Kevin Mitchell in the *Observer* was one of those who took the trouble to record the significance of the changing impact England fans made on the tournament. 'The real victory in Portugal has not been confined to the scorelines. It has been in the bars of Lisbon, in the streets, on the trains and on the faces of the England fans, the hitherto feared band of brigands who are rightly regarded as both the best and the worst in the world.' Adding a well-aimed jibe at those who build up the most negative side of our reputation in the expectation of how things will end up, he wrote of, 'The real hooligans, those all-knowing and cheap-shot commentators, people who would have liked nothing better than a riot to go with the pain of defeat.'

While Oliver Holt had been writing his warm words of appreciation, recording all the good things England fans were getting up to, elsewhere in the *Daily Mirror* page after page of photos and breathless on-the-spot reporting made the Albufeira trouble a huge story. Why make trouble involving a few hundred out of the tens of thousands of fans in Portugal the main newspaper event? Oliver sadly admits the reason: 'Good news isn't usually particularly attractive. Think of Iraq – we only ever read about the suicide bombings, what about the people going about their lives quite normally?' And he adds, 'Of course, we can't ignore incidents either, it is inevitable they will be covered. Especially as all the papers send reporters and journalists specifically to cover hooligan violence. What will be interesting is what they will find to write about in its absence.'

Oliver's point, about comparing the countervailing value of Euro 2004 good and bad news stories to how a story like Iraq is covered, reminded me of the railway station in Coimbra after the

England game there. The match had been magnificent. Rooney had turned over the Swiss, and the atmosphere had been brilliant too. Not even a hint of trouble in this small, quietish university town, which is a sort of Portuguese Oxford and most certainly not used to hosting thousands of England fans. As we made our way on to the platform I spotted Ben Brown of BBC TV news cowering in the corner of the station entrance hall with his camera crew. Over the past few months Ben had been embedded with British troops in Basra and all over Iraq. As soon as there was a bombing, assassination, kidnapping or soldier shot, Ben would be on the box. He's the BBC trouble-spots expert, and it was perfectly obvious why he and his colleagues were looking so miserable. Flown across Europe to broadcast the latest 'England raze town to the ground' story, all they had seen was happy, smiling faces having a good time, and nothing therefore to report. This is the problem. If the news agenda is to seek out trouble, what do you put in its place when there is none?

Oliver is convinced that the focus will only shift from trouble-searching to good-news reporting when more football journalists make the effort to find out what it's like to be an England fan, but the reality has to be a good one if we want to receive positive coverage. 'Part of me had always wanted to believe there was some good in England fans,' he says, but he admits his fear before Portugal was that as soon as he wrote something positive it would be contradicted the next day by the latest outrage involving some of our fans. 'What is different now is that Portugal has bought the fans a bit of credit. Next time there's trouble we have the chance to put it into a bit of perspective, to refer back to all the good things that came out of Portugal. And the really bad times aren't so long ago that we can't point out the difference that has been made.'

Mick Dennis in the *Daily Express* was writing regular reports from Portugal giving a sense of what it was really like to be with

The Blame Game

England's travelling support. He was one of an increasing number of journalists capable of providing a bit of context alongside the wall-to-wall coverage of the two nights of fighting in Albufeira. 'It is important to state that there are English fans of whom you would be proud back home. A number of supporters' groups have organized goodwill events here, including visits to schools, collections for children's homes and the clearing of litter from beaches.'

Mark Hetherington was very pleased to read that the efforts of the group he was involved with, NorthWestEnglandFans, were noticed by the media. 'We had come up with this idea that a bunch of England fans would spend a morning cleaning up a local beach.' With shovels and brooms in their rubber-gloved hands, Mark and his mates looked quite a picture on the Sky News report that covered their efforts. 'The Portuguese and the English media both gave us loads of coverage. We had been a bit worried whether we should go ahead after the trouble but the pictures of us, plus the kids' treasure hunt we organized, represented a real alternative to all the stuff about fighting and smashed-up bars.'

No one can pretend that most fans will ever give up their lie-in to turn out to sweep the pebbles and sand clean, but the fact that some do, and that they are committed fans who follow their national team wherever they play, offers the beginnings of a different way to report on, and read about, England abroad. But the cynics might say there's no point when most of us are written off as yobs. Mark is having none of this, 'We either do something about it or we accept that the way we're written about will never change. The point is we do it in ways that everyone can get involved with. And then if what we do gets covered you see something grow. There's no choice, we have to get the media on our side.'

The activities Mark and his group organized in Albufeira had never been tried before at a tournament – it was the start of something new. Mark describes how NorthWestEnglandFans take getting their message across in their local media back home seriously. 'Right from the start we had talked about improving our image and we felt that the papers and radio stations that cover our region would be key. The *Lancashire Evening Post* and *Manchester Evening News* were really glad that we contacted them. They don't have the resources to send reporters on England away trips or to tournaments, so we could provide them not only with an angle on what after all is a huge media event, but one which was local too.' And the same went for local radio. Thanks to Mark providing the contacts, BBC Radio Lancashire and BBC Radio Merseyside both carried regular interviews with local fans out in Portugal. 'It just took a bit of effort. The fact that we were from the Northwest was the key.'

Mark feels the good coverage they received is starting to make a difference. 'I know that for me it was important that I felt finally someone was taking an interest in what being an England fan means to myself and most England fans I know. It was a great opportunity to have our voices heard. This means a lot. It's constantly underestimated how important it is that the peaceful majority, not the violent minority, are taken notice of.'

When the FA refused to take up their ticket allocation for the away Euro 2004 qualifiers with Macedonia and Turkey in autumn 2003, many loyal, committed and nonviolent England fans were furious. But few in the media wanted to listen; instead the entire focus was on how by punishing the majority for a threat posed by a minority the greater cause of a peaceful football match was being served. Most fans would grudgingly accept that the risks of trouble in Istanbul warranted the travel ban, but when Macedonia was added our patience snapped. Paul Kelso, sports-news correspondent on the *Guardian*, was one of the few journalists who took the trouble to find out why. His piece on some England fans who defied the FA instructions not to go to Skopje caught their mood and predicament. 'For a decade the hooligan minority has largely overshadowed the good behaviour of the majority who go to extraordinary lengths and expense to follow their side. Alan and his friends have been following England home and away for more than twenty years and have never been involved in trouble. They despise the hooligan minority but are angry about the FA decision not to take tickets for Macedonia.'

When he is sent to cover a major tournament, Paul is there mainly to report on the fans. He always hopes he can find something positive to write about. 'Journalists are under incredible pressure to deliver. We have to produce copy, that's what we're there for. We can swan around a bit, enjoying the all-expenses-paid trip of our lives, but there's a paranoia about being a journalist too, the knowledge that none of this will last if we can't come up with good stories. And the biggest nightmare is that we might miss something that another paper gets.'

Paul was based in Lisbon for most of Euro 2004. 'I was faced with essentially a non-story, the lack of trouble. At first I wasn't sure it would turn out like this – there was the fighting in Albufeira, which could have spread. But after the game against the Swiss in Coimbra all the sports-news journalists ended up at the same restaurant. We all agreed that there wasn't going to be any trouble and from that point on the coverage changed quite dramatically.' Paul found himself writing instead about the fan culture that develops around a tournament. He and other journalists wrote feel-good pieces about families on their camp sites, how the Portuguese were giving the English such a welcoming reception and interesting profiles of the rising number of Asian England fans. Simon Barnes in *The Times* summed up the all-round impact of England fans in Portugal: 'The miracle of Rooney was predictable enough; the miracle of the England fans was something of quite another order. There was very little misbehaviour. There was hardly even bad vibes. The bellicosity, the war chants, the sweaty, boozy atmosphere of constant threat, these had all vanished. Perhaps they just don't make hooligans like they used to.'

Before becoming a journalist Paul followed England as a fan at home, going to Wembley from the mid 1980s, then away for the first time to Italy in 1997 for the decisive World Cup qualifier, and on to France 98 the following year. The experiences he has had as a fan unashamedly influence his writing. 'I abhor prejudice and violence, actual or threatened. I detest it when it attaches itself to England.' Few would disagree with Paul penning a condemnation of violence caused by England fans; the issue is rather getting events out of proportion and depicting the entire community of fans as violent thugs. 'News tends to focus on covering the abnormal,' admits Paul, 'so outbreaks of mindless violence, however unrepresentative, do tend to get covered. What is required, though, and I always try to do this, is to speak to the fans, as well as the police and the FA, to find out the context in which any incident took place. This demands building up relationships with fans whose views you can trust.'

Alan Lee was one of the fans Paul met up with, and wrote about, in Macedonia. 'We had arranged to see him out there,' says Alan, 'to tell him exactly why we had travelled. He seemed to enjoy our company, finding out that we'd spent the day sightseeing and swimming in this huge lake. We told him everything we'd been up to, how important having a good time is to us.' Alan was really pleased how their experience was reported. 'Paul and some of the other journalists are willing to sit down and listen to us. But what is most frustrating is the type who has already written his report and just asks questions to confirm his own views, not interested in our answers, our experience at all.'

The Blame Game

Before World Cup 2002 Alan had contacted his local newspaper, the *Lincolnshire Echo*, with the idea of writing a fan's diary of the tournament. 'I'd helped form the fans group 4England and through this I'd been on BBC Radio Lincolnshire a few times, being on there gave me a bit of credibility. The editor I spoke to on the paper had heard me and really liked the idea of me writing this column.' Alan's diary was a mix of match reports and travel writing, but most of all was about what it was like as an England fan to be at the World Cup in faraway Japan. With the by-line 'Our Fan in Japan' and a photo of Alan grinning from ear to ear, his column told of both his experiences and the impact the behaviour of the fans was having on the Japanese. As the Argentina game approached his column caught the mood in Sapporo for his readers. 'The next few days are crucial for English football; not only have the players a task to perform, so too have the fans, who surely must behave while they are out here.'

It is the kind of sentiment we're used to reading from journalists. The fact that this time it was from a fan gave the piece added credence, especially when mixed up with Alan's tales of what he was eating, where he was sleeping, how to get hold of tickets and the like. 'The paper really appreciated the connection between this huge global story and somebody local. They had something a bit different rather than simply rewriting what the nationals were writing.' Chipping away at the stereotype through every possible outlet, fans like Alan are making a significant contribution to refashioning what it means to be an England fan for a public who for more than twenty years have been told there is only one way to be I-N-G-E-R-L-A-N-D.

Alan was fortunate enough to find a local paper that was interested in his story and gave him the outlets to tell it. In London, BBC Radio London's sports editor Pete Stevens has been covering the efforts of LondonEnglandFans, which I'm involved with, since we started. Invariably the presenter calling to find out what we've been up to is Tom Watt, for those of a certain soap-opera vintage 'Lofty' in *EastEnders*, now better known as a football writer and radio presenter. An Arsenal fan since he was ten years old, Tom grew up in and around Finsbury Park, where Highbury is located, and he's been a season-ticket holder since 1971. He's just the sort of friendly, sympathetic face we need to get our message across.

I remember Tom calling me for a live report in Vienna Airport after the incidents at the Bratislava game. He let me tell it how it was for the fans. Tom would add his own measured comments, having been in similar circumstances himself. The passion he shares with plenty of our fans that England away should represent something positive oozes through his interjections. Tom admits that being a fan himself affects him as a broadcaster: 'Absolutely and definitively. There are plenty of other presenters who know more about playing the game. I don't see the point pretending to be better informed than I am. But what it is to be a football supporter, that is something I can talk about.'

When he is covering England matches Tom draws on what it was like when he travelled to Rome for the Italy match in 1997, and Warsaw for the Euro 2000 qualifier against Poland. 'The reports I was reading didn't match what I was seeing. In Italy the police stood with their backs to the Italian fans. All this stuff was being chucked at the English and as soon as anybody reacted they piled straight into the England fans with their batons. In Poland the safety and security was of a standard that would have a ground closed down in England.' Tom is convinced that journalists have a responsibility to listen and learn, before they attempt to report and explain. 'What I will never do is suggest that England fans are always to blame. But I hope I don't come across as someone who says they're never to blame either. What I want to do is find out all the different elements that are going on. That means only speaking to the limits of your own experience. On radio we can get fans on telling us what they saw, speaking up for themselves.'

I'm one of those fans. Tom, or his editor Pete, will call me up before most games and we'll chat about the likely issues. I make the effort to be always available, and to come up with something or someone a bit unusual for them to cover. Mark in the Northwest, Alan in Lincolnshire and plenty of others have been doing the same thing: making contacts, giving interviews, feeding journalists with stories. It all adds up. But most significant has been the explosion of media outlets all desperate to fill pages or time with every conceivable angle during a major tournament. Radio 5 Live, TalkSPORT, Sky Sports News, the Web, daily sports supplements with nearly every newspaper – most of these didn't exist during the period of the worst excesses involving England: Euro 88, Italia 90 and Euro 92. Of course when things go wrong, such as Marseille at France 98 or Charleroi at Euro 2000, we will be treated to page after page, round-the-clock exhaustive hoolie-watching. But those pages and airtime have to be filled when things are going right too, and this has enabled a much more balanced reporting of what it is to be an England fan to emerge.

England versus Holland, Villa Park, February 2005. Following the widespread racist abuse of our players by the Spanish crowd at the Bernabeu during the previous November's friendly, a good number of supporters had posted messages on the FA's englandfans website about the need to make some sort of fans' antiracist statement at the next game. This open-access forum for all members of England's supporters' club gives an instant voice to fans who previously would never have been heard before. Backed up by other independent websites and email loops, messages and debates spread rapidly.

A few suggested a 'No to Racism' message and the obvious way to do this was with giant letters spelling the slogan out across the huge St George Cross flag I help organize at England home matches. The words would be formed by thousands of fans holding up blue plastic sheets amongst the mass of red and white ones that create the flag. It would be both unmissable and entirely down to fans' willing participation. The FA backed our proposal and we went ahead with all the preparations. None of this was done to simply serve the needs of the media, but to ignore the possibility of amplifying our message and reach millions more than just those in the stadium that night really would have been missing a trick.

BBC Radio London ran a preview piece the night before. Early morning on match day, as the volunteers assembled to lay out the sheets, the local BBC Radio WM did a phone interview with me. The BBC Asian network did another interview with one of the fans involved, Pritpal Tamber. In the stadium Sky Sports News filmed us putting out the sheets and did live interviews. Not just once, but for morning, lunchtime and afternoon shows, with a range of fans, including the Dutch fans we had with us helping out, Harry and Corne.

Harry is a football poet, and gave Sky and Channel 5 a short performance to record. The TV crews were stuck in the stadium all day; they had very little else to film apart from us. There were no players, and the management and coaching staff weren't around either; there was nobody on hand from the FA to interview. Instead it was us fans who provided them with their story. Fans saying no to racism, fans of two countries working together for the same message, fans having a good time doing something positive, and a dash of poetic eccentricity thrown in to spice the piece up. How many times have you heard a poem about football recited on Sky Sports News?

With the massive expansion of the number of media outlets, and channels like Sky Sports News having twenty-four hours of reports to fill, there is at least the possibility of fans getting a contrasting account to pictures of thuggery and violence reported. When trouble does break out and receives its customary saturation coverage, these other stories at least provide some semblance of balance and context.

Walking down Witton Lane on the way to having something to eat before kickoff, a group of us who have been laying out the sheets pass a burger stall. A few lads in the queue point and laugh. They point and shout at Harry, 'Here, you're that Dutch poet, we saw you on Sky, fair play to you, mate.' The verses of his poem *Football Karma* clearly had had some sort of an effect.

Chris Skudder had been doing all the interviews for Sky Sports News. Sky didn't have the broadcast rights to the match itself so anything they could film to add to their coverage of the fixture would be very welcome. It was the same in Portugal where BBC and ITV shared the live rights, as they always do for European Championships and World Cups. At Euro 2004 three crews from Sky Sports covered the tournament; two were based with the England team, and one would cover fan issues, but not specifically trouble. Sky News were expected to cover this, with one crew permanently based in the Algarve, another in Lisbon and a third geared up to travel to any outbreak.

On Sky Sports Andy Gray and Richard Keys anchored the football coverage, Chris provided the bulk of the news material from outside the England team camp, while Nick Collins would cover Sven and the players' press conferences. Chris has done this job for the past two tournaments, though in Portugal he was able to be much more mobile than previously. New technology enabled the cameras filming his reports to be cable-free for live broadcasts, so no longer was he stuck by a satellite truck. Instead he got out and about amongst the fans.

Chris explains the significance of his more portable camera and crew: 'The truck meant we would be stuck in some central location like Rossio Square in Lisbon, but with these new cameras we were able to film and report from far more locations. At the opening game with France there was a huge problem with fans getting access to the stadium. A crush was building up close to kickoff. If we'd stayed in our rooftop vantage point like in the old days the scene would have looked like a riot when we broadcasted it, but we were able to get really close up, do interviews with the fans affected, and it became obvious there was no trouble. Just inefficiency on the part of the stadium management, and fans getting angry that they wouldn't get in on time for kickoff.'

Having covered England matches for quite a few years now, Chris was a familiar face for many at the game and trapped in this pre-match predicament. 'The fans were really eloquent explaining the problems they were facing. It made a great bit of live TV and a superb vehicle for their complaints.' By the time England played at the Estadio da Luz again a week and a bit later all these problems had been sorted out. 'The reports were well received back at Sky, that's important too. We had picked up on a situation and provided coverage which the other TV channels had not.'

The technology means the focus may begin to move away from this single camera angle, inevitably a central square, which then dominates the coverage of England fans, often in a quite unrepresentative way. So why do so many TV cameras all end up in the same place? 'The crews gather where they think there's most likely to be trouble,' explains Chris. 'Charleroi at Euro 2000 was when I was ashamed to be a TV reporter. One small square, cameras pointing at the crowd of fans from every possible vantage point. All waiting for the main event. And of course some of the fans, German as well as English, duly obliged us.'

Chris is aiming for a different type of reporting, to search out all the different locations where fans can be found. 'Ours is a twenty-four-hour rolling TV station. Live coverage is the key, not pre-recorded stuff. The more we can be with the fans, reporting on them as things happen, the better.' What determines the nature of the coverage is down to a combination of existing news values and the fans' own recent record. 'The situation is changing. At Euro 2000 there was such an expectation of trouble – it was what we were all preparing to cover. But that has started to change, as match after match, tournament after tournament, passes off peacefully.'

Chris describes the mix he and his colleagues are expected to provide: 'First the players and management, second the fans, third the local environment.' If the fans are obviously friendly and the local environment pieces are about food to eat, beer or wine to drink and places to see rather than an interview with the chief of police, then the balance is changed quite dramatically. As fans we are not in control of that mix, but we can actively contribute to shifting it towards the positive. This is what was largely lacking before, but since Euro 2000 fans have helped make that change. Chris explains the importance of this contribution. 'News reporting is all about access. If we get the story first then others will feed off our headlines and it snowballs. Previously, for twenty years or more, the only fans' story we had access to was trouble. Now it is different and the reports are slowly changing.'

Apart from Sky Sports, BBC Radio Five Live is the other key media outlet for football coverage. If a fan's story appears on these two stations, plus TalkSPORT, there won't be too many supporters who won't hear it. When England played Portugal in February 2004 Lynn Smith was surprised to be invited to take part in a live item for Five Live's drive-time show. 'I'd taken part in a school visit the fans had organized with the British Council that morning, and afterwards Five Live was looking for someone to go on air and talk about it. It was only a short piece, but instead of talking about the expectation of trouble at the tournament, we were able to chat about all the good things fans were getting up to.' But does this make any difference? 'It must do. The presenter let me put my point across, she asked me sensible questions, most of all she wanted to hear about the atmosphere, which was of course tremendous, a big party.' Lynn doesn't have much time for those who say she shouldn't have bothered, that given half a chance the media will turn the good news we tell into bad news about us. 'I feel we can change things. There's a lot more opportunities now to get across fans' views in the media, and as many fans as possible should take advantage of that, not for ourselves, but for all fans.'

BBC Radio Five Live was only launched in 1994. Euro 96 was the first major tournament the station covered and ever since, every two years, a World Cup or a Euro has dominated its schedules for the best part of June. Add the build-up in the preceding months, plus the qualifying campaign stretching back another eighteen months or so, and it's clear that providing coverage of England, players and fans, is a big part of what Five Live is all about.

Haydn Parry is a producer on the midweek edition of Five Live's *Sport on Five*. During a tournament his job in the studio is to collate ideas for items on the show, make contacts, find contributors and take in reports from BBC journalists in various locations spread all over the country hosting the competition. The England match commentary team for Five Live typically consists of Alan Green and Mike Ingham. It is their priority to cover the matches and team matters, and only rarely will they report on the fans unless something particularly dramatic happens.

'In Japan we had Victoria Derbyshire set up in a bar in Saitama chatting to England, Sweden and local Japanese fans. That kind of thing works really well on Five Live,' says Haydn. He recognizes that as Five Live has evolved the coverage of fans has changed too. 'We were launched in 1994 in the aftermath of the "Italia 90 effect"; the missed penalties, Pavarotti, "Nessun Dorma" and a new audience for football. I worked on the Five Live phone-in at the first tournament we covered, Euro 96. As the tournament unfolded the nature of Five Live's particular type of coverage started to emerge too. There's a big audience going to football which is highly opinionated. We realized we could be an outlet for this and that meant we needed to come across as close as possible to the audience and its experience.'

For some tournaments both the breakfast show and morning show are based in the host country. 'This supplements the staple football coverage, the team news and press conferences. It is these shows which will mainly cover the fans' stories, and if we can find anything positive we'll definitely feature it,' Haydn confirms. 'We want to cover as many different angles as possible, offer that to the listeners and see how they react. Balance is really important to us too, a lot of thought goes in to the range of studio guests we have. We're always looking for new faces, but there's also the reliability of those you can trust to have something useful to say.'

The biggest change for Haydn since Euro 96 has been the accessibility of the station for its listeners. 'Today it's the fans coming to us with their stories much more than us searching them out. Stuff comes in via our website all the time, an editor or a producer like me will look into it and propose it to one of our daily editorial planning meetings. If everyone likes the story then one of us will follow it up, chat to the person who provided it, check that they are reasonably articulate and will be confident enough to put their story across on air. We'll establish all the facts as well, and then discuss how the story would be best presented – finding a way of doing this to maximize the interest for our audience is the key. The question we always ask ourselves when assessing to run a piece is, if we were listeners, would we stay tuned in?'

Gordon Farquhar is Five Live's sports-news correspondent; it is his job to find, and respond to, these fans' stories. 'My first tournament was France 98. We like to promote ourselves as a fan-friendly station and this heavily influences how we cover the England supporters. We'll talk to as many as we can, try to reflect their experiences, get out round the hotels, the camp sites, and check up on issues such as ticketing and security.' Gordon admits there is another story they can't afford not to cover either: 'Trouble. We try to provide the bigger picture but we will never ignore the hooliganism.' Gordon describes the coverage he has been responsible for providing. 'To be accurate you have to be there. That's crucial. You have to watch the build-up, but also what happens afterwards – the actual scale of any damage caused. To look for the reasons why violence erupted. Not being instantly judgemental, but to be as accurate as possible. And distinguish between the boisterous and the offensive.'

The BBC issues strict guidelines to Gordon and his colleagues on how such incidents are covered; one clause specifies: 'It is important for BBC people on the spot to make a judgement about whether apparently spontaneous activity is being staged for the benefit of the cameras. BBC people who suspect that their presence is inflaming a section of the crowd should withdraw at once.' And there is another about how irresponsible coverage can produce more trouble. 'Audiences are concerned about the possibility of people imitating behaviour they see or hear on television and radio. We should try to ensure that any life-threatening, antisocial, or criminal behaviour portrayed in BBC programmes does not encourage copycat actions.'

Gordon will often be the link between the station's sports and news coverage, as he explains: 'Alan Green and his team are really only interested in telling listeners how England won, lost or drew. The news coverage covers everything from Baghdad to Downing Street. I'm the guy in between.' There's a physical barrier between the commentary team and the fans too. 'From two hours before kickoff they'll be holed up in the commentary box at the stadium or thereabouts. They won't be around in town where the fans are gathering, and on the days before a big match they will often be with the team at their hotel, attending press conferences and training sessions.' Gordon's job is to be elsewhere, and this usually means being where the fans are. So what will determine whether a good news story gets covered or not? 'It will depend on a number of factors, most important of which is what else is happening that day. If there's a big news story breaking, football or otherwise, unfortunately this is the kind of item which will get squeezed out.'

When trouble does happen it is only right that Five Live will cover it. 'We will seek to be impartial, accurate and fair. It is incumbent on us to reflect all the different factors that contribute to a situation. We're there primarily as observers, not to pass judgement.' Gordon uses the Charleroi Euro 2000 example to illustrate how this mix of editorial commitments and responsibilities can cause problems. 'We had been broadcasting from the main square since nine a.m. We reflected how the English and German fans were mixing together peacefully. Then the tension started rising as the police became more heavy-handed, followed by a three-minute fight. But the editors were watching the TV-camera footage on their screens back in London. They were convinced this was a major public disorder breakdown and wanted to portray it as such.'

In Portugal the presence of Five Live reporters with the fans had a very different outcome. 'After the Croatia game we were on the buses back into town and wandering around Lisbon city centre. We did four or five reports on the fantastic atmosphere England supporters were creating, and the total lack of trouble. When the story came out of the fan tragically murdered by a pickpocket we were able to put that in context. It was a tragic act of petty criminality gone horribly wrong and nothing to do with crowd trouble. If we hadn't been out there in the town getting a feel of the mood of the fans we might have reported that story very differently, and quite wrongly.'

Gordon is convinced Five Live has made a difference. 'The kind of radio reporting we provide simply didn't exist at Euro 88, Italia 90 and Euro 92. We get our highest listening figures when we are able to create a sense of an event. A World Cup or European Championship is, in that sense, ideal for us to cover.' And the drama of a big occasion is surely going to benefit from good news surrounding that event rather than dread, fear and shame. This is what fans look to the media to help us generate. Not to cover up what might be wrong with our support, but neither should they criminalize us all.

On the day of the Germany–England match in September 2001 I was called in the Munich stadium by Five Live. John Motson wanted me on his lunch-time show to report on the fan-friendly initiative we had organized with a group of German fans. It was a great opportunity; the listening figures for Motty's pre-match build-up would be huge, so of course I agreed.

Motty started the item by asking me why we were in the stadium so early. Live, I replied, 'We're down by the pitch, John. We've got twenty England fans here. We're going to be laying out sheets on every England seat to form a huge St George's Cross when 'God Save the Queen' goes up. We've also got twenty young German fans here because the German FA were so impressed by the fact that we were going to lay out cards to form our national flag they said they wanted to do the same. But they hadn't got a clue how to organize it. So we said in the best new tradition of the friendly, fan ambassadors which we've got following England nowadays, we're going to organize it for them. But unlike on the Costa del Sol, we're going to get our flag down first!'

Motty liked that. He was laughing away and the item was going really well. There had been some trouble the night before and it was only fair he should ask me about that too. What did I think about it? This is live radio – you don't have too much time to consider what you're going to say. 'We're here for a good result and we're here for a good time. For the vast majority of fans that is the mentality. They're here to see the city, a lot of people sampling the beers, unsurprisingly, and sampling the odd bit of sausage and so on, as I'm sure you have been. We've got to ensure that's right at the forefront. Undoubtedly there will be some trouble. If you shifted ten thousand young English males to any city in the world you'd have a bit of trouble. But what you've got to ensure is that it becomes the sideshow rather than the main event. I was in the city last night, I'm sure you and your colleagues were, and I felt that the little bits of fighting there were very much the sideshow. It was a bit like the West End of London on a Saturday night.'

The short item finished and I thought nothing more about it. I couldn't believe it when the following Wednesday Michael Henderson devoted his entire *Daily Telegraph* column to denouncing 'Perryman and his squalid crew', accusing me of saying, 'there's nothing wrong with the odd skirmish' and declaring with all the self-confidence of a big-name columnist, 'There's no doubt about it: Perryman speaks for the English football supporter, in all his bigotry, aggression and cod-patriotism. They'll all be there at St James' Park tonight, singing those horrible songs and imitating the Dambusters, loathing the inhabitants of a country far more at ease with itself than this one is.'

Michael Henderson hadn't bothered to listen to what I had actually said in the interview. I was sure I hadn't said anything remotely resembling what he was accusing me of – the very opposite of what I'd been involved with in Munich. I phoned the station and obtained a tape. As I thought, Henderson had misquoted me. The exact words I had used in the interview perhaps could have been better chosen, but considering I had used most of the interview to describe England fans involved in a friendly initiative with German fans, surely it was as obvious as it could be that we were out in Munich doing something positive.

I wrote Michael Henderson a polite letter pointing out the errors in his report. He responded with a grudging admission that he had reported my words second-hand, and excused his description of my supposed bigotry, aggression and cod-patriotism as a collective noun. Denouncing the entire support, using me merely as a figurehead, apparently made it all right. He finished with at least some words of encouragement, though, wishing me luck for what he considered must be a 'lonely task', suggesting he didn't have much faith we would succeed.

This kind of thing, thankfully, doesn't happen too often, but what it reveals is that for some journalists no explanation for England abroad will ever satisfy them. We can never be as good as they seem to think they are. This is what frames their demonization of us, and is why they deride us for wanting something better.

World Cup 2002, which was so fondly written up afterwards as a great fans' experience, was still being predicted right up to the Argentine game as the next stop on the orgy of destruction that I-N-G-E-R-L-A-N-D had become. 'British soccer hooligans are secretly plotting to wreck the World Cup,' claimed the *Sunday Mirror*. Two years later, prior to Euro 2004, it was another kind of story that previewed the tournament in the London *Evening*

The Blame Game

Standard. The paper devoted its front-page lead a month before kickoff to a piece headlined: ROBOCOPS AWAIT ENGLAND FANS. It went on: 'English football fans heading to Euro 2004 were warned today they face a force of hi-tech "robocops". Portuguese police have spent £8 million on an armoury to crush hooliganism at the tournament and will have on standby a rapid-reaction-force of specially trained riot officers. The list of how the money has been spent shows the scale of preparations for the arrival of 1.2 million fans on 12 June. It includes 17,640 pepper sprays, 1,465 riot truncheons, and 40 stun-grenade launchers.'

It would be irresponsible to pretend this kind of coverage is an excuse, or even an explanation, for what sometimes follows. But to imagine it doesn't feature at all as a contributory factor would be equally foolhardy. It is part of a potent mix that combines universal condemnation with reckless forecasting of certain trouble, and draws this together in the way any actual outrages are reported. After yet another night of fighting involving groups of England fans at Euro 88 the *Daily Mail* let loose with all its pent-up editorial exasperation: 'It is ironic that, as we remember with distaste that appeasement of fifty years ago against the street gangs of murderous organized yobbery of the Nazis, there is a shameful parallel of appeasement towards our own barbarism which is growing in menace every day. Football hooliganism is merely the spearhead.' Strong words, but we must seriously doubt the author's sense of proportion. However bad the trouble, were those involved really about to inflict a blitzkrieg across Europe as the writer seems to suggest? Neither exaggeration nor generalization are any help in developing an accurate picture of the scale and nature of the problem we face. Rather they represent a real obstacle for those actually seeking solutions.

During World Cup 2002 *Guardian* journalist Joseph Harker complained about all the overenthusiastic reporting of England fans in Japan. 'I know everyone's talking about how well behaved the fans have been this time, but it only takes an England defeat for it all to change. Remember Euro 2000? England lost to Portugal: the fans rioted. They lost to Romania: they rioted again.' Joseph's article was a well-argued piece about the racism that has deterred him from supporting England, but that's no excuse for getting his facts so hopelessly wrong. There was no trouble when England suffered those two defeats in 2000. Yet his impression that there must have been was so strong he felt he didn't need to bother to check the details. I-N-G-E-R-L-A-N-D spelled trouble, that was all Joseph needed to know to write his comment piece.

Steve Beauchampe was there at the beginning when fans first tried to turn this situation around. He can enjoy his England trips now, but back at Euro 88 it was very different. 'As England fans we were the media's folk-devils. One week it would be rottweiler dogs and the next, us. They never had to justify their coverage. We made such an easy target for everything they wanted to write.' Things got worse two years later at Italia 90. 'It was like they were making up a photo-fit picture of hooliganism, and then put our faces in the frame. For months on end the papers were full of stories about the threat we posed, the black-market tickets we'd get hold of, how the police were preparing for us, and the minister for sport, Colin Moynihan, would be talking up the risk of trouble and how we were all hooligans too.'

The impact on the Italians was something Steve has never forgotten. 'I can remember going into shops and the shopkeepers would cheerfully greet us in broken English: '"Ello, English hooligan?" They genuinely thought there was no such word as fan in our vocabulary.' But Steve knew only too well that a different kind of fan did exist. 'I was one of them. We enjoyed our football, but we wanted a holiday too. This was before the era of budget airlines – the World Cup was our one trip abroad of the year and we were determined to enjoy ourselves. We had no interest in the trouble, it wrecked our chances of having a good time. But the media never seemed to notice us.'

Steve was an activist with the newly formed Football Supporters' Association. Fairly quickly Steve found himself fielding numerous interview requests from journalists. He was forced to explain the trouble and the violence that the media claimed was always the fault of the English. 'Looking back on it we excused away too much. There *was* trouble caused by some England fans but we were just so fed up with only ever being a bad-news story. We knew that you could go to Italy, follow England and see no violence, and nobody was listening.'

Steve is surprised it has taken so long for things to get better. 'Back home Italia 90 was huge, Gazza's tears and all that. Yet the way the media portrayed the fans hardly changed. This contributed to narrowing the appeal of following England to a hardened few. There was still only a small support out in Sweden for Euro 92. Not much more than four thousand, the same kind of numbers that were in Italy for most of the World Cup. Even for the semifinal against the Germans only ten thousand made it out to Turin.'

Euro 96 was what made the difference for Steve. A tournament at home with the biggest numbers since 1966 following England, and little or no trouble. Certainly none in and around Wembley, where all of England's games were played. 'It was France 98 where the Euro 96 effect had its impact. How many went over to France, twenty-five thousand? Thirty thousand? Maybe more. It was just so obvious that most weren't there to fight, and there was a diversity too. More women than had ever followed England abroad before, families and a small but growing number of black and Asian fans. The vast majority had never been to a tournament overseas. With the much smaller numbers out in Germany, Italy and Sweden those who wanted to cause trouble were much more noticeable. It was easier for them to dominate, but not in France with this much broader support. When there was trouble in Marseille and Lens it became harder for the media to ignore the very obvious fact that it was only a minority involved.'

Decades' worth of gross overgeneralizations that all England fans were ignorant thugs was also consistently accompanied by the regular exaggerating of the situation. In one edition during Euro 88 the *Daily Mirror* declared, 'We'll use guns – Rommel's city cops get tough' and then three days later added, 'The knowledge that Englishmen abroad are terrifying innocent German families horrifies us.' Of course most Englishmen terrified nobody, and thankfully no German guns were fired either, with or without instructions from Stuttgart's mayor, Rommel's grandson, but the impression stuck.

The broadsheets, particularly the liberal ones, are never quite sure what to do with the combination of pride, and the occasional dash of prejudice that is I-N-G-E-R-L-A-N-D. At Italia 90 Matthew Engel in the *Guardian* expressed his contradictory appreciation of what he was witnessing at England versus Holland. 'It would be premature to say one attended a football match and felt proud to be English, but one did not feel actively ashamed. "Rule Britannia" took over. If they added "Jerusalem" and the Henry Wood sea shanties to their repertoire, these evenings might become quite agreeable.' There's a certain snobbishness about Engel's comments but at least he was trying to understand what was going on, not writing off those he stood with as xenophobes and bigots just because the team they support is the national side.

The *Daily Mirror* was less interested than Matthew Engel and other journalists at this tournament who, for the first time, filed reports that began to speculate whether there was something to be admired about our fans' dogged determination as they supported England through the highs, lows and final exit of a World Cup. WE

The Blame Game

FACE A WAR IF ENGLAND WIN was the garish front-page headline of the *Mirror* the day before England's 1990 semifinal with Germany. It was a quote from the Mayor of Turin who had expressed in reckless terms the city's fears of disorder. It was a story that needed reporting, but was a front-page splash really necessary?

With England hosting Euro 96 some continued to doubted our ability to join in all the fun of a tournament even on home soil. Ian Wooldridge in the *Daily Mail* wrote: 'Far from anticipating a carnival, millions are cringing in apprehension of what further indignities will befall us in the name of sport in the next three weeks. How real is the threat to bring Euro 96 to a violent halt by the hooligans who have got their hooks into football?' Not very real at all, Ian, as most other journalists quickly appreciated once the tournament began. The *Daily Mirror* captured this mood well: 'There is a new spirit. It really is remarkable. It will not disappear throughout the rest of Euro 96. It shows there is still the old feeling, the old sense of community. And the old sense of pride.'

But misgivings remained. Not about how the fans behaved but the emotions which were being released. It began with the Dutch, as the *Daily Mirror* implored its readers to 'Pull up the tulips, and throw out any Edam cheese in the fridge'. So ludicrous a declaration was never going to be taken seriously, and with no obvious history of rivalry off the pitch we could safely dismiss the consequences and have a good chuckle. Particularly when the finest night at Wembley since 1966 saw Holland dispatched 4–1 by England.

Things turned uglier with the prospect of playing Spain in the quarterfinal. Did the *Daily Mirror* really do anybody any favours by starting their preview of the match with '10 Nasties Spain's given Europe' topped by 'Syphilis, Spanish Flu and Carpet bombing', an extraordinary third choice given the carnage and destruction suffered by the Spanish citizens of Guernica.

183

And then, of course, with the Spanish knocked out by Pearce's decisive penalty, the Germans awaited us and the *Daily Mirror* editor, Piers Morgan, threw any remaining caution, and conscience, where he'd presumably deposited his Edam cheese.

'Achtung! Surrender! For you, Fritz, ze Euro 96 Championship is over. Last night the *Daily Mirror*'s ambassador in Berlin handed the German Government a final note stating that unless we heard from them by eleven o'clock that they were prepared at once to withdraw their football team from Wembley, a state of soccer war would exist between us.' And just in case we missed the point, across two pages inside the paper added, 'England's old enemy – defeated in two World Wars and one World Cup – formally announced that they would stand firm on the historic battlefield in north London.'

And afterwards these selfsame journalists pontificate about why the pride we take in our team so often comes with an unwelcome amount of prejudice against the opposition. However, when we blame the media for making such an unhelpful contribution we shouldn't make the mistake of overstating their influence either. Those papers which commented on the fantastic atmosphere of the Wembley crowds during Euro 96 weren't simply scoring points at the expense of the *Daily Mirror* for its error in seeking to make sales out of bashing assorted Johnny Foreigners. They were also paying tribute to their readers' well-worn ability not to believe all that journalists write. Paul Hayward in the *Daily Telegraph* recorded the friendly mood of the crowd, so removed from the temper of much of the press. 'For once we could dispute the idea that newspapers are a mirror held up to society. This was not about hating another country but supporting an England team who have surpassed all rational expectations.'

Four years after the *Daily Mirror* had so spectacularly misread the mood before England–Germany at Euro 96 the paper previewed the match between the two countries at Euro 2000. 'The *Mirror* has had a few problems covering this fixture in the past, so we won't try and squeeze in any clever little jokes about you know what. All we will say is this. The kickoff is at 19.45. Time for victory, boys.' They couldn't resist it could they? Whether it is journalists or fans mistaking world cups for world wars, or confusing their number three for our 3 Para, it is a mix-up we could well do without.

Of course, those who take the intent of these kinds of headlines too seriously have more than the papers to blame for their attitude problem. As an academic expert in media analysis, Emma Poulton takes more time reading the papers than most. 'We mustn't invest too much cultural power in newspaper coverage, the tabloids particularly. They don't create confrontations. At the same time they're not blameless.' Emma is keen to emphasize that outcomes, violent or otherwise, are not inevitable as a result of this coverage. 'The press coverage doesn't make people behave in a certain way, it would be crass to suggest that. It's more a case of the media being responsible for helping create a heightened level of expectancy before tournaments that we're going to do so much better than previous history would suggest, and if and when that overzealous, euphoric bubble bursts, there can sometimes be a negative reaction from some supporters.' This is a shared responsibility. The trouble is that too many from each side want to hold the other entirely to blame.

Emma has researched the media coverage of England for over ten years and picks two key moments to illustrate how things have changed. 'Euro 96 was when there was a genuine sense of popular outrage at the press going too far with their jingoism. Of course it still happens, Germany in 2000 and 2001, Argentina in 2002, Turkey in 2003, but there is now some sense of awareness of the limits too. The coverage has become at least a little more measured and responsible. And Euro 2004 – after the big splashes the papers ran on the two or three nights of trouble in Albufeira the press agreed with what the police, the FA, UEFA, the Portuguese authorities were saying. That it wasn't to do with the football. They calmed their coverage down and ended up saying a lot of good things about the fans.' This could represent a breakthrough, she argues: 'Before every previous tournament the papers have been full of predictions of trouble, forecasting with certainty where it will occur. That has slowly been lessened and the positive reviews of the fans in Portugal should hopefully help this develop.'

Amy Lawrence was in Portugal covering Euro 2004 for the *Observer*. She is a football journalist, writing match reports and previews, interviewing the players, profiling the teams. She doesn't cover much of what goes on outside the stadiums and the training camps, but she's very aware of how the fans help shape the tournament she is writing about. 'I'm a fan who happens to be a journalist. And I hope that comes across in my writing. I feel incredibly privileged, getting paid to cover a sport I love.'

Amy started off penning articles for *The Gooner*, the Arsenal fanzine, then became involved with the FSA before helping launch *FourFourTwo* as one of their main writers. 'That era, the late 1980s when the fanzines really took off, has become very influential in terms of how football is covered today. There was a self-mocking humour. We didn't take ourselves too seriously but at the same time there was a space to discuss the issues that did matter. Hillsborough, commercialization, racism and what did, and didn't, cause hooliganism. We were irreverent but not irresponsible, and we helped force the national press to recognize that fan culture was changing.'

This has undoubtedly had an impact on how England fans are covered by the media too. When the trouble was at its worst the outlets that might have added some context, listen to explanations, or give the other side of the story, hardly existed. But as they did emerge, Sky, Five Live, TalkSPORT and a great variety of websites, they were shaped by the influence of what Amy was part of. This affected the press too. The tabloids started to seek fan comments and stories, while the broadsheets recruited former fanzine writers and added sports supplements where a greater range of accounts and explanations would feature.

'The horror stories the front pages carried during Euro 88, Italia 90 and Euro 92 were slowly being eroded by what we were writing about in the fanzines, a very different account of what it was to be a fan.' According to Amy, what really changed everything, though it wasn't immediately apparent, was Italia 90. She went there as a fan of world football, and deliberately avoided England games. 'As a teenager I'd always felt alienated by the national team. But Gazza's tears, the incredible joy at what the team achieved, those memorable scenes after the third-place play-off with our fans dancing in the stands, the team joining in too, all this struck a chord. It turned the fearful image on its head, made me feel incredibly good and gave me some faith that following England could be positive. And it became impossible for the media to ignore this.'

Nevertheless she remained cautious, unsure whether this happy way of following England could outlast all she felt had gone before it. 'When you see the other horrible side of this support it knocks you back, makes you question the game that you love. How can you rationalize that kind of behaviour? How can you begin to explain it?'

Unless there is a major incident of trouble inside the stadium – and even in the worst of times this was rare – the football writers rarely write about the fans. Nor do they often comment about the positive contribution of the fans to the tournament's atmosphere. News of this type tends to appear elsewhere in the paper, but not on the back pages. Amy explains why: 'We don't have the time to cover anything apart from the match and the team's performance.

Our job is to produce one thousand words almost as soon as the final whistle is blown. We're writing away while the game is being played, shut off inside the press box, concentrating on the game, nothing else.' Amy admits, though, that the whole media package does construct a particular image of fans. 'Not all fans are demons, and not all journalists are mischievous either. Neither of us have exactly covered ourselves in glory over the years. Now we have the opportunity to change how we write about the fans. If football journalists don't do that, then we'll be to blame.'

The blame game, we all like to play it. The media have never had a good word for us and vice versa. Except, given half a chance, plenty of journalists would prefer to write a positive story about England off the pitch every bit as much as they'd like to carry a World Cup victory splashed across back, front and most pages in-between. Euro 96, World Cup 2002 and Euro 2004 began to disprove that pessimistic press adage: bad news sells, good news doesn't. While we failed to win on the pitch, the stories and pictures of our fans told us I-N-G-E-R-L-A-N-D was starting to change, to mean something different. All national identities need stories, what sociologists call a 'grand narrative'.

As Englishness rediscovers itself it will draw on stories ancient, 1066 and all that, as well as modern, 1966 and all that. Euro 96 marked the start of a decade's worth of England qualifying, if not yet winning, every tournament going. Add the 2003 rugby world cup win and the 2005 Ashes victory to the mix and the past ten years have seen plenty of opportunities for friendly bouts of flag-waving to fill our screens and front pages. As the excesses and stereotypes that saturated the media coverage of England away of an earlier era start to subside in favour of something bordering on human interest, then quite a different story gets a chance to be written. Home truths from football, read all about it.

7

Out of Order

Clifford Stott isn't someone who sticks out in a crowd of fans. He slips into the background unnoticed, quietly observing and recording what the rest of us are getting up to. In the fields surrounding Liechtenstein's tiny Vaduz stadium when England played their Euro 2004 qualifier there Clifford was taking notes. He was feeling a bit battered and bruised following an awkward encounter the night before in one of the seedier parts of Zurich with a particularly nasty bunch of what he thinks were Bristol City fans.

The allocation of tickets for England fans for this match had been very small, less than a thousand. The total stadium capacity was barely three thousand. A weekend game, a meaningful qualifier, in a part of Europe cheap and easy to reach by budget airline; all this meant England's following was considerably larger than the tickets provided for.

All through the day the numbers mount up. To police the crowd Liechtenstein, a country which doesn't add up to much more than one not very long valley, has borrowed vehicles, riot shields, helmets, batons and police officers from neighbouring countries. The ground is surrounded by fields, with barbed wire hurriedly strung across the wide-open spaces and pockets of policemen with snarling dogs patrolling where cows and sheep normally roam. They are intent on repelling any invasion by the ticketless.

As kickoff approaches quite a crush builds up on the road outside the single entry point where our invaluable tickets will be carefully scrutinized for any telltale signs of forgery. The fences which pen us in as we wait start rocking as some try to force their way in. This is making the security guards edgy and as the size of the crowd grows a few manage to push down the fences and scramble across the fields, with police in a mud-splattered rural equivalent of hot pursuit. A handful of fans make it into the ground and the security, probably sensibly, decide it's safer to never mind the losses and leave them to their own devices. Most, though, are caught and marched off in handcuffs and half-nelsons. Clifford has his designer-jacket collar turned up, quietly, anonymously taking all this in. Carefully identifying where the police have stationed themselves, doing his best to measure the mood of the crowd, catching conversations where he can, asking questions of faces he recognizes and trusts for their opinion on what is going on.

Liechtenstein away. The night before the match a few smashed-up bars with some arrests in one part of Zurich. Fans chased across fields trying to break into a game they didn't have tickets for. An average sort of trip.

Clifford Stott packs away his observations of how the weekend has passed off and travels back home. Another phase in gathering together a detailed picture of the dynamics of the I-N-G-E-R-L-A-N-D crowd completed. In Zurich, he felt the policing went too easily from one inappropriate extreme to another. 'The policing was all or nothing. For hours England fans who were clearly up for trouble were left to provoke and confront with no police intervention. Yet at other times when there was nothing going on the police were walking about firing tear gas and then withdrawing. This had the effect of drawing confrontational fans out of the bars into the street, by which time the police had withdrawn. If the police had been more proactive they could have set limits much earlier in the day and it is likely that had they done so none of the later events in Zurich, including the smashing-up of a kebab shop, would ever have happened.'

In Liechtenstein, again, according to Clifford, a situation had been allowed to develop which could have been prevented. 'Up at the ground it was obvious what was going to happen. These fans who didn't have tickets and like a ruck do as they always try to do. They create a public-safety issue at the entrance to build up pressure. This forces the authorities to let the crowd through without adequate checking because, if they don't, people in the crowd could be crushed. They did this and some of those fans got in without a ticket. What the police and security should have done is structured the entrance in ways that didn't allow such pressure to build up.'

Clifford is very clear how he would like to see England fans policed. 'What I want the police and stadium stewards to do is act earlier, with less force, and direct their attention not at England fans in general, but specifically at those fans that deserve to be arrested because they are actually doing something wrong at that time.'

Clifford is a social psychologist. He has been following England fans to games since Italia 90, trying to understand what turns one group of fans violent while another remains peaceful. At first his views were treated as a tad barmy; not many in anything resembling positions of influence would even give him a hearing. Give our fans the right conditions and nothing will happen? This was entirely different from the consensus of blame and criminalization which just about everyone else offered up as common sense. It took fourteen years of nothing very much getting better until Clifford was finally taken seriously.

After Euro 2000 the government introduced the legislation that imposed banning orders. At the same time the Home Office agreed to back Clifford's research in order to develop some sort of under-standing of the processes that caused the violence that had followed in I-N-G-E-R-L-A-N-D's wake for so long. Clifford explains how Euro 2000 proved a turning point: 'Policing likes to deal with fixed categories, but most of those who got into trouble had no previous record. They weren't known hooligans – blaming it all on a band of tightly organized "generals" and their troops just didn't add up.' There was an increasing realization that the tough new laws on their own would not be enough; something else had to change as well – policing practice.

'Marseilles in 1998 was all about a particular expression of what it means to be an England fan becoming dominant,' says Clifford. 'A group of fans felt under threat by the locals, and unprotected. Violence as a response became legitimized, and those with a willingness to be violent empowered.'

Marseilles was by no means an isolated example. Warsaw, September 1999, England v Poland, our final qualifying match of a frankly dismal Euro 2000 campaign. Poland has been a frequent away destination for England over the years and is renowned as a risky place to be if you don't know enough to spot the warning signs of trouble heading in your direction. Anne and I made it to the ground nice and early – we do this to avoid any of the hassle when the crowd getting into the stadium builds up close to kickoff time.

As the night darkened and more fans arrived there were tales of assaults in the park area at the back of the ground. Up the front of our section was a large group of our fans, hoods up, scarves round their faces, forsaking their seats to stand immediately in front of the cage penning us in. I was just beginning to wish they'd sit down like the rest of us so I could get a decent view of the pitch when the first flare was fired into the seats behind me by the Poles. These were rockets – if you were caught by one of these you'd be left with a very nasty burn, or maybe something worse.

Anne was terrified, and I wasn't feeling too chirpy either. A lot of the fans around us left immediately, perhaps not the best thing to do with the park outside to face and goodness knows who lurking behind the trees and bushes. The Polish police and stewards were doing nothing about those firing the flares. It was a nightmare. And then those lads who I'd felt uneasy about, and kept my distance from, climbed over the fence between us and the Poles. In large numbers they swarmed over the seats, pushing the Poles back, forcing the security men into some kind of action to create a safe zone between us and them. It didn't make me feel particularly good, but the physical response of those fans had helped save the day for the rest of us.

This is the kind of situation that Clifford is convinced contributes to the formation of a violent culture, which in certain circumstances will move from minority to majority status. 'A perceived vulnerability can lead to antagonism towards others,' he says. A kind of defence mechanism in other words, often resulting in offensive consequences. Events are allowed to develop that permit a violent response to be agreed to, acted upon and supported by more than those simply looking to cause trouble.

In a report on the Marseilles trouble at World Cup 98 he co-wrote with fellow researchers John Drury and Paul Hutchinson, Clifford established a line of reasoning that would influence all his future investigations: 'As they arrived in Marseilles, increasing numbers of English supporters understood themselves as being confronted by persistent taunts, threats and at times unprovoked violence, from large groups of local youths. They also experienced policing that appeared to go from one extreme to another; from police inactivity during situations of provocation and violence to "heavy-handed" indiscriminate intervention in situations of English retaliation or defence. Those supporters not directly witnessing these events soon came into contact with those who had.'

His conclusion established the very real dangers to public order that could follow if such an attitude that supports a violent reaction is allowed to take over: 'English supporters who had not previously been engaged in conflict came to understand violence as a proper social action and then gathered together, particularly with those that were prepared to confront, and therefore provide defence from, local youths.'

While Clifford was completing his report on France 98, Otto Adang, Professor of Public Order Management at the Netherlands Police Academy, was preparing for the likelihood of similar scenes should England qualify for Euro 2000. The trouble in the main square of Charleroi when England played Germany at this tournament has become a symbol of all that is wrong with I-N-G-E-R-L-A-N-D. There was a very real threat from UEFA that the team would be expelled from the championships.

One immediate consequence was the wrecking of what remained of England's ill-fated, but high-prestige, bid to host World Cup 2006. For these reasons Euro 2000 is not remembered with much fondness, which means that what happened in Eindhoven, for England's opening match with Portugal (losing 2–3 after the rosy glow of being 2–0 up) is often forgotten. The city was packed with almost as many England fans as Charleroi a few days later – many would be the same individuals. Yet not a hint of trouble, even though we lost.

Otto's mission was to investigate and explain the contrast in order to create a policing strategy that the Dutch could share with police forces for future tournaments. He came up with the neat phrase 'friendly but firm' to describe what he found was the answer.

The job of Otto and his team of observers during Euro 2000 was to try to identify what kind of police and crowd behaviour would be most likely to produce a peaceful outcome. Otto's final report listed these key factors: 'The participation of fans in safe and festive circumstances. Any police intervention should be preventative rather than late and excessively repressive. Maintain a visible yet discreet permanent police presence, in all places, linked to the possibility of fast proportional intervention.'

Based on what he had seen work at Euro 2000, Otto outlined the basic tactics of how in future to police a football crowd: 'Small surveillance units in regular uniform, who are easily approachable and actively contact fans. Decentralized intervention units are kept away from the street scene for as long as possible. Fast information flow and use of the knowledge and skills of the foreign police services.'

Does all this add up to wishy-washy Dutch liberalism unable to cope when things get dangerously out of hand? Otto doesn't think so. 'It is important to emphasize that the "friendly but firm" policing style is not a "laissez-faire" approach: it involves officers actively responding at an early stage to relatively minor infractions of the pre-set tolerance limits. The results show that it is possible to maintain public order effectively in this way without creating a siege situation.'

As our own Home Office started to look around for similar long-term solutions to the problems caused by hooliganism, Clifford Stott found his ideas – backed up now by something similar from Holland – received some sort of hearing from those who mattered. Clifford and Otto were both invited to advise not only the British police responsible for dealing with public disorder caused by England fans, but crucially the Portuguese police who would be responsible for policing Euro 2004. 'We were offering a scientific method to officers desperate to find the most effective ways to police fans with the minimum of public disruption,' explains Clifford. 'Our approach worked because we had access to the authorities; we could influence their approach while retaining the trust of fan groups who knew what we were up to, and interested parts of the media supported us as well.'

With Euro 2004 over and the widespread public disorder failing to materialize, Clifford is able to assess precisely what had been achieved. 'The Portuguese police recognized that in order to prevent violence they needed to differentiate. They have to observe and communicate what they see. Any intervention must be both timely and focused.'

Clifford believes riots are avoided when police actions are perceived as appropriate. Most crowds are naturally law-abiding. If the police are clearly acting to protect our security they will have our support, however grudging. This leaves the hooligan element isolated, while the rest of us avoid the sites of conflict, practising whatever level of self-policing responsibilities that suit us best. If police actions are widely regarded as inappropriate, hitting out indiscriminately, posing a threat rather than offering protection, then the mood of aggression becomes universal. Resistance is widely supported and the conditions for conflict take over.

Clifford consults his Euro 2004 field notes to recount a story which for him sums up the shifts he observed in the bars and on the pavements around Rossio Square in Lisbon. 'When England played Croatia, a large number of lads were gathered in a bar and one of them spotted some Croatians who were coming their way and definitely looking for trouble. He went over and warned the police that if they didn't do something fast there could be savage consequences.' Clifford asked the fan who'd requested the police to act why he'd done so, and he replied, 'This is fantastic. This is England away. But if something kicks off we'll get the blame and it's fucking wrong. If somebody has a go at our country we've been bred for the last two thousand years to fight back. I saw them Croatian lads coming and it was fucking obvious that they were going to have a go. So I got up and did something about it, to get the police to move the Croatians before the England boys sussed out what was going on. If they had it would have gone off.'

Portugal was different from previous tournaments. A non-violent and friendly fandom dominated becauses the causes that might legitimize a violent reaction beyond the most hardcore troublemakers were either not present or eliminated. The policing was low-profile, widely accepted and appropriate. An identification with fans of other nations through what we had in common, football, began to emerge. Hooliganism and violence was treated as extreme, opposed to all that we were enjoying so much.

The mainstream view for the past twenty years or more has paid hardly any heed to this kind of approach. The liberal-minded *New Statesman* suggested during Euro 2000: 'What the authorities should have done from the moment the first beer-bellied lout stepped on to Continental soil to give his first two-fingered salute: send the English ingloriously home.' No differentiation, rather clampdown and expulsion. 'The simple answer, when football matches are thought likely to cause mayhem, is to ban them as a threat to public order.' That's right, don't just give up on the fans, abandon the entire sport too.

As Euro 2004 approached this kind of thinking gained increasing currency, especially after the FA sought to prevent fans from travelling to the September and October 2003 qualifiers in Macedonia and Turkey. Simon Barnes, who in his column in *The*

Times had shown a real grasp of the double-sided nature of the passion that filled the Stadium of Light a few months earlier, used the imposition of this one-off ban to call for more drastic measures.

> The FA should follow this excellent precedent and refuse to sell tickets to England fans for any other overseas fixture. England fans should be banned on aesthetic grounds, on the grounds of noise abatement, on the grounds of taste, on the grounds of racism, on the grounds of threatening behaviour, on the grounds of vilely invasive demeanour. And that's before the trouble starts. There will beyond question be trouble if England qualify for the European Championship in Portugal next summer. I don't care about the minority of self-styled 'decent' England supporters. They exist, but there aren't enough of them and they lack the moral force to influence the majority.

On the grounds of racism and threatening behaviour? Absolutely right, bans should be handed out left, right and centre on those who offend on this count. But because we're noisy, or we wear a different designer label to Simon Barnes' liking? He is mixing up good grounds for condemnation with a surly mix of snobbery and proclamations that everybody in an England shirt is guilty until proven innocent. This leaves the friendly fans, who Barnes and others don't count as worth the effort supporting, exposed and marginalized.

All of this, and worse, has dogged I-N-G-E-R-L-A-N-D since the early 1980s. Like Clifford Stott, John Williams is a keen observer of England abroad. John is Head of the Centre for the Sociology of Sport and has been compiling reports on England fans for government organizations over the past twenty years. 'I'd been a fan myself since the 1960s, Liverpool home and away. I was interested in understanding how this shoddy list of incidents had become so closely associated in the public mind with England fans. Club fans might cause trouble as well, but by the 1980s it was England's following that had become the focal point of popular and political anxiety.'

From the 1982 World Cup in Spain onwards John has followed England to most of the major tournaments, and a fair number of qualifiers too. The changes in England's support during this period have been huge. 'In the 1980s the hooligans felt England belonged to them. They were unchallenged by the rest, they dominated. Today that is no longer the case. The hooligans are swamped. That's down to wider changes underway in the game which has made following England abroad a much more attractive proposition than ever before.'

Those who now make the away trips, especially to big tournaments, are very different to the fans who travelled to Spain and Germany in the 1980s. 'Back then there were large numbers of young men, seventeen or eighteen years old, following England away. They were active fans, but unused to overseas travel, and often went without either tickets or accommodation. A plastic bag with a spare set of clothes was about all that they took with them. They didn't carry flags or wear England shirts. They just turned up, and invariably somehow found their way into the matches they were travelling to see.'

Since France 98 much of this has altered. 'Today's England fans are that much bit older. There's a significant number taking children with them. Many seem more willing to try out the unfamiliar in the countries they visit. They fix up their travel arrangements in advance.'

John is unconvinced there is an ongoing cycle of violence to be broken, rather there are particular triggers that switch it on and off. 'The question I always ask is whether a group of people can come together to make trouble happen.' In his view the authorities can only have a limited impact on the outcome. 'There are four factors that will create the conditions for such a group to assemble. First, the history: is there a long-standing rivalry that needs accounting for? Second, have there been recent incidents of trouble involving one, or both, sets of fans? Third, is there a local opposition, how will they react and respond to the arrival of England fans in their territory? Fourth, are the hooligans able to define the situation? What are the rest of the fans like, will the troublemakers have sufficient numbers to back them up, to provide cover?'

John is convinced that what determines how these different factors unfold is the fans' reaction to the away location. 'The key moment is the beginning of an event, the first few days of "occupation". This will help determine how fans see their own situation. There is a natural sense of excitement, of being there. They want their presence to be memorable, and this is expressed in particularly intense expressions of what it means to be English.' John was out in the main square of Lisbon watching as the first forty-eight hours of England in Portugal took shape. 'There were moments when things could have gone horribly wrong. The sheer numbers, the exuberance, the drinking, it all added up. When the fans filled up the roads, blocked the traffic, the police could have cleared people out of the way in a manner that would have spread fear and panic. Instead they took a risk. They dealt with the crowd in segments, didn't rush at them all. They prevented a conflict arising and fairly soon the fans drifted away, point made, allowing traffic to move again.'

Many of those seeking some sort of explanation why situations like this in Portugal didn't descend into violent conflict, credited not just the local policing tactics but also legislation which banned known English troublemakers from reaching Portugal. David Bohannan, head of the Football Disorder Unit at the Home Office is one of the most determined advocates of the effectiveness of the football banning orders. Football hooliganism associated with England isn't exactly a new phenomenon. If these bans are the answer, why has the legislation to impose them taken so long to be introduced? 'Laws designed to tackle football disorder were introduced from 1986 onwards, but they were piecemeal and never really tackled the problem. Moreover, there was not an effective football disorder strategy in place – in truth, there appears to have been a limited understanding of the evolving dynamic and character of the phenomenon. The approach tended to be based on superficial and, in some cases, wrong assumptions: like football hooligans are not true fans, and that the problems are caused by people travelling to tournaments overseas without authorized tickets. To be effective, the strategy and the law needed to be far more sophisticated.'

It was the trouble involving England fans at Euro 2000 that finally forced the government to act decisively. 'That disorder changed the political climate. It resulted in the Home Office being tasked to prepare a multi-agency strategy and to co-ordinate multi-agency preparations for overseas tournaments. Before, the preparations of the various agencies had been quite extensive but not co-ordinated or complementary. Some good work was being done but it remained fragmentary.'

When the Home Office took over, David and his staff started to redefine football hooliganism in judicial terms. An impressive armoury of laws and police powers already appeared to exist to deal with the problem. Yet twenty years or more of failure, despite the regular demands after every supposed outrage for the most extreme measures to be taken, suggested that they were in fact both ineffectual and inappropriate. 'After Euro 2000, our extended role enabled us to analyse the dynamic of football disorder and set about moulding a judicial response.'

However, it was recognized from the start that a response that concentrated solely on new laws would be inadequate. 'In terms of trouble abroad, we knew that to make any sort of impact we had to change the environment in which disorder occurred,' says David. 'In isolation, tough policing and tough criminal sanctions wouldn't work. Contrary to media reporting, most football hooligans are passionate about football and the team they follow. The key question centred on why do some individuals demonstrate their passion for football in a violent or antisocial way, and why so many people who never cause problems at domestic matches get drawn into the problem when they follow England overseas. It was in this wider context that banning orders would be the key to tackling the problem, not least because those who cause or get involved in trouble truly fear being denied access to football.'

David Bohannan recognizes here why fans who travel abroad with England are suspicious of police efforts to control the violent minority. 'Up to and including Euro 2000, attention centred on thousands of England fans travelling to tournaments overseas in the expectation of being treated as potential hooligans. This generated a kind of self-fulfilling prophecy with host police tactics being designed around the inevitability of mass English disorder, and treating all England fans with suspicion or hostility. This made fans feel excluded and defensive which, in turn, increased the tension and sometimes prompted a heavy and disproportionate policing response to minor problems. We had to try and break that cycle and we felt that the football banning orders would offer the primary means.'

The Football Disorder Act 2000 introduced as a completely new procedure 'a banning order on complaint', rather than conviction. Clause 14b makes scary reading, describing a legitimate case for an order as follows: 'An application for a banning order in respect of any person made by the chief officer of police for the area in which the person resides or appears to reside, if it appears to the officer that the condition below is met. That condition is that the respondent has at any time caused or contributed to any violence or disorder in the United Kingdom or elsewhere.' With disorder defined as including 'displaying any writing or other thing which is threatening, abusive or insulting', there is more than a hint of a catch-all clause. To secure the support of fans and soften any suspicion of bans being slapped on all and sundry, the police need to be seen to be fair, just and targeted in their approach.

David is certain this is the case. 'The tough banning order legislation was designed to prevent people with a track record of causing problems from travelling to matches overseas. This was a reasonable and proportionate response to the legacy of major incidents and we ensured that the process would include a number of safeguards intended to minimize the impact on basic human rights like freedom of movement. For example, any court being asked to impose a banning order has to be satisfied that banning an individual will help to prevent violence and disorder in connection with football. That places the burden on the police to gather evidence at home and abroad that will demonstrate to the court's satisfaction that an individual poses a threat to public order. Once banned, the travel restriction only comes into effect when matches are played overseas. Otherwise there is no impediment to travel. Even during the period of a tournament, a banned individual can seek an exemption if they can demonstrate that they have to travel for personal or employment reasons. Each case is treated on its merits.'

David's argument is that fans who have (sometimes legitimate) doubts about the banning orders applied and the airport checks carried out need to appreciate the overall impact. 'The banning orders have helped change that experience of fans who travel to tournaments. Host police and other authorities now recognize that the UK has taken responsibility for preventing the export of its domestic football problems, and perceive that there will be fewer risk fans to deal with. As a result, they are far more inclined to give England fans the benefit of the doubt. In Japan and Portugal, England fans were welcomed and responded magnificently. In the build-up to the tournaments, England fans were given the opportunity to visit host cities and pursue their own communication and goodwill initiatives. We give a high priority to supporting this work and to bringing host police spokespeople over to the UK to talk to fans. It is all about empowering fans to help influence host perceptions and expectations. And it works! I have no doubt that the progress on all fronts would not have been so great if it was not for our tough banning order legislation.'

Fans like Lynda Copson appreciate the reasoning behind the bans and the results: 'I've already agreed to the FA vetting me in order to be admitted into the supporters' club. My application to join was subject to a police check. If the banning orders are another way of stopping those out to cause trouble ending up at the same match as me, great. But a hand raised in joy can easily resemble a hand raised in anger when a photo is taken. The police have to be certain they're catching the right people for the right reasons.'

Lynda is typical of a significant opinion amongst England fans. Not naturally anti-authoritarian, yet their experience of being policed, at domestic club games as well as on trips abroad, has on occasion brought them face to face with the full force of the law, deserved or not. The trust they place in the banning orders and their acceptance of being the target of intelligence-gathering operations remains provisional.

David Bohannan seems to be aware of the delicacy of the situation. 'There must be, and there are, checks and balances, the most important of which is adjudication by a court of law. Unless the magistrate approves the complaint, and not all do, the ban cannot be imposed.' Nevertheless, David's view remains unequivocal. 'Football banning orders are a positive measure. Government and the police must do everything we can to help create a non-threatening, inclusive environment at tournaments: one in which fans can demonstrate their loyalty and support in a passionate way but also have a good time, irrespective of the result. To that end, we must prevent and deter known troublemakers from spoiling the experience, while at the same time doing everything we can to encourage the host police to treat England fans on their behaviour rather than reputation. Ultimately, we all know that self-policing is the best policing and the impact of banning orders undoubtedly empowers fans in this and other ways.'

It can be a bit daunting for fans to sit down with senior civil servants, high-ranking police officers and FA officials to discuss how to avoid disorder and the misery for all concerned that comes with it. But what David Bohannan describes as a 'multi-agency approach, not seeking to deal with trouble in isolation' is beginning to work. The authorities are listening to us. They are being seen to act, largely in favour of our interests, and the pressure from within our own fan culture on those who threaten to ruin things for the rest of us is becoming much more obvious than before.

As Euro 2004 approached, England fan groups from around the country were invited by the Home Office to offer ideas on how we could help ensure a fan-friendly tournament, not just for ourselves, but for the hosts and the supporters of the countries we played against as well. From 2003–2005 Deputy Chief Constable David Swift was the Association of Chief Police Officers' (ACPO) representative responsible for policing England matches. In this role he was keen to be working with, rather than against, the fans. 'It had been a good few years since football had been part of my direct operational responsibilities, so I wanted to listen, to find out what those involved had to say, including the fans.' The conversations started to make sense: 'Trying to stop those travelling without tickets clearly didn't work, and segregation isn't an issue either. England fans end up all over the stadium wherever England play with no obvious problems. We needed to change our focus to other tactics that mattered far more.'

The new strategy was based around four key elements. 'Firstly, the successful imposition of football banning orders. Secondly, engage with and influence the host police force. At Euro 2004 we fully supported the Portuguese approach of being visible but low profile. We were convinced this was the best way to police our fans. Thirdly, encourage balanced media coverage of any trouble. Fourthly, support the fans to police themselves.' This was a very different approach to what England fans had been used to before, but as David Swift acknowledges, 'We were starting to realize that it is only very rarely that confrontational policing will happen without causing problems.'

This approach was to be founded on the police 'national intelligence model'. With this the police seek to develop target profiles of individuals who are known to them as proven troublemakers, and identify situations in which they might be able to exert undue influence on others. The police attempt to locate places on away trips where crowds might build up and cause disruption. They establish how this might be dealt with without it leading to confrontation. The strategic assessment would be the result of a better understanding of the majority of fans, identifying factors which will help fans move towards self-policing without the need for police intervention.

To help him with the implementation of this strategy David

developed a sort of instant-recognition formula. 'First there's the "shirts". We want to maximize their numbers, encourage, include, advise and protect them. They amount to sixty per cent of the fans. The "lads" we tolerate, manage, control. They account for a further thirty-five per cent. The remaining five per cent are the "Yobs". These we want to exclude, disrupt, isolate.'

Plenty will have quibbles with David's definition criteria. Personally bri-nylon has never done me any fashion favours, so wearing the official shirt doesn't appeal, yet I'm quite certain David's officers would include me amongst the 'shirts'. But the overall balance does seem about right. The recognition that the majority require a combination of crowd safety and management measures and not much more is very welcome. According to David's assessment the 'lads' and the 'yobs' pose two different policing problems. 'The lads will react if they feel they are being policed in an inappropriate way, and if they are provoked by the opposition supporters. The yobs are actively seeking to cause trouble but need the cover of the lads for their actions.'

David Swift's long-term ambition for how England fans should be policed is quite clear: 'We want to include the good, and exclude the bad. The number of banning orders will inevitably rise. There is no evidence that the problem will completely disappear, but what our actions will impact upon is how our fans are policed overseas, for the better.' And he is equally certain what will happen if foreign policing fails to account for the change in our fans. 'If the policing is bad then the yobs will be allowed by the rest to do what they want, and this will deter the good fans from going.'

David Swift makes the distinction between the 20 per cent who cause 80 per cent of the problems he has to deal with, and the rest who cause none. 'Eighty per cent never get overexcited. Twenty per cent are prone to get overexuberant.' And, he argues, only about a fifth of the 'overexuberant' are potential troublemakers.

'That means no more than four per cent of the total number of fans travelling are the real problem.' As with his shirts, lads and yobs distinction, we can argue the toss over David Swift's calculations, but the basic principle is surely sound. Target the minority while leaving the majority to their own devices and they will neither come to, nor cause, any harm.

In order to ensure this can happen David identifies a table of tolerance levels. 'As numbers gather there is invariably increasing drunkenness and consequent changes of behaviour. The crowd gets noisy, there is shouting, singing and chanting. Some dancing might follow, then obstructing the pavements and roads, trespassing, bantering and taunting, jockeying for position and finally fighting.' The issue is at what point should the police intervene, and how, to prevent the tolerable escalating into the intolerable. 'If the police are recognized by the shirts as doing a legitimate job, then that will be a key factor in preventative policing. We have to show that we understand the problems faced by the general population of fans. We must project an absolute clarity of objectives and use our intelligence process to highlight risks. Then we can establish agreed tolerance levels, enforced by consistent and predictable policing styles combined with effective communication.' This means a kind of change of previous policing priorities, 'Listening to fans, becoming familiar with them, understanding what they want, their views on what we do. All of this will help in establishing boundaries, preventing fans being treated as one homogeneous mass, enabling us to remove those who deserve to be excluded and encourage the remainder towards self-policing.'

Tony Conniford is the head of intelligence and operational delivery at the UK Football Policy Unit. 'I soon realized how important it is to dispel the myths about what we are trying to achieve,' he says. He is also keen to emphasize the positive impact of the work his unit is carrying out. 'We can never eradicate the problem of football hooliganism but we can take actions to minimize it.'

Within football intelligence, supporters are classed in one of three groups: Category A, peaceful, genuine supporters; Category B, possible risk of disorder, especially alcohol related; or Category C, violent supporters, and organizers of violence. Tony outlines his targeting priorities for intelligence-gathering and banning orders: 'We never lose sight of the Cat C's, in fact some of these feature in other areas of criminality, but they are relatively small in number. It is the Cat B's who are predominant and cause the majority of the problems.'

Tony is uncomfortable with the rigidity of the categorization, and while the classifications are common throughout Europe the interpretations can vary alarmingly, causing inconsistent policing styles. 'I prefer the categorization of "risk" and "non-risk" fans, and the emphasis should always be on the recognition that the majority of England fans are non-risk.' Security visits ahead of England fixtures overseas seek to ensure the host police fully understand this. 'What we try to avoid is policing on reputation, where police forces are influenced by historical events, meeting the fans with riot police and snarling dogs.'

Hooliganism, according to Tony, is something like a professional pastime for some. 'They practise week in week out, game after game. Most clubs have a risk group like this. These are the ones we want to stop and get banned. Those who make this country ashamed.' Each football club has a police Football Intelligence Officer attached to it, appointed by the host force. One of their main roles is to identify those risk supporters who regularly engage in hooligan activities. Evidence is gathered and, if warranted, the individual is profiled and a football banning order sought. Tony believes it is these banning orders obtained 'on complaint' that have proved most effective in combating hooliganism.

'There are those whom we don't catch committing offences but who regularly form part of the risk group. They act in an intimidating, threatening manner and always seem to be in the vicinity of disorder. It is these people that we use this procedure against.'

By mid-2005 some 322 individuals had received a banning order 'on complaint'. Tony insists the targeting procedure is correct. 'Those persons that regularly feature within the risk groups causing problems and those who commit violent and public-order offences remain our focus. We would not be doing our job properly if we failed to target these individuals and try to prevent disorder.'

In addition to the football banning order legislation, the other major asset for the police in preventing football-associated criminality since 2000 has been the provision of additional government funding. Tony explains: 'Burglary, motor theft, violent crime, these are the offences by which individual police forces are normally judged. In terms of policing priorities, football never used to feature. The extra funding, in the region of five million pounds, has enabled our policing and intelligence strategy to be enhanced far beyond what was previously known.' Before, without the nationwide operations Tony and his colleagues are now able to administer, the police would face the same problems with disorder repeated on a similar scale over and over again wherever a high-risk match was being played. 'This would not happen in other areas of crime. We would have set out to target offenders and stop the repetition. Thanks to our increased budget we can now do this.'

The same applies to British police activities overseas when England are playing away. 'We travel to assist the host police and offer them advice on English supporter behaviour and suggest appropriate ways to respond to this.' Tony's team of spotters monitor our fans' behaviour, filming, and gathering evidence to possibly use in the future. 'We don't just rely on involvement in a solitary incident beside a segregation fence, for example, although if an individual's actions warrant an application for a ban we will certainly pursue it. More often what we witness is the final part of a jigsaw for a banning order application. We will also be trying to establish why some supporters are acting in this manner, while most are not. We want to help prevent future such incidents. The truth is that if fans don't cause any problems then we won't be interested in them.'

The peculiarity of English hooliganism is its record of close association with the national team, and at major tournaments. This is what has provided the unwelcome reputation that often goes before England fans. It makes it difficult to dismiss – even where countries have a similar history of trouble it tends to be confined to the domestic league or home matches of the national side. According to Tony this remains a key issue. 'It is the reputation of the England fans that often causes a response rather than actual events.' There are plenty of fans who would agree and it is on this basis that many accept the intrusion of Tony's evidence-gathering teams and the imposition of banning orders on those who deserve them. It is a form of insurance, but if it isn't accompanied by pro-tection of the innocent our support will quickly ebb away.

What Dale Hyde and many others had to endure at England's away match with Slovakia in October 2002 has to be properly dealt with by the authorities, domestic and foreign. This is not a reason for inaction against those amongst our own hellbent on causing trouble. But if legitimate fears and anxieties aren't taken equally seriously, major obstacles will remain in the way of estab-lishing a shared interest in finding solutions.

Dale recounts the episode when he was battered by the Slovakian riot police. 'I saw them coming. With just a second to make up my mind I decided to stay where I was. I was not a troublemaker. In a packed-out England away section I just happened to be sitting in the seats next to the home fans. The police would surely pick out the guys who had been aggressively shaking the segregation fence between our fans and theirs. Bad decision. I was whacked around the head and fell to the ground, where they continued to strike me. I took around twenty blows. After a couple of minutes I noticed that several women had sought refuge in the first row of the second tier, so I went there as well. The police had by this time retreated, but after a while they were baited by a few of our idiots, quite a big group. This gave the police the excuse to charge again. It's these guys who should be spotted in the videos and properly dealt with. Although they didn't start the original incident, the Slovakians' racist chanting caused that, it is their type who stop England being able to travel without trouble.'

Dale was treated by a first-aid unit at the ground. While he was having his hand bandaged he witnessed the sad consequences of this kind of experience. 'I saw dozens of England fans leaving the game early. Many were couples, just about every woman was crying, but also many groups of ordinary lads left who just said it wasn't worth staying.' In the treatment room Dale was joined by another England fan, handcuffed to a policeman. 'He was saying he'd been shaking the fence for a bit of fun, then some of the police had hit us for a bit of fun. He really didn't seem to realize what grief his "fun" had resulted in.'

Tirana, Albania, March 2001. Anne and I had enjoyed a great few days in the sunshine of this previously most inaccessible of East European capitals. Great food, friendly people, and lots of sights to see that mixed Balkan history, the remnants of Enver Hoxha's regime and the leftovers of the Ottoman Empire. Not a huge number travelled to Albania, but enough for there to be an obvious I-N-G-E-R-L-A-N-D presence in the main square on match day.

Out of Order

The Albanians seemed happy enough to see us, their main fear being apparently that we might be carriers of foot-and-mouth, which at the time was sweeping through English cattle herds. The *Albanian Daily News* announced what would face us at the airport in the arrivals lounge: 'The England supporters will all walk on disinfected carpets and they will be searched for food. They will not be allowed to bring any food into Albania.' Our cheese-and-pickle sandwiches posed the kind of international public-health threat that left the odd bit of hooliganism shrinking in comparison.

On the day of the match as the crowds grew in the city centre, the mood shifted from the happy-go-lucky tourism of the last forty-eight hours to a rising expectancy that one of the biggest footballing nations on earth was about to play one of the smallest. England might not have won anything of significance for the best part of forty years, but abroad we remain the Man United of international football, on and off the pitch. We brought some of the world's most famous players, playing for some of the most famous clubs, and more supporters than are likely to accompany any other country to Albania. This had been made vividly apparent to me on the morning of the match when a group of us spent an hour or so at a local school on a goodwill visit. Inviting the kids to ask some questions about our team so they could practise their English, a hand shot up at the front of the class. 'Why does your team captain wear his wife's underwear and skirt?' The fame of David Beckham's fashion taste is certainly global.

Anne and I got to the ground early. In a place like this there's unlikely to be the care and attention paid to crowd safety we're used to back home. Settled down in our seats, we looked around and spotted a few friendly faces to have a chat with. The game was one of those where we expect to win by a wide margin but end up waiting until the second half to actually hit the back of the net.

With England finally 1–0 up we were looking forward to the

remaining twenty minutes of the match with something bordering on confidence, and when Scholes put England's second goal away, our end erupted. Nothing to worry about, but as some surged forward to taunt the Albanians beneath us, a few idiots started chucking coins too.

One of these hit Anne. At first she was just numb with shock. Then the blood started to flow and she was screaming with panic. I was furious, desperate to get her out of the ground and receive some medical attention. Fans around us were full of sympathy and helped me get her to the aisle. The armed police, however, looked bemused. Equipped with machine guns (for goodness knows what purpose), some basic first-aid remained well beyond their capabilities. We finally made our way out of the stadium and somehow found a doctor to treat Anne's badly cut head.

The Albanians were streaming past us – after the second goal they were doing what fans the world over do, give up on their team, get out the ground early and hope they'll be first out the car park as a result. Then Albania scored a late goal. They're back in the game and the same crowds were rushing back past us to the places in the stands they'd only just left. It was chaos: no lighting, no stewards, hundreds of Albania supporters running around in different directions, along boulder-strewn tracks.

Andy Cole finished off their dreams with a decisive third goal and almost immediately the whistle was blown for full time. Anne was still being bandaged up, when above us a few of our fans started pelting the Albanians below, and us, with seats, flagpoles and coins again. Most who went to Tirana had nothing but having a good time on their mind. But thanks to the actions of a few, harm was caused and prejudices reinforced, including, I admit, some of my own. It is the arrogant presumption that we can do what we want, where we want, and stuff the consequences that permits football violence to survive. Fans have more of a responsibility than most to deal with this particular part of the hooliganism equation.

Nic Banner is involved with the fans' group 4England. Nic is as against the violence as I am, but he has serious reservations about the overwhelming pressure to condemn it. 'We need to get away from all that. To swing things round to a different conversation.' He is unconvinced that simply by saying we're opposed to trouble we can do much good, in fact he fears the opposite effect. 'I would much rather talk about the positive things that fans do. When every interview turns to hooliganism it just encourages some into thinking this is what supporting England is all about.'

Nic has been following England at home since 1981. 'It's not just England that has changed since the 1980s, the whole of football has changed. I can still remember when bananas would be chucked at black players. That kind of thing really shook people up. I don't like all this political correctness stuff, it can be taken too far, but everybody understands that the kind of racism that went on then would never be tolerated today. It's the same with hooliganism inside the ground, though there's still places outside where trouble can be found.'

In September and October 2003 England were due to play away games in Macedonia and Turkey. Following the heavy fine imposed on the FA by UEFA for the racist abuse and crowd invasions at the Turkey home match in April, there was a real fear that another incident would result in England's expulsion from the Euro 2004 qualifying campaign. The FA decided to deal with the issue by banning fans from travelling to the two matches. As Paul Barber, FA director of marketing and communications explained in press interviews: 'We do accept that the minority of people that cause us problems have now become too large a minority.' He then linked this concern with the desire to alter

England's core support. 'We want to change the demographic of those who follow England.'

Whether it was intended or not, the message was read by fans like Nic that they were no longer welcome. Made to feel expendable, Nic and his friends decided to defy the first of the two travel bans. 'The FA tried to spread these scare stories that Macedonia was a dangerous place to visit, but if it was such a risky trip, why on earth would they send a team out there to play?' Nic seriously doubted the warnings. Dressed in a smart suit with a letter from his local MP in his pocket declaring him a solid citizen whose right to support his national team was being endangered by the actions of the FA, Nic swept through customs and on to his flight without once being questioned about his reasons for travel.

'In Skopje we received a great welcome. It didn't matter where we went, everybody was pleased to see us. No danger at all. Best away trip I've been on in years.' Five hundred fans did the same as Nic, and there was not a hint of bother. To be fair, the FA had faced a genuine predicament. If there had been trouble, and if in UEFA's view they had failed to do their utmost to prevent it, then expulsion from Euro 2004 was a serious possibility. But by penalizing all fans, issuing ill-thought-out scare stories to deter them, and appearing to be happy and willing to alienate those most committed to a positive England, the Macedonia ban failed to convince.

Doug Hopkins and Graham White work as crowd-control advisers for the FA. Doug was formerly match commander at Highbury for five years, while Graham did the same job at Old Trafford. They are hugely experienced in the policing of football crowds. In large part Doug and Graham's task is to create the conditions which would make imposing the kind of blanket ban the FA imposed over Macedonia unnecessary. Graham explains their role: 'We observe. The stewarding, policing, the state of the ground's infrastructure and surrounding areas. We advise. Though sometimes that advice, particularly overseas, will be ignored. We develop policy, establishing best practice for ground safety, and liaise with fans to seek their support for changes in crowd management.'

For an away match this role requires advance preparation. 'We always visit the match venue, we meet with the authorities, attend briefings with UEFA and FIFA personnel, and afterwards submit a report to the FA.' Doug was previously in charge of the Metropolitan Police's Special Patrol Group. In that role he has policed everything from demonstrations by the National Front to royal weddings. 'These are all public events. To that extent football is no different. There is the potential for disorder in all of these situations. At a football match the key is crowd management, which means reducing congestion and ensuring there are no hold-ups with getting people into and away from the ground. What does make football different is the prevalence of low-level criminality; drunk and disorderly offences, causing an obstruction, abusive behaviour.'

To reduce these kinds of problems building up into something more serious on away trips, the FA's crowd-control advisers provide vital information for domestic and overseas police forces. Graham outlines the preparations for each away match. 'We inform the host authorities how many of our fans will travel, the routes they will take, ways and means of getting to the ground. All this is compiled for the relevant authorities, home and abroad. And the members of the supporters' club subjected to a full criminal record check before every away match and tournament.'

On match day Doug, Graham and their colleagues will more

often than not be found around the turnstiles for the England section, checking to see nothing is being done wrong which a bit of helpful advice might be able to correct. But Doug admits that's not always so easy. 'We've no powers as such, it's up to them whether they're willing to listen to what we have to say.'

The job of reducing the chances of trouble is made immeasurably harder when a majority of our fans feel badly served by poor stadium management, inadequate crowd safety provision and brutal policing. Doug agrees: 'The best way to get our fans to behave is to provide them with good conditions.'

Crystal Palace fan Ade Clarke is thirty-two and travels to England away games with his dad Nigel. England's November 2004 friendly in Madrid was intended to be a relaxing end to a busy footballing year. 'We met up with friends before the game. People who we'd got to know in Portugal at Euro 2004 and now make an effort to have a drink with wherever England are playing.'

There has always been a strong sense of community about England away, but the Internet, mobile phones and the increasing variety of fan groups and events has undoubtedly strengthened this. Where once the most organized were the hooligan gangs, fans like Ade are now part of a counter fan-culture with no intent apart from enjoying their trips. 'We enjoyed our tapas and then made our way to the Bernabeu a good few hours before kickoff to avoid any last-minute crush. We stopped off at a bar right next to the ground and met up with Ann and Martyn Justice.'

Ann had an extra reason to want to get into the ground before the big crowds. Martyn is disabled and uses an electric wheelchair. They had tried to get into the ground to avoid any hassle but the gates were still locked. Ann describes the atmosphere in the bar: 'There were lots of Spanish enjoying a drink after work. We were all mixed in together, no trouble. We couldn't get inside with Martyn's wheelchair, so we joined those drinking outside on the pavement. Every so often the England fans would start up a singsong, nothing offensive, absolutely without malice. Nigel had gone inside to get another round in when suddenly there was this surge of people from the bar pushing their way out on to the street. Martyn was tipped over, it was only the fact that his fall was stopped by a wall that prevented him falling out of his wheelchair and seriously injuring himself.'

What had happened? 'The police in riot gear with helmets on and visors down had entered the bar from the other side and were hitting out with their batons.' The incident caused panic, as Ann recalls: 'People were covered in blood, it was like a battlefield, and the police caused it all.'

Like everyone else, Ann was shocked by what was happening. 'There was no sort of warning. No one had told us that they wanted the bar closed down or for us to leave. We had no idea why we were being treated like this.'

Ade was determined that the story of this incident was told. He believed if fans felt their concerns weren't being taken seriously then there was a very real danger there would be a retreat into the 'no one likes us' siege mentality. 'All the time and effort we'd put in with so much success to build up a positive England at Euro 2004 when everyone else expected us to be expelled for misbe-haviour could be ruined by this kind of policing. And there was no media there to witness how we had been treated.'

Quite rightly, the press coverage of the match focused on the appalling treatment of our players by the Spanish fans with their loud and continual racist monkey chants. But there was no mention of what had happened to Ade and his friends. 'It would have been typically English of us to have kept quiet, not done anything about it, and then waited for the next time. I felt something had to be done. We had too much to lose if we didn't at least try to stop something like this happening again.'

Ade helped the Football Supporters' Federation (as the FSA had become by then) compile a dossier containing an incredible seventy-four detailed accounts of incidents of brutal policing. These recorded not just the event at the bar where Ade had been drinking, but similar violent mistreatment of fans by the Spanish police: at other bars around the stadium, as fans queued to enter the ground, in the stands, and as they left. What impressed Ade was not just the determination of fans to force some sort of response but also the reaction of the authorities. 'The FA, the Home Office, ACPO, they all supported us, our case was even taken up at ministerial level, the first time apparently. Key to this was that British Police spotters were there when the Spanish police attacked our fans. They directly experienced what we experienced. Some of them were even hit, just like us.'

Ade recognizes the change that this episode and the aftermath represented. 'The England away crowd will always be different. We're not sexy Latins or cartoon orange characters. Our support is huge in numbers, and just that can be threatening enough. But now people when they see us, meet us, they're no longer frightened. Nor should they be. The way we were treated in Spain was completely unacceptable, and at last those with the power to do something about it agreed with us.'

John Walsh and Gordon Taylor like to dress well. Stone Island, Paul & Shark, Henri Lloyd, Aquascutum, Giorgio Armani, they wear designer gear from baseball caps to trainers. Before one away match Gordon popped out on a lunch-time shopping trip to stock up on the latest lines from his favourite labels. Back at work he reeled off to one of the office girls what he'd bought. 'Oh, so you're one of those hooligans, are you?' she retorted or, as Jim

White put it in the *Guardian*, 'The chosen attire for the brain-dead everywhere.' This kind of lazy thinking stinks.

'Proper fans go to the shitty games,' is how Gordon describes his dedication to the England cause. Club and country, he's followed both for years, whether to success or failure, his dedication always the same. 'A lot of those who turn out for the tournaments, they haven't a clue about what following their country means. For them England didn't exist before Euro 96 happened along.' He can sound resentful, jealous of others spoiling the exclusivity of his passion, but this isn't his intention. 'I just don't want football sanitized, cleaned up, others telling me what I can and can't do as a fan. Being at a match will never be the same as watching it in your living room. The piss-taking, the rivalry, it's real – we mustn't ever lose that.'

What about those who are seeking out violence? John is certain there aren't that many. 'Only a few, and not at every game either. If something kicks off, though, somebody has a pop at us, then there are plenty more who won't back down. That's a lot more than those who go away just to find another set of fans to have a row with. The "mobs" are largely a myth, the only time I can remember a big bunch of lads came together like this was Warsaw in '99, and that was to protect ourselves from the Poles.' He dismisses those who copy their support from what they've read about England hooliganism: 'They buy up all the gear to wear and sing "No Surrender" just because they think it's the thing to do. They're horrible little fucks in this country, and not much better abroad.'

Gordon has been a regular at the LondonEnglandFans forums since they first started and he's been to meetings with the FA to discuss ticketing issues, tournament preparations and the like. 'I'll never paint my face. I hate Mexican waves. I haven't helped out with "Raise the Flag" or been on a goodwill visit to a school.

Before, I felt the FA weren't interested in fans like me, that they wouldn't let me fit in, but this has started to change.' Gordon wasn't convinced at first that anything useful would come from the fans getting organized. 'I was suspicious. I mistrusted the motives behind it. I wasn't interested in the sort of set-up where someone speaks out claiming to represent me. But I've been surprised; on most things we all have the same opinions. I feel as much a part of it as anyone. And the lads I travel with appreciate the info I pick up, it gets spread around.'

John and Gordon don't fit the comfortable stereotypes of those who only judge fans by the clothes we wear. Nor do they fit into the cosy slot of middle-class bandwagon jumpers that some presume make up the audience for a fans' travel forum. Here, plans are made to see as much of Japan as we can fit into the two or three weeks of a World Cup trip. 'Mount Fuji, Hiroshima, Kyoto, we did the lot,' Gordon proudly boasts, and in South Africa when England played a friendly there, 'Table Mountain and Robben Island to see where Nelson Mandela was locked up for all those years.' If, instead of blaming this pair and the many others who dress like them for their reaction when a push becomes a shove, more asked how to prevent what invariably follows, then we'd learn something else too. 'It's the English who never back down,' says Gordon. 'Maybe because we're an island race. Whatever the reason, if someone else has a go we have to fight back. When the police can prevent that happening in the first place, like they did in Portugal, then nothing happens. And this has been more or less the way it's been since World Cup 2002.'

Bans, border checks, riot police out in force, baton charges and water cannon have all been tried and tested over the past twenty years or more in the battle to curb the worst excesses of English hooliganism abroad. Each effort has certainly had a partial effect, but very often in facing down one problem these actions have simply created another. The worst knock-on effect has been to narrow those who will follow England abroad to at best the brave, and at worst the foolhardy, while legitimizing in the minds of many the most ferocious response to the way we are being treated. Portugal 2004 was part of a process of proving to ourselves and to others that it doesn't have to be like this. Many different agencies, a lot of anonymous individuals, and most of all the vast majority of fans, played their part in what happened.

But one person stood out – Dame Glynn Evans. Like Gordon and John, she is a fan of designer labels, though her Burberry and Aquascutum is more likely to be an elegant evening dress than a baseball cap. Dame Glynn was Her Majesty's Ambassador to Portugal at the time of Euro 2004, and she had some serious concerns about what England's massive fan presence might mean for the friendly Anglo-Portuguese relationship she was responsible for safeguarding. 'When we started our preparations all we knew about was the potential for fans making trouble.'

Portugal is the country with which England has had its longest period of unbroken peace, dating all the way back to the 1386 Treaty of Windsor. A few hundred rioting in Rossio Square wouldn't represent a state of war, but the consequences were nevertheless recognized as serious. 'The Portuguese were scared off by our fans' reputation. We knew that if the impression was allowed to be created that all our fans would be both drunk and violent this would have a devastating impact on our relations with Portugal. Factual or not, this was the perception we feared the most.'

Approaching retirement, not knowing a great deal about football, it would have hardly been surprising if Glynn had shied away from the task, but on the contrary: 'For a year it must have taken up half my time. The Portuguese were really impressed that I personally took such an interest in the facilities they were providing for our fans, everything from accommodation pricing to how to pre-book long-distance train tickets. We established with them that we all wanted the tournament to be a success.' And central to this for Glynn was involving the fans.

Glynn was a newcomer to all this, but the painstaking time spent by her staff clearing up local issues – which, if mishandled, could have become major incidents causing grief, panic and then trouble – was crucial. Tickets, transport to and away from matches, personal safety at the ground: these three matters concern fans more than anything else and in large measure Portugal got all three right. Much of this was thanks to Dame Glynn's persistent prodding. The closest most of us get to the inside of an embassy or meeting an ambassador is an advert for the posh chocolate sweets Ferrero Rocher. When fans gathered together to seek answers to their problems Dame Glynn cut an admittedly incongruous figure draped in her expensive-looking pashmina, and many who travelled to Euro 2004 wouldn't be aware of what the ambassador and her colleagues did to help ensure we were policed in a manner we would be happy with. Yet the fact that they were there to help, and that more and more fans did hear about this determination – and by an institution as previously alien to us as the Foreign Office – to assist us in avoiding the root causes of conflict made a huge difference.

Nobody can deny that some England fans are intent on causing trouble. A combination of factors have ensured that on too many occasions larger numbers have found themselves involved in the resulting violence rather than getting themselves out of the way. Reducing the factors that help determine aggressive participation instead of peaceful evacuation is key. The preventative policing of banning orders and intelligence gathering is widely accepted by fans as a necessary element contributing towards this. It's not very nice having video cameras track our movements, our particulars taken down, asked to explain our reasons for travel, dates of departure and destination, but it's something we put up with for the common good.

The author of *Football Hooligans*, Gary Armstrong, expresses a serious concern about what we are accepting when we endorse these measures, which admittedly represent a deeper infringement of civil liberties than most of the population are expected to put up with. 'Football hooliganism has legitimized promoting and extending the tactics and ideology of a pervasive and intrusive surveillance culture.' The police have earned widespread endorsement for this intrusion by supporters because we have accepted the necessity of improving our reputation; being seen to co-operate with the measures are a form of insurance policy. But if these measures are used to simply intimidate and coerce the majority, without any targeting aimed at obvious offenders, this goodwill will certainly, and quite correctly, disappear.

The bare legislation makes frightening reading. As we queue up for our flights, ferries or trains to follow England abroad, the police have an almost unlimited remit to stop us. 'During any control period in relation to a regulated football match outside England and Wales, if a constable in uniform has reasonable grounds to believe that making a banning order would help to prevent violence or disorder at or in connection with any regulated football matches the constable may detain the person in his custody until he has decided whether or not to issue a notice.' If we are forced to miss our plane or boat, in all likelihood we'd not make it to the match. The more punitive amongst our critics would smile to themselves and think 'problem solved'.

Thankfully the police have more common sense and these measures are very sparingly used. Of the tens of thousands passing through airports, docks and railways stations on their way to Portugal for Euro 2004, just 126 were subject to six hours' detention.

Of these, ninety-one were sent to court within twenty-four hours to have the case heard against them for a banning order. Fifty-four received a ban and were prevented from travelling, the rest made it out to Portugal, bothered by the imposition, no doubt, but glad to be free to travel. Not a very pleasant experience for those held up, but the figures do indicate that the catch-all tendency isn't as strong amongst either police or judges as we might have expected. In just one case an individual was cleared by the English court but stopped by the Portuguese authorities from entering the country. They weren't far wrong in doing so – the next season this same individual was caught offending again and is now subject to a three-year banning order.

The same careful targeting, rather than careless policing, must apply to those who receive a banning order 'on complaint' rather than because they have been found guilty of an offence. Of the 2,548 banning orders in operation in October 2004 only 322 had been imposed via this route, and 96 per cent of those subject to a banning order on complaint had a previous conviction. The remainder received their bans on the basis of violent behaviour caught on video footage at overseas matches. All of those who have received their bans as part of a conviction did so because they had committed a football-related offence.

The legislation and the policing aren't perfect. But they are not being used in an indiscriminate manner which fires up resentment and allows a violent reaction to flourish. The contention of the police and the Home Office, universally supported by media enthusiasm, is that the banning orders have significantly reduced the risk of football violence at England away matches. Only effective in their current form since after Euro 2000, the tournaments affected (World Cup 2002 in Japan and Euro 2004 in Portugal) were largely trouble-free, with English arrests massively reduced. There were just ninety in Portugal, of which fifty-three were for violent disorder, and only one of these took place at or close to an England match. The violence that did take place was limited to two nights, hundreds of miles away from where England were playing. In Japan there were just eleven arrests, and not a single one for a public order offence, rather petty theft and the like. Compare this to Euro 88 when fifty fans were arrested for trouble just at the first match, and a further thirty when England's campaign came to a humiliating halt after defeat by Marco Van Basten and his Dutch team-mates. At Italia 90 the worst incident, after the quarterfinal victory over Belgium, resulted in the deportation of 247 fans. The figures, however, don't necessarily tell us very much about how bad, or good it was in those days. Without any obvious irony the *Sun* commented on the conditions under which the 247 were arrested and deported from Italy. 'Police said they would not bring charges because they were unable to sort out the innocent from the guilty.'

Nevertheless, combined with the increasingly evident changes in England's own support a decline in the number of arrests is obviously welcome. The bans, which the police expect to continue to increase in number, are a deterrent. And they appear to be effective. The Football Banning Orders Authority reported 96 per cent compliance, which involves the surrender of their passport by those subject to a ban, during Euro 2004. This compares favourably with Anti-Social Behaviour Orders, the notorious ASBO. The government admits compliance with these is as low as 66 per cent.

The law-and-order conversation in England, whether about football or whatever the latest moral panic happens to be, is invariably founded on fear. It has been much the same for twenty years. As Italia 90 began the *Sun* warned its readers of their fate as they headed off to Spain and Portugal for their hols: 'If you don't fancy playing "Spot the Lager Lout" on the beach it's worth finding out exactly where you *shouldn't* be heading this summer.'

Ingerland

Albufeira was listed as a place to avoid. Fourteen years later it was featured in news reports again, this time as the location for the two nights of trouble involving England fans at Euro 2004. To pretend this violence involving our fans has nothing to do with football won't wash. Whether inside the stadium, a square in the host city or a beach resort hundreds of miles down the coast, of course the fighting has a lot to do with football and the emotions we invest in it. But it also has a lot to do with the fact that the Foreign Office reports around 2,000 UK residents are detained or arrested every single summer by the Spanish police for drunken violence and disorder along the Costa del Sol alone.

It is a sobering fact that almost a third of the adult male population have caused some sort of bother. The most common offences are drink-related, resulting in driving offences, public disorder or criminal damage. Most of us who follow football never get involved in or cause any trouble, but some do. The figures speak for themselves. A majority reach adulthood without coming into conflict with the law of the land, but a significant minority do, committing offences which, if they were done at or close to a match, would rapidly be labelled football hooliganism.

There may well be trouble involving England again. The problem has been moderated rather than eliminated, and a set of factors can come together to provide the unwelcome conditions that favour conflict. When it happens we can be certain we'll be treated to the same response as before. For two decades the calls for a vicious crackdown have been amplified by every section of the media, supported by politicians, encouraged and enforced by football authorities and the police. And to no good effect – in fact, the opposite. Instead, to find some sort of solution a very English quiet revolution has had to take place, founded on recognizing common-sense principles, key agencies listening to each other and everybody willing to compromize. The answers will satisfy neither the demands of law-and-order moralists nor the concerns of civil-liberty guardians. Both have been found wanting when we came to call. Our forty years' worth of hurt on the pitch have been made worse by what – and never mind the reason – was happening off it. The combination meant I-N-G-E-R-L-A-N-D was forced into representing a particular version of dilapidated national pride, and nobody seemed to know how to make it better. We thought it was all over – it's not now.

8

When Saturday's Been

Since England's qualification for France 98 the FA had sought to establish some sort of consultative body with representation from the travelling England fans. A rather complicated system of regional committees was formed, with individuals putting themselves forward to the FA for selection. Those chosen were then invited to attend various meetings. The effort was well meaning but lacked any connection between these supporters and those they were supposed to speak for. To make matters worse the purpose of listening to the fans was never properly spelled out, so discussions would range from ticket prices to playing strips, security matters and transport arrangements, without either firm conclusions being reached or a sense of whether the fans' views were of any worth at all. After a couple of years of investing time and effort in this way, neither the fans nor the FA were satisfied.

Euro 2000 forced the FA to review what they were seeking to achieve with this process. With memories of the fighting in Marseilles etched into its collective consciousness the FA was running scared of any sort of repeat performance. Some of the fan representatives, including me, were invited to join goodwill visits to Eindhoven, Brussels and Charleroi. With cameramen and photographers in tow, we toured these host cities, met up with local dignitaries, received briefings from their police and said all the right things to the Dutch and Belgian media. A few sympathetic column inches were earned, though the cynicism of Charlie Whelan writing in the *Observer* was probably a more accurate emotional measure of how most regarded the effort: 'We are told that England fans are to go on a charm offensive. Are they trying to insult our intelligence?'

Whelan was both right and wrong. A 'charm offensive' led by the FA, manufactured by their officials, and then dished out for the poor bloody fans to put into practice in a foreign land, stretches the credibility of a fan-friendly England beyond breaking point. But Whelan also refused to believe any of us could enjoy ourselves in the same kind of manner he presumably would be on his own expenses-paid Euro 2000 trip. 'The fans will be given a guide to restaurants, museums and other cultural attractions. This, we are told, will encourage them to sample life in the towns and cities they visit. Who are they kidding?'

A couple of months before Euro 2000 I met up with the handful of others who were supposed to be representing London's England fans to the FA. We knew there were several thousand from the capital intending to travel to Euro 2000. We couldn't reach all of them but maybe we could connect with a decent-sized number, find out what they expected of the tournament and create a platform for our hopes and fears. This would hopefully challenge the idea of Charlie Whelan and other critics that England fans are incapable of appreciating the country and the culture we find ourselves in abroad.

Some FA officials were aghast at the idea. They tried to warn us off our efforts. The place will be wrecked, they said, a slanging match, a punch-up in front of the cameras. We thought it at least worth a try. Representatives from the Belgium and Holland Tourist Boards both came along; Cathy Long, who would be organizing the FSA fan embassies joined us; and Jill Smith, responsible for ticketing at the FA, also came. Most important of all, nearly a hundred fans packed the room solid, attracted by the fact that these representatives were willing to meet with us and listen to our concerns. Here were the beginnings of some sort of sense of community.

ITV London turned up too. They filmed us and recorded an interview with me, which was nice. We were getting our message across to a wider public, but that wasn't the reason for this venture. The reason was the crowd we formed and the conversation we were beginning to have, both with each other and with those in authority who would listen.

Jill Smith was already well known amongst regular away travellers with England. Wherever England played she would set up her mobile FA office in whatever space was provided and try to deal with as many queries and complaints from the fans as she could. Back home, before we set off it would be Jill who would sort out our queries about tickets which had gone missing in the post.

Jill is a fan who ended up working for the FA. 'I first travelled abroad with my club Arsenal in 1970 for the first leg of the Fairs Cup final against Anderlecht in Brussels. In the 1970s I was one of their volunteer couriers on away trips for a couple of years. This was the era of football specials; helping to look after six hundred fans on a train journey from London to Manchester was quite something in those days.'

Apart from following Arsenal and helping out at the club as a courier, Jill's 'proper' job then was a secretary. In 1978 she landed a dream career move, combining her love of football with her flair for administration. She became secretary to the FA deputy secretary at their then headquarters in Lancaster Gate. As Italia 90 approached, the FA had the good sense to realize that Jill was the ideal member of staff to make preparations for the several thousand fans expected to travel to Italy. 'I was given the title Assistant Travel Manager for the England Travel Club – it was what the supporters' club was called in those days. I had been looking after the members' ticketing arrangements for home games, but this World Cup was a much bigger venture. Everybody knew that if there was trouble the English clubs banned from Europe after Heysel would have their expulsion continued. I was sent out to Italy to set up a temporary FA office and see what could be done to help the fans, sort out their problems and reduce the risk of things going wrong.'

This was before the days when England's tournament support numbered many tens of thousands. Computerized vetting systems, cross-referencing ticket applications from the supporters'-club members against criminal records, wasn't available either. Jill saw her job as simply getting those fans in Italy into the games and off the streets. 'We carried loads of spare tickets with us and the fans could sign up to join the Travel Club on the day of a match. Membership entitled them to buy their tickets from us. In theory we had a sort of blacklist of known hooligans, but our systems in those days were pretty basic. We just had these long lists of names who we weren't supposed to let have tickets, but no way of checking that others didn't pass their tickets on to them.'

The innovation of the FA being seen publicly to be available at a tournament to help fans was welcome, though at the time it didn't feel as if there was very much appreciation for what Jill was trying to do. 'The first week was amongst the most depressing seven days of my life. Loads and loads of fans were being robbed of everything they had. They came to us with these incredibly miserable tales. But there wasn't very much we could do to help.

Then others turned up just to abuse us. It was the high prices they were expected to pay for the tickets that enraged them. Not our fault, but we had to face their anger.'

When England made it through their qualifying group and on to the knockout stages Jill followed team and supporters to the Italian mainland from Sardinia where they had all been based. 'Our so-called office was a caravan in the middle of a field. We would open up at nine-thirty in the morning, but by eight o'clock the field was already full of England supporters. Some had camped out there all night. When we arrived to open up hundreds of fans got on their feet as we picked our way between them to get to the caravan. I always hung around for a chat. I think people realized that I was a supporter just like they were. If it got a bit too threatening there was always someone around who told those who didn't know me to stop and listen to what news I had for them.'

Jill was one of the pioneers of a new FA approach to working with the fans: not everyone was convinced. 'I was very supporter-minded compared to a lot who worked at the FA. There weren't many there who had ever travelled on a football special, experienced what it was like to endure what fans have to put up with; the fact that for most of the train journey we were working out the safest way to get from the station to the stadium without being battered.' Fortunately for Jill her boss, Pat Smith, shared her opinion of what needed to be done in terms of working with the fans. 'She was the energy behind getting things moving at the FA for the fans. Pat was the one who always made sure that I was involved because she could see you had to have someone dealing with the fans who knew what it was like to be a supporter.'

After Italia 90, under pressure from Pat Smith, the FA agreed to sanction a similar mobile-office operation staffed by Jill and others at Euro 92 in Sweden. 'It was brilliant to start off with. In Malmö the Swedish police were really good-natured. They had just the right attitude to coping with our fans. There was this one main square where the numbers gathering, mainly to drink, were growing night after night. But on our last evening in the city I went out for a meal with some friends and I could sense there was going to be trouble. I was right. We hid in shop doorways as we made our way back to our hotel, with police chasing fans, then fans chasing the police, back and forth.'

Even after an episode like this Jill wasn't willing to give up the cause. 'I wanted us to be seen to be assisting those fans who most needed our help.' The biggest issue for England's support in Sweden had been finding reasonably priced accommodation. The best option proved to be camping, and the FA negotiated with various landowners for our fans to use their camp sites. 'After the trouble in Malmö the site owners became really worried about the risk of trouble,' Jill explains. 'None of the FA security people wanted to go out and meet the fans to try to calm things down, so it was left to me. The scene I was met with was appalling. Three or four hundred fans were bedded down in these huge marquees. At first when they saw me arrive there was a hush, then came this wave of abuse. There was so much "effing so-and-so's" I couldn't hear what was being said. I asked the fans to nominate ten of their number so we could try and thrash out some solutions.'

It was the simple things that Jill found made a difference: 'The fans were stuck out by this beautiful lake, surrounded by trees, but there was no transport back into Stockholm where the bars were, places to visit and, most important, the next match. That night we made arrangements for a shuttle-bus service and moved the tents away from the gravel-like surface which in the sun was creating a horrible red-dust haze which covered everybody and everything in its way. A lot of fans knew me and the fact that we could work together to make a difference started to get through.'

It was thanks to Jill's work at Euro 92 that the FA began to develop the beginnings of some sort of basis for consulting with England fans. 'It just made sense, it was so much easier to communicate if the fans were involved.' Jill recognizes that a certain tension remained: 'Supporters can't stand being preached at; they are naturally suspicious of being looked down upon. And there is a resistance to putting too much structure in place as well.' None of this sat very easily with the FA's customary way of working.

Laura Allen was one of the supporters who volunteered to take part in these early faltering attempts by the FA to work with England fans. She was surprised by the haphazard way the FA approached the entire venture. 'They were so unprofessional. There was no effort to establish how representative the fans were that they met.' By appealing for volunteer committee members the FA attracted mainly those sorts like Laura and me, who were used to serving on these kinds of bodies. Laura remained suspicious of the FA's motives. 'I wasn't convinced that as an organization they were all that committed to it. Individuals were, but it seemed they were left to get on with it, while any wider impact was minimal.'

The FA didn't seem to be taking much notice of all this so-called consultation, and our fellow supporters weren't exactly moved by it either. Me, Laura and the other London fans on the regional consultative committee the FA had set up, realized after a year or so that we were getting nowhere. Called into the FA offices every three months or so when they decided they wanted to meet us, we had no means of influencing their agenda. We just ended up talking about what they wanted us to discuss, then disappeared off home again until the next time. Consultation over: but who did we represent apart from ourselves, and what did the FA do as a result of what they'd heard anyway?

Years after they first kicked up a fuss with the FA, Anne-Marie Mockridge still describes herself and her friend Ceri as 'a pair of ringleaders'. The two of them have followed England everywhere and had from time to time made it their business to complain to the FA about how they were treated. Like others they had volunteered to be fan representatives on these new regional consultative committees; theirs was for the Northwest.

'It was the simple things we thought we could change,' says Anne-Marie, 'like travel advice. A map of the stadium so you knew where you would be sitting, how to get there, tourist information for the city where we were playing.' These were the kinds of suggestions that Anne-Marie and Ceri started making. 'Before each meeting we met up with the other fans on the committee. We all came up with ideas to propose to the FA.' When they did so they often found themselves disappointed. 'The FA seemed to think we were a pair of daft women. The simplest proposals we put forward, like the maps and travel advice, the FA either couldn't or wouldn't implement.' Much closer to the fans than the FA officials, Anne-Marie and Ceri knew what a big difference small changes like this could make.

It is always easy to knock the FA. Caught between the twin stereotypes of blazered old farts and sharp-suited marketing types, they make for an obvious target. Since the early 1990s, as political, economic and social pressures built up to deal with the fans' rapidly worsening reputation, the FA had tried to respond. But it did so in a piecemeal, partial and sometimes unhelpful fashion. Euro 96 offered a glimpse of what might be possible without public disorder being dragged into fan matters. But as Back, Crabbe and Solomos suggest in *The Changing Face of Football*, by simply celebrating the culture of the 'new fans' the FA could be seen to be excluding those who remained the national team's most committed supporters: 'The appreciation of larger attendances at Wembley, greater passion and displays of patriotism are countered by the unwanted and potentially divisive pressure to moderate behaviour in a more family and feminized environment.'

This pressure from the FA, and loudly supported by sections of the media and politicians, misread what was going on. Part of the appeal of Wembley at Euro 96 was the very intensity, passion and loyalty that with the slightest change of circumstances can so easily generate a much nastier, and hugely unattractive, spectacle.

It was after the trouble at Euro 2000 that the pressure for some sort of change became irresistible. Investigating and quantifying the precise scale of the physical intimidation, racist abuse and fighting by our fans hardly seemed to matter. Instead what counted was that UEFA and the Blair government were no longer willing to wait for the FA to act. The FA would either take notice or face the inevitable, and dire, consequences of suspension or expulsion.

After Euro 96, Paul Barber was asked by the FA to join an informal group of unpaid advisers with relevant skills to help the FA with their World Cup 2006 bid. As director of communications at Barclays Bank, and a Spurs season-ticket holder, the combination made his marketing advice invaluable. Although in the end the bid was startlingly unsuccessful, the packaging of the submission to FIFA indicated a new professionalism about the FA's public-affairs strategy, something which Paul was partly responsible for. In 2000 the invitation to join Adam Crozier, whose professional background was similar to Paul's, in the high command of the FA was too tempting to resist and he became the organization's director of marketing and communications.

Paul regarded this as a unique opportunity in the increasingly marketized world of football. 'What is unique about England is the coming together of fans of all these different clubs to back one team. In marketing terms this was a target audience which the FA was failing to capitalize on. The biggest reason for this was the image problem caused by hooliganism associated with following the national team.'

Whether we liked to admit it or not, the new market-driven FA shared a not dissimilar agenda with those fans who wanted an England everybody could be happy, and proud, to support. But for that commonality to have any sort of foundation the FA had to understand the reasons why fans became such committed supporters of England. It was our hardcore commitment, both the good and bad sides of it, which would shape the emergence of a more soft-core support. If the FA misunderstood this relationship then Paul Barber's efforts to open up England's support to all would be read as simply a moneymaking device at the expense of supporter interests.

John Walsh is one of many who remain intensely suspicious of the FA's motives. 'We are supporters. The sooner the FA take into account that we support and don't just "like" England the better. That might go some way to make them realize the resource they are dealing with and the potential a large support has in helping the FA achieve things.'

Paul's first meeting with England fans, most of whom shared John Walsh's suspicions, was immediately after Euro 2000. He was in for a shock. 'I can remember we handed out a new FA merchandising catalogue. It was almost physically thrown back in our faces. They just didn't want to know.'

I was at the same meeting. The brochure represented our worst fears of an FA that wanted to treat those of us who follow England as just another commercial property. Yet there was a contradiction too. Most of us were wearing the products being advertised. But for the FA to reduce our relationship with team and country to just another mail-order transaction would be a huge error. They have their objectives; sometimes these coincide with the fans' interests, sometimes not. But if the organization could prove in practice that it would at least consider the views of fans, the relations with us would take a huge step forward.

'I adopted the policy of replying to every single email the supporters sent me,' says Paul. 'These were really frank exchanges – many valid points were made. I had total respect for those who were willing to discuss things, even when we disagreed.' As Paul learned more about the fans he began to appreciate what following England involved. 'It's like a mini-industry. Getting the tickets is just part of it. Booking time off work, often at the expense of holidays, finding the cheapest travel, places to stay, sometimes going as a family or with a group of mates.' This was a far bigger matter than simply buying an England shirt at your local sports store.

In London, after meeting together before Euro 2000 we now needed to try to influence the changes the FA were seeking to impose on how we supported England. Wembley was about to close and our access to home tickets was under threat, with games due to be played at grounds with significantly lower capacities. The fear was the FA would use this opportunity to exclude existing fans and replace us with ones closer to the FA's marketing model. More casual supporters, who would come for one match, buy up all the merchandising, then be replaced with another lot next time who would do just the same. Meanwhile legislation was being introduced to ban known hooligans. Again, we feared the FA might use it as an excuse to simply get rid of those whom it didn't like the look of: white, male, twenty-something working-class males.

Combined with cost-cutting and out-sourcing services to members of the England supporters' club, it did begin to look as if the current fans were being dumped in favour of Paul Barber's new target audience. These were the ones who watched England on the box, partied their way through Euro 96, and painted their face with the St George Cross, but who weren't currently giving the FA their cash in return for any of this.

In May 2003, UEFA issued the FA with a huge fine and a final warning following the racist abuse and two pitch invasions at the

April home game against Turkey. The FA announced it might refuse to take up their ticket allocation for that autumn's away games in Macedonia and Turkey – effectively, a ban on England fans travelling to these matches.

At the Slovakia match in June Paul Barber was in the stadium on the morning of the game while a large number of fans laid out the 'Raise the Flag' sheets which that night, just before the kick-off, would be held up to spell out the slogan 'No to Racism'. Paul Barber's message to the fans attending that evening's game was printed on the back of the FA posters we also put on every seat. It was uncompromising: 'Far too often decent fans stay silent allowing the game to be ruined by a small number of bigots. Some even think it's all part of football. It isn't.' The statement linked the urgent need to take a stand with the broadening of England's support. 'We've been making good progress in attracting families, women, children and people from different cultures. Football is a game for everyone – let's not spoil it.'

For researcher Tim Crabbe, the connection Paul Barber made between excluding some and including others was symptomatic of the FA's entire approach post-Euro 2000 to the 'problem' of the fans. In an article he wrote for the academic journal *Leisure Studies* Tim described in terms fans would readily recognize the FA's strategy: 'A desire to prevent forms of disruptive behaviour which were seen as highly media-sensitive and damaging to the game's public image and commercial appeal. Accordingly, after the 2000 European football championships, an increasingly sophisticated effort was made to actively reshape the forms and representation of support for the team.'

As we laid out our sheets on the seats a few of us talked to Paul about our anxieties at the FA threat to ban us from away travel. Sean Branton has been taking his son, Sean junior, to England games, home and abroad, since he was eleven years old. The two of them were planning to travel to Macedonia and couldn't understand why the FA should want to stop them. 'Paul Barber did listen to us. I was surprised. I didn't think he would be interested in what we had to say, but he was. And he was honest too about the situation the FA was in. I think he was amazed at the lengths we have to go to in order to see a game.'

But weeks later, the ban was formally announced. Sean was disappointed; the FA had listened but they hadn't changed their minds. 'Why us? The FA couldn't wish for a better bunch of fans.' Sean, and the others who went over and chatted to Paul Barber that afternoon, had been on loads of away trips. All were keen volunteers for any fan-friendly initiatives going, they were advocates of dialogue with the FA when others said it was a waste of time, and most of them took their kids, the next generation of England fans, to the matches with them too.

The morning after the Slovakia game, the front page of the local Teesside paper the *Northern Echo* told the story of what the vast majority of England fans had achieved the night before: 'Fans lead the way on night of victory'. The piece recounted one key sign of that achievement. 'The passionate fans played their part by remaining silent for Slovakia's national anthem – and even applauding it.' Of course, the UEFA warning, the FA posters, the big-screen appeal by David Beckham all helped but none of this would have amounted to very much if the fans themselves hadn't actively wanted this to happen.

Paul Barber recognizes the impact the ban had. 'It caused a huge amount of grief.' In London Paul attended a packed meeting of fans to explain his actions. The FA provided him with security, worried things might get out of hand. At the start of the evening I asked for a show of hands, and almost everyone in the room disagreed with the ban. But by the end of the evening, while we still opposed what the FA was doing, most of us expressed a degree of understanding for the predicament the FA was in. At the very least we were confident that if such a constructive dialogue could continue with the FA it would make it less likely such drastic action would be resorted to again.

We had helped to establish that if the FA was serious about improving the reception and impact of England fans it had to work with the fans who shared that ambition, rather than against us. As for the security, none was needed. Instead we bought Paul a pint after, with more than grudging admiration for his willingness to come and meet us. A decent number did travel to Macedonia, but most didn't, so did this mean the FA had won the argument? Paul doesn't like to see it in those terms. 'It wasn't a question of winning. It was about restoring our reputation, with others. The gradual dying-down of the booing of the opposition's national anthem, the support for the antiracism message, the sense amongst so many fans that something had to change. This was what that period was all about, not just the travel ban on those two matches.'

There was also a recognition by the FA of the scale of the problem they faced. 'We started saying it was a significant minority. We couldn't pretend after the Turkey match that it was tens or hundreds, it was more like a few thousand. We had to say, "Enough". I sat through those meetings with UEFA; they simply weren't going to stand for it any more. This was no hollow threat, expulsion was a very real possibility.'

Recognition and resolution are two very different matters. The FA had to find a way to involve the majority of fans. Those who, however sickened by racism and shamed by the violence of their fellow fans, also expressed a deep-seated resentment at the lack of recognition that they themselves were neither racist nor violent. 'We recognized that the fans have a voice, and we could only see it getting more powerful. The media is only too willing to listen to what the fans have to say.' This is what the FA fears more than anything – bad publicity. But if as fans we make the mistake of heaping this upon them with no good cause except to make the odd entertaining news-paper headline at the FA's expense, we will be suckered by the insubstantial world of media matters. Instead we must address the need for meaningful, and ongoing, dialogue with the FA.

After 1996, changes in England's support were already starting to happen at home games. With Wembley closed from October 2000 as the new stadium was being built, England games were held all around the country. An international was no longer a long trek to London; the commitment and expense involved in going was less for large parts of the country when the game was played in their region.

During World Cup 2002 the performance of the fans off the pitch had an even more dramatic effect on the numbers and types of fans who wanted to identify with and support the national team. None of this made much difference in terms of those willing to travel to Baku, Katowice or Tirana on a Wednesday night. England's away matches, be they friendlies or qualifiers, are the Continental equivalent of my club Spurs playing Middlesborough or Blackburn in a midweek league game with nothing more than three points at stake. Only the most committed will travel, dwarfed by those who fill White Hart Lane most Saturdays.

Of course when England play away at a weekend, in a familiar and accessible part of Western Europe, there is a much larger demand for tickets, which becomes even bigger for tournaments. The reasons why England's regular away support is of a particular type are the same that shape most clubs' away support. It takes effort in terms of time off from work and money plus the willing-ness and ability to take some risks. Many won't have family responsibilities to worry about, or maybe some shirk the ones they do have. Occupations or income are of a sort that allow a lot of these short breaks. Individuals sometimes have to be willing to put up with a one-day round trip and very little sleep over the course of twenty-four hours for the joy, and sometimes despair, of ninety minutes' worth of international football.

Yes, we are still mainly white, male, with no kids in tow. Away travel, for club or country, has a much narrower appeal than going to home games. Our gender and race doesn't mean we're all brutish chauvinists or racists. The FA seemed to be unfairly targeting us as the problem preventing others joining in, while ignoring all the other factors involved.

Jonathan Arana was appointed FA customer relations manager in October 2001. Almost immediately he appreciated how important it was to improve the very poor relationship the FA had with the fans if England's support was ever to become something the wider public could be proud of. And, vitally for the FA's commercial ambitions, want to become a part of too. 'We had to change our entire approach. We started to understand that any initiatives to change what it means to support England for the better must be fan-led. This meant developing a relationship with those fans likely to initiate and support this process.'

This wasn't made easy by the organizational culture within the FA. 'You have to appreciate just how conservative this organization is, sometimes with good reason,' Jonathan points out. 'Any mistakes we make aren't just turned into back-page stories, they can make the front pages as well. The natural tendency when it comes to making a decision is risk-aversion – avoid bad publicity at all costs.' What helped Jonathan's case was that the fans committed to a positive England didn't have to bother with any of this. While the FA waited, we just got on with it, and our successes enabled those at the FA who supported what we were doing to win the confidence of others.

In London we had continued to meet together regularly after our first effort at a forum just before Euro 2000. The group slowly grew, and the media started to listen to what we had to say. But the anger with the FA remained. Jonathan remembers the first time he attended one of our meetings: 'The relationship was so awful it could only get better. It was difficult to imagine it could get any worse. But anything we promised to do had to be achievable, otherwise nobody would have any faith in us.'

Jonathan understood that an important step forward would be for the FA to listen to what the fans had to say, even if both parties continued to disagree. 'It kept coming up, the fans wanted their voices to be heard. If we supported any initiatives organized by the fans to make this happen maybe things would improve. Before, the FA had always presumed it knew what the fans wanted – this was quite a big change.'

For four years until he left the FA in April 2005 Jonathan spent a huge amount of his time attending forums with fans all across the country. He became the person we would contact with our proposals for fan-friendly events on away trips, he would help secure FA support for our efforts to improve our image, and respond to our ideas to give England fans a better deal from the FA as well. The result was a much better dialogue than the bitter disagreement we had started with in 2000. So has an irreversible shift in FA attitudes occurred? Jonathan is unconvinced: 'Not everybody is sure this is the right way to go, not yet. There are different pressures: security, marketing, ticketing.' This caution is the legacy of a negative reputation, and mishandled relationships, built up over decades. 'When things are going right, everybody will back this fan-led approach, they can see it works. Euro 2004 was a huge success for the fans, and the way the FA supported the fans, but we've only had the recognition afterwards. The doubts remained right up to, and during, the tournament.'

Jonathan remains optimistic that the FA has sufficient appreciation for what has been achieved so far to give this kind of approach the opportunity to develop. 'If things do go wrong the consequences for the FA are enormous commercially: lost sponsorship, decreasing income from TV deals. The self-interest helps the fans – the FA is being forced to give anything that reduces the possibility of trouble a go. If the fan-led approach is seen to work the FA will back it.'

The backing is most likely to continue while it serves to aid the FA's three core ambitions for the development of England's support. Jonathan summarizes these: 'Firstly, to appeal to as many fans as possible, and a diversity too. This isn't just about those who go to games, but everybody who might think of themselves as an England fan. Secondly, the security of those who do go, particularly on away trips. Eliminating any problems caused by disorder remains the FA's prime objective. Thirdly, making the England team the most attractive commercial proposition, both to sponsors and the football market.'

The Independent Football Commission (IFC) has limited regulatory powers and enjoys a near nonexistent profile beyond those already employed in the governance of the sport. But for individuals like Jonathan Arana, what the IFC had to say about their work was hugely encouraging. In their report on Euro 2004 the IFC detected 'a feeling, often voiced, that the FA is starting to be "more transparent" and "more willing to recognize what fans put into football" and a respect – though criticisms remain – for the FA's changing relations with supporters'. The England supporter groups which had worked with the FA for a fan-friendly Euro 2004 could also celebrate the same report's recognition that 'a supporter majority ready to take its own initiatives to rectify the problems associated with England fans abroad was one of a number of shifts that was starting to transform the supporter landscape'.

But there is a very real danger if fan involvement in this process becomes bureaucratized, immersed in formality and detached from the football culture representatives claim to speak for.

Tim Crabbe is both an academic and a hugely experienced fan activist, including a period when he chaired the Football Supporters' Association. He believes that maintaining this balance between fans being well-enough organized to get recognition without becoming separated from the vast majority of fans is incredibly difficult. 'There are models, but none are universal. What is most important is that each form of organization is able to communicate with each other. They also need to avoid depending on a few personalities; instead they should be plural and have a range of people speaking to the TV, radio or the press.'

In 1985 Liverpool fan Rogan Taylor was involved in helping to found the FSA. The impetus had been the Heysel Stadium tragedy when rioting Liverpool and Juventus supporters combined with a shoddy stadium and poor policing, left thirty-nine Juve supporters dead. Rogan was amongst a small group who decided something had to be done. 'It wasn't enough to just sit and talk. That match and what happened was a symbol of everything that was wrong with the game.'

The FSA grew quickly, particularly on Merseyside where Liverpool and Everton fans came together for the common cause. Their aim was to eliminate the factors that had created an environment in which supporters' lives could be put at risk and finally, at Heysel, lost. A year later the first ever FA Cup Final between Liverpool and Everton took place. Rogan remembers the nightmarish way in which the fans were treated. 'Several generations of both sets of supporters had waited for this match to happen but the organization at Wembley was disastrous. The FSA prepared a report, the authorities were surprised how sensible our suggestions were, but they just didn't seem to understand what we were trying to do, how serious and committed we were.'

The seriousness of the issues the FSA raised was proved tragically correct in 1989 at Hillsborough. Ninety-six Liverpool fans lost their lives that day as a result of a near total lack of crowd-control management. Rogan, as both a Liverpool fan and the main FSA spokesman, became hugely involved in the inquiry into the tragedy. He helped ensure the fans' experiences were heard, along with proposed solutions framed by those experiences.

After Heysel all English club sides had been withdrawn from European competition. Domestically the Thatcher government's favoured solution to hooliganism was an ID card that would have to be carried by all football supporters. The FSA was implacably opposed to the proposal – Rogan explains why: 'The ID card's purpose was to exclude, to keep supporters out, rather than encourage supporters to join.' The intention was to narrow and regiment football's support, never to include, consult and involve. The FA might not have been in favour of the latter, but to reduce football's support was certainly not in their interests. Without making a huge public deal of it they backed the campaign by Rogan and the FSA against the proposal.

But in the end what finished off supporter ID cards was Hillsborough, and the Taylor Report into the tragedy. Rogan remembers the impact the FSA had on Lord Justice Taylor: 'Our submission to the inquiry was vital. We presented a sophisticated critique of the football industry centred on the fact that the fans were so badly looked after. The modernization of the game which then came about as a result wasn't entirely good, but the Football Licensing Authority at least meant that our safety would never be ignored again.'

Crowd management and stadium security issues were a central concern for England fans too. At Italia 90 the FSA launched its Fans Embassy service to try to ensure that at least some of this would be addressed. Rogan remembers the reasons for the initiative: 'I'd been to Euro 88 and seen the way our fans were treated. It made me think there must be some sort of service that could be provided, run by the supporters themselves, with the backing of the World Cup organizers, and recognized by the media as a source of the fans' side of any story.' At Italia 90 Rogan observed one crucial and enduring factor, which he identified in a magazine article afterwards: 'The alienating experience of being an English supporter in Europe – arriving after months of media hype to be met by ranks of armed police – still concentrates the tolerant and the racist fans together.' Rogan had an understanding that different types of fans don't occupy arbitrarily opposing positions – they will mix and merge depending on circumstances.

Since 1998 Kevin Miles has been responsible for organizing the FSA (now the FSF) Fans Embassy service at all England's away games and tournaments. 'The basic proposition remains the same as back at the start in 1990. Supporters organizing to help other supporters. The aim is to ensure we can all enjoy ourselves by providing practical help with travel and accommodation advice, representing fans' interests to official bodies, and sharing any positive experiences.'

Kevin believes the embassy's success depends on hard-earned credibility. 'Nowadays there is a lot of recognition for what we do, from both fans and official bodies. We've become quite a familiar sight for those who travel away regularly, and most will know that we will be there to speak out if our fans are being badly treated.' Kevin and his helpers not only provide a mobile advice service to be found wherever England play, but also produce a free fanzine, *Free Lions*, for each game, home and away, distributed to as many supporters as they can reach. Plus they publish a well-researched tournament handbook for World Cups and European Championships. All this adds up to an extraordinary facility, one which has acquired official recognition, and some funding, as different bodies have appreciated the communication the Fans Embassy provides with a broad swathe of England supporters. Kevin is proud of this achievement – he is a highly effective operator and spokesperson that few in authority aren't impressed by, but he isn't seduced or softened by any of this either. 'Our independence remains crucial.' And impartiality too: 'We're not there to preach or pass judgement,' he reminds me.

After Euro 2000 the pressure was on anybody concerned with England's support abroad not only to pass judgement but to come up with some answers. At first the FA's motives were treated with suspicion. Angela Cox, writing in *Free Lions*, was one of those unimpressed with what the FA was doing:

> It seems to me a short-sighted approach to dismiss the feelings of your most loyal customers. Treat them fairly, make them feel part of a club ethos and you will have a group of people prepared to unite to show the acceptable face of England fans. These people will do their best to influence others and marginalize those hellbent on behaving anti-socially. The change will not come overnight. It will be a slow process but the FA should start to value their members and work with them, as they are a powerful resource in the fight for a better-behaved England.

In London our group of away travellers started to meet together. It was most important that we had chosen a positive rather than a negative focus for why we met. The defining characteristic of an active England fan is international travel. Not even supporters of Champions League clubs will travel to as many countries as we do, and our trips aren't limited to Europe either. This is what makes us different. Increasingly there were fans for whom, while the result was the most important part of their trips, enjoying the places visited came a very close second. Instead of organizing around our enthusiasm for an opposition to violence or racism we organized primarily around increasing the pleasure of these trips.

An FA representative attending an open meeting with fans was, in those early days, still something rare. They preferred either committee meetings with fan representatives who had no obvious contact with other fans, or staged forums where the FA selected the audience and controlled the agenda. We knew we couldn't guarantee any outcomes, but maybe we could get the FA to understand that by alienating England's core support they would be losing the co-operation of their most likely allies. Our meetings were lively and loud. We were a football crowd, and most had never been part of a process like this before. The case we made, however, was reasoned, based on years of experience, and our proposals were mostly constructive. The FA started to appreciate what we were trying to do; they realized what a resource we could be, and started to understand how disastrous it would be if they succeeded in turning us into their implacable opponents.

Some fans remained suspicious of the motives. They saw us as just another bunch of tub-thumpers and spotlight-seekers, one-man bands purporting to speak on others' behalf. And for fans in the rest of the country the fact that all of this at first took place in London, right on the FA's doorstep, didn't help either. None of this was surprising. While the fan embassies have provided an outstanding service at tournaments from Italia 90 onwards, never before had we England fans organized amongst ourselves. What convinced those that came along that we were involved in something worthwhile was the modesty and practicality of our ambition. We were a group of London-based fans who follow England. We wanted a better deal for England fans and a support we can all feel proud to be a part of. We expected the FA to help, not hinder, that process. We believed, as fans, we are best placed to lead the process. And we didn't want to overload ourselves with bureaucracy and formality as a result.

It became obvious from the start that certain elements of the FA's policy on organizing England fans would remain unchanged. But at the fringes they responded. When each small suggestion was acted upon we gained the confidence of others that we were right to make the effort to push the FA along in the right direction. The most important sign of an evolving recognition of what we were trying to achieve was that the FA became willing to publicize to all members of the supporters' club what we were trying to do. After Euro 2000 and the reorganization, when the supporters' club was rebranded as 'englandfans', it became mainly web-based in terms of communication, with the FA finally setting up a dedicated website for all members to access and contribute to.

In an instant the club acquired that sometimes-hazy democratic credential, 'transparency'. Our LondonEnglandFans meetings were advertised to the entire membership, with full uncensored reports of the points we raised with the FA, as well as their responses. At the same time hundreds of fans would clog up the members' message board with angry complaints about how they felt their support of England was being mismanaged. None of this had been possible before. What pressures there had been on the FA had come from outside: the FSA, the fanzine *When Saturday Comes* and various academic reports, plus the occasional piece in the broadsheet press. Never a loud and consistent voice from the England fans themselves; not because those voices didn't exist, they had always been there. But there was no platform for them, no place where the fans could express themselves, and force the FA to take notice.

Emma Kirkham is typical of those who turn up to the London forums. For Emma the attraction was simple enough. 'To start off with it was that contact with the FA. If they could be bothered to turn up then it was surely our job to get them to listen to what we have to say. But then the forums started to provide information on trips, the places we were going to. The kind of people who came along to talk about this, from *Lonely Planet*, tourist boards, foreign embassies, you knew this was really valid advice, well worth having.'

It was World Cup 2002 that really established the LondonEnglandFans group and convinced us that we were taking part in something really quite significant. Japan was a country few of us had visited before, and we knew very little about the culture. We expected few Japanese outside Tokyo to speak English, and were wary of what they would think about having English fans in their country.

From the start of 2002 until we flew out to Japan in early June we met each month. Everything we could think of was covered in our travel forums, including a film show about the host cities from the Japanese Tourist Board, a security briefing by Stuart Jack, deputy head of mission at the British Embassy in Japan, and a Japanese football journalist who came along to find about what England fans were really like. With a few weeks to go before we departed the final forum was held. Nearly two hundred fans packed into Sportspages bookshop for a saki and sushi tasting followed by a Japanese language lesson. There we all stood practising our 'thank you very much', '*Arrigatoh Gozaimas*', for all we were worth. The Japanese TV crew in attendance thought they were in football heaven. Was this really what the dreaded England fans were like?

After the tournament was over I counted up how many had come along; it was something like five hundred fans in the course of the six-month build-up. Add the many hundreds more who would read our email reports, and the thousands who saw the reports carried on the FA website news page, plus the fact most of the forums were covered by Sky Sports News, Five Live, BBC Radio London and others. This sort of media coverage would extend our reach to millions. It was an incredible achievement in a short space of time. Of course we were just one part of what contributed to such a successful performance by our fans off the pitch in Japan. But we had helped create a popular and participative way for ourselves as fans to contribute towards ensuring a fan-friendly tournament.

In October 2002 the Bratislava away trip was pretty horrible for most of us who went, with nonexistent stadium safety plus riot police lashing out at all and sundry. Hardly any of this was reported in the press, just the return of a troublesome England away trip after the cessation of hostilities during our summer visit to Japan. We decided to hold a forum to review what had gone wrong. Senior staff from the Home Office and British Police officers who had been out in Bratislava agreed to attend, along with Ian Murphy, responsible for ticketing at the FA, and Clifford Stott, who was just beginning his research into the policing of England fans abroad.

The room was packed out with fans who had suffered at the hands of the Slovakian riot police. The Home Office and police explained the limits to their jurisdiction abroad and the extent to which their careful advice had been ignored. The FA agreed to take up our complaints with UEFA. BBC news cameras filmed fans as they explained the injuries the riot police had caused them. Trust still wasn't guaranteed but for Emma, who had been sexually harassed by stewards as she entered the Bratislava ground, the meeting did make a difference. 'I hate the word but I did feel "empowered". The forum had given us all a voice with which we could report what had gone on and, right there in front of us, people in positions of responsibility were listening to us.'

It is the balance between meeting to complain and seek redress, and a determination to create the conditions in which we can enjoy ourselves that gives the group its appeal. Emma believes it is the latter that ensures the variety of different sorts of fans who come along. 'Most places we travel to we stay there for forty-eight hours or thereabouts. Take Baku in Azerbaijan; how many wouldn't want to visit the Maiden Tower, the oilfields, the carpet market, if they knew about them?' Of course, a forum isn't the only way to find out about these Azeri sights. But to do so at one of our forums with others who are making the trip, and hear from Welsh fans how they had made the best of their few days in Baku a month before us, plus meet some representatives from the Azerbaijan Embassy keen to wish us well (and, more bizarrely, pass on the details of where to find the counterfeit DVD shops) all adds to making following England special.

As Euro 2004 approached, similar groups to the one in London started meeting in the Northwest, Yorkshire and the South Coast. Pete Nicholas went to the first forum of NorthWestEnglandFans. 'People were complaining bitterly about how they were being treated by the FA, but all they really wanted was to be listened to. I was new to travelling abroad with England, what was best was just this opportunity to meet other fans, to hear their stories, learn from their experiences.' It is a welcoming, friendly group. 'There's no cliques. People want to help. We always arrange to meet up in the place we're going to.'

Pete represented the NorthWestEnglandFans group at a meeting the IFC organized after Euro 2004 between all the regional EnglandFans groups and David Davies, one of the FA's most senior officials. 'At first I was a bit worried. I didn't want to make a fool of myself. But I soon got into it. I realized he wanted to hear about my experiences as an England fan, what the FA could do to help improve that experience. I went away thinking yes, he has taken some notice, we are making some sort of a difference.'

In London we were ready for Euro 2004 with an approach that had worked well for Japan, but could we do even better this time round? Japan had been special – none of us had been there so the appetite for travel and tourist information was obvious. But in the meantime we had continued to meet, learned to get on with each other, and established friendships. We also practised an openness that meant newcomers were made to feel welcome, with seasoned away travellers always pleased to be able to pass on an answer to any question. The FA and other authorities increasingly appreci-ated the constructive and communicative role we sought, which enabled them to meet fans and views to be exchanged.

We ran a similar series to our World Cup 2002 build-up with panels of influential speakers. When the Deputy Chief Constable responsible for policing England fans is joined by the Lisbon Match Commander in front of nearly a hundred England fans seeking assurances that they will be policed in a friendly if firm manner, then it is surely possible to claim that our interests are being at least considered. And that was just one meeting. Month after month our panellists included the likes of the British Ambassador to Lisbon, the chief sports writer on the *Daily Mirror*, the technical director of the FA and the director of the British Council in Portugal. We were being taken seriously, recognized as vital partners, our views valued.

There isn't one model for how this outcome might be achieved, though Martin O'Hara, who is involved in the Yorkshire England Supporters' group, agrees an informal approach is vital. 'I'd never been involved in anything like this before. There's a stage of get-ting to know each other which is important.' The Yorkshire group have been meeting since just before Euro 2004. Already Martin can see a rapid rate of development. 'We needed to discuss what we were trying to do. Even now we're not always sure and sometimes the problem is we have the wrong expectations of what the FA can do for us. Although when they manage to be both arrogant and incompetent they deserve all the complaints they get. However, as we have got to know the FA staff, things have certainly improved. Our group receiving a kind of recognition has been really important.'

After Euro 2004 the FA examined once more the way it organized the England supporters' club. All those forums set up by the fans in London, Manchester, Doncaster and elsewhere had succeeded in earning us a fair hearing. The FA had listened. Much of what we had been complaining about for the past two years was taken notice of when the new membership scheme was announced.

The most bitter complaint had been about the FA's abandonment of the loyalty points scheme for ticket allocations. The demand for tickets when England qualifies for a tournament is enormous, and increasingly the same applies for quite a number of away qualifiers and friendlies. The FA had long recognized that the fairest way to allocate tickets when supply is vastly outnumbered by demand was by a loyalty system. Each game attended earned a fan a 'cap'. But in 2002 they took the decision to zero these points after the Japan finals. Long-standing fans were devastated. They had earned their right to be at the front of the queue, but now all that effort and sacrifice was to be discarded, and tickets would become an unregulated free-for-all. The impression that England's existing support was the FA's enemy within, to be targeted and got rid of, was disastrously reinforced. After two years of arguing, patiently making our case, the FA in 2004 finally agreed with us that points gained from away trips of one qualifying campaign would be carried over to the next. Not for every match we'd ever attended – that was fair enough as this made it nearly impossible for new fans to ever catch up – but credit was given for at least some of our length of service in the cause of England. In the process the FA recognized the value of this loyalty.

The first time the FA had tried to turn the negatives of our support into positives it hand-picked a few fans to join its staff on a couple of goodwill visits to French host cities ahead of France 98. As preparations began for World Cup 2006 eight years later the approach could not have been more different. It was the fan groups, organized by the supporters themselves, who were invited by the Home Office and the British Embassy in Berlin to meet German officials, plan forums for fans across Britain ahead of the tournament and propose ideas for fan-friendly activities in Germany wherever England played. These aren't representative of all fans and they have never claimed to be. But they are in touch with a growing chunk of like-minded supporters who want to enjoy themselves, to be well received and looked after, and make a contribution to the one big party that, at its best, a World Cup or European Championships becomes.

What made us England fans in the first place? Not content with just watching the team on the TV, we've travelled to a home game, bought the shirt, flown the flag. And some of us have become so infected with what we saw to think nothing of jetting off to all parts foreign to see England play. We wouldn't do it if we didn't enjoy it. Our fandom is wrapped up in the pride we have for all that is good about being an England fan; not *against* this, that or the other, but in favour of being fan-friendly. This is a value grounded in the everyday, sometimes incredible, experience of travelling England fans.

By organizing around our enthusiasm as fans we not only marginalize those who would hinder our enjoyment of all of this, but we also defy the tendency to bureaucratize and formalize our fandom. It is a simple process we are involved in but one remarkably rare in what passes for civil society. At our fan forums those in powerful positions to affect how we watch our football are called to public account. How many ordinary citizens have a dialogue with the Home Office, the Foreign Office, the police? Or as fans, have the opportunity to quiz those who run the game? We are all readers of newspapers, viewers of TV programmes, listeners to radio stations, but when do most of us get to meet the journalists and reporters who create all of this? A fan-led movement has helped create these conversations. However huge the market-research budget, the simple matter of putting those in charge in front of those they seek to manage remains the most dynamic communication imaginable, because it tells us something about the regard in which we are held.

None of this would be possible if fans didn't want to be a part of the conversation. We invest time, effort and some of our supporter identity in this process. The appeal lies in treating our support as full of positives rather than simply concentrating on the negatives, working together to ensure our England fan culture is something everyone can be proud of. This is a process no committee could ever achieve, no marketing campaign could ever initiate, no governing body could ever lead. Because it is our enthusiasm that keeps us going when Saturday comes, and goes. Enthusiasm brings out the best in us: loyalty, commitment, passion, knowledge of our team and theirs, a sense of being part of a community. And mostly a willingness to include, not exclude, all those who share this enthusiasm.

England fans have a lot to be proud of, and a little to be ashamed of. Liberate, listen to and give due recognition to our enthusiasm and we can start to make the difference.

9

If It Wasn't for the English

Ben Forgey is a fan of the Major League Soccer (MLS) side Chicago Fire, and a season-ticket holder since the club was founded in 1998. Ben plays too, a sport he calls soccer to distinguish it from a game involving blokes in helmets, shoulder pads and tights chasing something which looks remarkably like a rugby ball to me.

Ben explains why soccer has always appealed to him: 'I started playing when I was five years old, in a recreational league, like most kids at that age.' American children play soccer in enormous numbers, boys and girls, but by the time they reach high school the principal US sports claim the majority of allegiances: basketball, baseball and American Football. 'I knew I'd never be tall enough to compete at basketball, and I didn't have the bulk to play American Football. My mum didn't want me to play either, the risk of injury is too high for a lot of parents.' So Ben stuck with soccer, eventually securing a college scholarship. Now in his mid-twenties, he still plays most weekends in a Sunday league. While the US media remains dominated by the nation's other major team sports, participation in soccer is growing, outlasting what was previously just kicks for kids.

I met up with Ben and his girlfriend Sommer to see England play the USA at Chicago's Soldier Field stadium in May 2005. The first thing that strikes me is the near total absence of police on duty, not only at the ground but on any of the approach roads either. Don't they know England are in town? Ben isn't surprised, though. 'It's the same when the two Chicago baseball sides play each other, White Sox versus the Cubs.' The idea of crowd trouble is almost entirely alien to US sports culture and they're unwilling to accept that the English are about to change all that. Once in the stadium our support is sitting back and continuing to enjoy the kind of hospitality we are entirely unfamiliar with. Beer, served in our seats – these Americans really do know how to treat fans properly, and no exception is being made for the English either.

The game? A lot more meaningful than most had expected, with Kieran Richardson scoring twice on his debut, and Michael Carrick controlling the midfield in a manner many Spurs fans, based on his past season's performance, would never have suspected him capable of. The team is playing a friendly with a determination that suggests some of the players realize this is their big chance to impress the manager and possibly make it into the World Cup 2006 squad.

In the stands our fans start to stoke up the atmosphere in the only way we know. We sing 'Ingerland! Ingerland! Ingerland!' We make plenty of noise, though what passes for our soundtrack hardly refers to football. Scotland get a mention of course: 'Are you Scotland in disguise?' when the USA go 2–0 down. There are precious few songs about the team, past victories or individual players; instead the favourites are 'Rule Britannia', the occasional 'No Surrender to the IRA' and most of all today, 'Ten German Bombers'. Sung to the tune of 'She'll Be Coming Round the Mountain', it has become increasingly popular over the past year. Each of the German bombers is dealt with in the same way, those joining in singing loudly, 'And the RAF from England shot them down.'

What has all this to do with the football? Not much, though it has plenty to do with our anything but dormant obsession with our nation's martial past. For most the song is what it sounds like. A nursery rhyme to cheer themselves up and wind up the other lot. The degree of meaningless motivation behind most of those singing the song is revealed by what turns out to be the most popular song of the day: 'We're on the piss and havin' a laugh'.

Does that make the song OK, the fact that most of those who sing it don't mean any particular malice? What about the song's gloating inaccuracy? The RAF fought the Battle of Britain, never the 'Battle of England', and a significant number of pilots and aircrew came from the Empire or were escapees from occupied Europe as well. Personally I find 'Ten German Bombers', the *Dambusters* theme and 'Two World Wars and One World Cup' tiresome, out of place and, on occasion, downright offensive. Many feel the same way, so we don't join in, but lots do. Anti-German feeling isn't exactly a minority trend in our popular culture. Is it such a surprise that with more than our fair share of penalty shoot-out defeats at their hands we have a habit of reminding the Germans of another sort of defeat we inflicted upon them at almost every opportunity?

This has a habit of getting wrapped up in a set of attitudes to our history and others' cultures that leaves England fans sounding as if we belong on the outer fringes of extremism. For the most part this would be an unfair and inaccurate representation, though when the far-right loyalist chant 'No Surrender to the IRA' strikes up it does start to feel like the kind of place I'd rather not be. How many of those singing it know the sectarian heritage of the song? Looking at the faces, the ages, the teenage Asian I stood beside in

Liechtenstein as he bellowed it out for all he was worth, I would hazard a guess precious few. Supporters of Irish Republicanism in the shape of Gerry Adams, Martin McGuinness and their Sinn Fein pals are few and far between amongst England's support, but that doesn't mean the UDA, UVF and Orange Order are signing many up to march behind their flutes and drums to celebrate the Battle of the Boyne either. Instead the IRA simply represent a more recent armed threat to England than the Germans, and so are given the same sort of verbal treatment. England fans are anything but political – in part football is our way of escaping from the daily claptrap of parliament – so why 'No Surrender'? I'm not a big fan of what this and previous governments have done to our railways, and most of our public services too, but I don't go along to an England game to sing 'No Privatization' and I'd get some very funny looks if I did. But 'No Surrender' is every bit as political, so why do others get away with singing it? Because, to some, any threat to our national identity is fair game for a match-day singsong.

Two days later we are in New York, the day before the second of our summer tour matches, against Colombia. A big group of England fans gathers together on a playground in Manhattan. In March I had met Hugh Cosman and his 12-year-old son Haden at White Hart Lane. They were in the UK for a few days with the intention of taking in as many games as possible. Spurs versus Manchester City would be followed the next day by the Merseyside derby, then Luton against Barnsley for a touch of lower-division variety, and it would be rounded off by seeing Arsenal thrash Norwich.

Hugh had first been introduced to football by his uncle, Hans Keller, an Austrian Jew living in Hampstead, North London. Hans had managed to escape from Austria just before the Nazi Anschluss and was a huge fan of English football. In the 1960s

Hugh spent his summer vacations with Uncle Hans, who by now was a keen follower of Jimmy Greaves. Under his uncle's influence, Hugh did his best back in the USA to keep up with the fluctuating fortunes of Jimmy's various clubs, Chelsea, Spurs and West Ham. After the collapse in the mid-1980s of the North American Soccer League and his local club New York Cosmos, football became less important to Hugh. Haden has reignited his dad's interest. Together they watch as many Premiership games as they can catch on the TV, and Haden turns out for his local side, the Manhattan Soccer Club. As we chatted following the Spurs game, I tentatively enquired about the possibility of a bunch of our fans who were going to New York for the May friendly with Colombia getting together with Americans like Hugh and Haden who love our football; they might fancy a game too.

Hugh put me in touch with the Manhattan Soccer Club; they liked the idea, and MetroNation, the supporters' club of the New York MLS side MetroStars, wanted to meet up with us too. In New York there's a huge expatriate English community. David Witchard runs a website and publishes a weekly fanzine, *First Touch*, which provides these exiles with all the vital up-to-date listings on which league matches are being shown, and where. He was keen to help out as well and offered to organize a bar and a Colombian band for a party after the game, and recruit some American teams for us to play against.

This kind of venture has become an increasingly regular feature on England away trips. Sharing what we have in common with others, football, while never shying away from our differences either. More and more fans are keen to be involved. Not exactly 'do-gooders' – most would bristle at the suggestion – but doing some good nonetheless. We're not special, everyone can do their bit: swapping a pin badge with an opposing fan, leaving a St George postcard in a bar where we've been well received, or spending an afternoon in Manhattan turning out for a game and a party afterwards. The common, vital ingredient is we enjoy mixing with others, rather than sticking just with our own.

These fan-friendly initiatives are organized by fans, for fans. The FA don't seek to control or interfere with what we do. What they do is provide publicity. Nicola Jones in the supporters' club office makes sure the details are sent out to everyone travelling, and provides a huge bag of England badges, pens and key rings for us to give away. This is just the sort of support we need, and it is much appreciated.

Jamie Craig runs the supporters' club section of the FA website. Posting the information about what has been organized on the site ensures we reach not just those fans going to the USA, but the many thousands more members who wish they were and are interested to hear what we'll be getting up to. I had dubbed our event 'Becks and the City' and jokingly suggested to Jamie that a pic of Sarah Jessica Parker accompanying the notice about the event will probably boost the numbers responding. I'm not sure if it was the sexy photo of SJP or my sparky copy, but almost two hundred fans sign up by email to meet up in New York for the game and party. The idea of playing a game against some Americans, talking with MLS fans, finding out a bit more about the popularity of football in the USA and mixing with other England fans who share a similar sort of positive outlook has a certain appeal. Hugh, Haden, David and Marc Bernaducci from the MetroNation have assured us of a good reception, a pitch and some opposition to play against, but it's all been arranged by email, and I've never met most of the fans who have said they'll come. Who knows if it will work?

Hugh had booked the Frederick Douglas Playground in Manhattan's upper west side, an AstroTurf pitch used for both football and baseball, surrounded by blocks of council housing in a mainly Hispanic, working-class neighbourhood. This is a part of

New York few tourists will visit. As the kids playing baseball on what will shortly be our pitch finish off their game, the friend Hugh has recruited to provide the afternoon picnic, Naomi, unloads her car, packed full with genuine New York deli sarnies, and a Mexican speciality, tamales. The organization at the US end has been faultless.

We have two Manhattan kids' teams to play against our under-11s, and a scratch team of Americans with a few ex-pats making up the numbers, to play our seniors and vets. Marc from the MetroNation is here, joined by staff from the MetroStars and their MetroGirlz, the club's cheerleaders, sadly minus any pompoms. Amongst the crowd of England fans who have turned up are regulars who have come along to previous events I've helped organize on previous trips – they are always looking for something to do.

There are plenty of new faces as well. Linda Murray is on her first trip abroad for an England game with husband Mike and their ten-year-old son Chris. 'We'd joined the supporters' club at the end of 2004. We go regularly to England home games, we're passionate about our football and joining up seemed a way to become part of a community.' Chris plays for a kids' team, the Chineham Tigers Under-11s. The idea of him lining up in an England shirt representing England Fans' Children against Haden's Manhattan Soccer Club was hugely attractive.

Linda admits she had had her reservations about how England away might turn out: 'I wanted to be part of this community but at the same time there's something about the group mentality that put me off. But that afternoon Chris was able to play, and meet, children of his own age, American and English, in another country. For Chris it made the trip real. Mike and myself also met other fans who were travelling with their children. Everybody was so friendly, passing on helpful advice to us. We didn't feel we were on our own even though we were so new to all of this.'

Another of Hugh's friends, Andrei, has volunteered to referee for us. Dave Beverley, who we'd brought along as our ref, has come all dressed up as a properly qualified man in black. Dave swaps his official referee's jersey with Andrei, who is really impressed. He's never worn one before, and can't get over that in Dave's shirt pocket are genuine yellow and red cards for him to flash at any of the seniors or vets who might give him any bother. After the game Andrei turns to me and asks, 'But where are the hooligans? This is a one-hundred-and-eighty degree turn.' I couldn't have put it better. Of course we shouldn't have to make this extra effort to dispel what are sometimes unfair illusions. That's just how it is, and if we do it in a fun way that fans new and old, ours and theirs, enjoy, then is that such a chore?

At these gatherings we normally challenge our opponents to a pub quiz, with the added twist that we answer questions on the opposition country, and they do the same about England. Cheating is rife, and actively encouraged. This results in co-operation, conversation and useless bits of swapped trivia such as the two English League clubs with the nickname 'The Pilgrims' (after the USA's Pilgrim Fathers) or the name of the Brazilian town where England lost to the USA 1–0 at the 1950 World Cup. Ouch! (The answers are, of course, Boston United and Plymouth Argyle, and Belo Horizonte was the scene of the USA's giant-killing at our expense.)

The Americans impress us with their knowledge of English football and we award them with their prizes, a T-shirt that the company I co-founded, Philosophy Football has produced for fans making the trip. The script on the front seeks to sort out our minor linguistic misunderstanding: 'Football: A field sport, played by two teams with a round, inflated ball. The people's game, invented by the English and exported the world over. Never knowingly called "soccer", a word used by many Americans to describe twenty-two foreigners in funny shorts.' A dash of humour to explain away our differences, and similarities.

Marc and his MetroNation mates are certainly glad they turned up. The following day they introduce hundreds more of our fans to another American tradition. There are no pubs or bars near the New York Giants stadium in Meadowlands, New Jersey, just vast concrete car parks, and it is here the US tradition of 'tailgating' has grown up. Cold beers, a barbecue grill and, rather bizarrely, a karaoke machine are all provided by our American hosts.

'We wanted to introduce the England fans to one of our match-day traditions and leave you all with a lasting, positive memory of soccer in America,' says Marc. It is precisely the same sentiments that had been behind our own venture in Manhattan the day before. 'We'd never met any of you before. We didn't know what to expect. But the great thing about football is the commonality. That is what binds us together.' Of course Marc has loyalties of his own too. 'The best part of the afternoon in Manhattan with you all? Heading the assist for Team USA's first goal against your lot.' Two very different fan cultures have come into contact with each other. Marc is certain what he and his fellow American fans got out of it: 'As America and Major League Soccer establishes itself in the game on both the world and domestic stages, we will be aspiring to achieve the exemplary loyalty, passion and pride of England fans.'

Ian Black would never aspire to be anything remotely resembling an England fan. Ian has followed Scotland since the late 1940s. He can still remember being stowed in the luggage rack as a convenient place for a young lad to sleep on the long journey south of the border to take on the Auld Enemy at Wembley. 1974 was his first World Cup with Scotland, and apart from missing Argentina in 1978 he has been to just about every Scotland away match since.

When Ian started his travels Scotland had a reputation for trouble every bit as fearsome as the English. Today the 1977 Wembley pitch invasion by the Scots and them smashing up our goalposts may be just a harmless part of tartan folklore. At the time it represented the hate and fear they were determined to impose upon others. As the Scots started to shift away from the worst of this excess, they were continually confused by foreign hosts with their near neighbours, the English. This is what really riled them, and still does. Neither of us would ever mistake ourselves for the other, but for the rest of the world Scots, English, Brits, we're all much of a national muchness.

Ian dates the shift back to the 1982 World Cup in Spain. 'Thirty thousand Scots had made it out there for the game against Brazil. My wife and children came with me. Lots of fans were doing the same, making the trip a family holiday. We scored first, the Brazilians won 4–1.' No change there then, the plucky Scots suffering a heavy defeat, ha! It was what the Scots sang as they streamed out of the stadium which, for Ian, represented the change that was going on: '"The best team won! The best team won!" We sang the same line over and over again. It had never happened before, and not since either. At that moment and quite spontaneously we all realized we'd just watched a great game of football and if we weren't here to enjoy ourselves what were we doing out here?'

With England also in the tournament and our reputation for hooliganism as bad then as it has ever been, one of the ways the Scots distinguished themselves was by behaving in an entirely different way. 'It was our standard insult to anybody about to cause any mischief: "You're acting like the English".' Ian admits to a certain Scottish smugness about all the plaudits they have been awarded for what the Tartan Army have achieved, more often than not in comparison with all the negatives heaped upon England fans. He is well aware that, with their history, it could very easily have been them in our place. 'Our fans have done something similar to yours in the past.' A crucial difference for the Tartan Army has been the way the often nationalist-inclined Scots media, including their tabloids, has vigorously championed their cause. It isn't that the tam-o'-shanter, kilts and ginger wigs are a media myth. Rather it is that this image has been pushed to the foreground as the number-one image of Scottish fans abroad, leaving anything less savoury in the margins.

The Tartan Army are friendly to everyone with one notable exception – us. The Scots don't like the English and vice versa. When Ian travelled with the Tartan Army to Dortmund in September 2003 for Scotland's Euro 2004 qualifier against Germany, he and his mates were dumbfounded by what the opposing fans sang at them. 'The Germans taunted us by chanting, "We hate the English more than you". That threw us, but after a quick huddle we responded by singing, "You only fought the bastards once". It well and truly shut them up.'

The Scots and the English aren't alone in their apparent inability to get along. The Dutch don't like the Germans yet, like the Scots, are widely lauded as carnival fans, held up as representing everything we're not. Corne Aarts is part of Holland's huge travelling support and describes what it means to him to follow his national team. 'The atmosphere is amazing, one huge family, no hint of trouble. And away, even better. Only the most committed fans travel, and the big attraction for us is the countries we visit, the cultures we encounter.'

The Dutch have their orange parade but have this rivalry with Germany to deal with too. An English writer who has written extensively on Dutch football, Simon Kuper, described in his book *Football Against the Enemy* what Holland's Euro 88 semifinal victory over West Germany meant. 'The Dutch players were the

Resistance, and the Germans the Wehrmacht – these comparisons are absurd, but they occurred to most Dutchmen.'

Corne remembers both the 1988 game and the 1974 defeat by West Germany in the World Cup final. '1974 was a national trauma, 1988 a national recovery. 1974 was about revenge for the war, 1988 revenge again for the war and the 1974 defeat too.' Hopelessly mixing up world history, national identity and the more minor matter of putting the ball in the back of the net, this confusion isn't unique to the English. Though we are sometimes made to feel it is by a combination of our parochialism and the pride, or the shame, we share.

Patrick Mignon is the head of research at France's National Institute for Sport and Physical Education. He specializes in investigating the contribution football makes to shaping contemporary French national identity, a task made considerably more interesting after France's 1998 World Cup victory was swiftly followed by their success in winning Euro 2000. 'I never believed our two victories, won of course by a multiracial team, represented what we think of as the "real" France. They were great results, and created new possibilities for integration and harmony, but sport really isn't as important to us as it is to the English and some other nationalities.'

The French retain a sense of proportion, detaching one context from another. The fact that their football success is relatively recent and does not depend on the superlatives of heightened national expectation helps. Waterloo and Trafalgar are kept for the history books, rather than revenge sought for them on the football pitch whenever France play England. Likewise, the Common Agricultural Policy and EU Constitution they leave to Monsieurs Chirac and Blair to argue over instead of expecting Thuram and Vieira to settle France's quarrels with other nations. Zidane scoring a last-minute winner against the English is just that, a symbol of nothing more than the magnificence of his skill as a footballer. 'When he conjures up some magic we praise Zidane for his football,' comments Patrick, 'not his Frenchness.'

France 98 left some kind of popular legacy, of course. Time and again commentators compared the dancing in the streets of the Champs-Elysées when France defeated Brazil in the final to similar scenes when Paris was liberated in 1944. Patrick remembers the moment: 'It was good to be French. We were proud and with a team that came from everywhere.' Two years later the rest of Europe was shocked when 20 per cent of French voters backed the fascist Front National's Jean Marie Le Pen in the presidential election runoff against Chirac. The pride and the celebration of their multicultural team, which Patrick and millions of other French men and women shared, only meant so much. 'Most of those who vote for Le Pen don't have a problem with Zidane or Vieira, rather they have been convinced by the racists that the immigrant community in our towns and cities are all criminals and pose a direct threat to the survival of our nation, particularly the Muslims.'

If parts of French society are not integrated, producing fear and insecurity exacerbated by the wave of anxiety post-9/11, then even winning the World Cup and European Championship in quick succession isn't going to clear all that up in a hurry. In 2005, just five years after the Euro 2000 victors *Les Bleus* were being hailed as symbolizing how French multiculturalism was now triumphant, French cities burned when a wave of riots swept the nation. Political disintegration and a violent disaffected immigrant youth, in part motivated by a demand to be recognized and listened to, suggested anything but France united. That doesn't mean football cannot help the French, the English or any other nationality transform the meaning of their national identity. But it won't complete the task on its own; all it can do is perhaps get the process started.

After World Cup 2002 the distinguished Daiwa Anglo-Japanese Foundation in London hosted a discussion rather grandly entitled 'Sport, the Media and Mutual Perceptions'. Christopher Hood, director of the Japanese Studies Centre, wasn't in any doubt that England's three weeks in Japan had been of considerable significance: 'It is fair to say that one man has done more than any other in the past hundred years to help Anglo-Japanese relations: David Beckham.'

According to Christopher, the impact wasn't just on the Japanese but on ourselves too. 'Without doubt Beckham has helped to create a different, softer and more modern image of Britain.' Of course he meant England, but we'll let that customary confusion pass. I sat in on Christopher's talk as an interested observer and I left agreeing with much of what he had to say. He was certainly right about Becks, but he had missed something – what England fans in Japan had contributed to those changed perceptions.

Englishman Trevor Ballance has lived and worked in Japan for seventeen years. A Manchester United supporter, he keeps his love of football alive far from home by following the Urawa Reds, one of the top J-League teams who in the aftermath of the 2002 World Cup were able to attract crowds of over 40,000. Trevor recounted the fear before the tournament of what our fans would do amongst his Japanese friends and workmates. 'They were anxious, scared even. There had been TV programmes supposedly revealing what the English hooligan was like. Mickey Francis, who had written this book *Guv'nors*, was widely featured. It was the most extreme stereotype you could possibly imagine.'

Guv'nors, a hoolie-lit classic, was even translated into Japanese and became required reading for Japan's police force. 'There was a big focus on the preparations being made, lots of shots of the police in large-scale outdoor martial-arts training sessions, and these Spiderman-style nets which would be fired from cannons over the heads of groups of troublemakers to trap them.'

The Japanese are a different colour to most of the England fans who travelled out there. The sum total of our knowledge of their culture amounts to Sony, sushi and sumo. They have slanty eyes, were on the wrong side in the Second World War and their major corporations have successfully put out of business significant sectors of our manufacturing base.

None of this would suggest we'd end up best friends. Yet the Japanese detected something in the English they admired, with an intensity few of our fans can have ever experienced before. We were that much-sought-after commercial property, the real thing. It was obvious we weren't just in their country for a holiday; ending those years of hurt really meant something to us. Football was leaving home. Our infamy became something to celebrate rather than to fear. In Sapporo's Odori Park the afternoon before our game with Argentina, we tied our flags to the trees and the Japanese came in their thousands. First to look, then to politely ask if they could take a photo; in the evening after we had won they came back to join us for a party. Congaing up and down the streets, with chorus after chorus of the *Great Escape* theme, the police and onlooking media were hopelessly confused.

They had been warned what to expect when England and Argentina clashed, that much they were prepared for. What they hadn't expected was that the Japanese would embrace our riotous assembly as if it was their own, soften its ugly excesses and help turn it into a heaving, happy mass of mixed-up nationalities. Of course, Englishness has for a long time been a bit of a fad for the Japanese. One middle-ranking '70s punk band even half-jokingly named themselves after the phenomenon, 'Big in Japan'. The Japanese adore Fred Perry shirts, read *Harry Potter*, bring home souvenirs by the bagful from Harrods, our boy bands play sell-out concerts at the Budokan, while Japan's more hip youths get into Radiohead or Fat Boy Slim. But our fan culture wasn't until now such an obvious candidate to export to widespread Japanese acclaim and mimicry.

Japan is hemmed in on one side by the might of American culture, while on the other is the emergence of post-Communist China. The Japanese are engaged in a struggle to defend and define their own sense of identity and authenticity. They have a troubled relationship with the rest of Asia and the USA not dissimilar to our own with Europe and America. Put all this together with an awkwardness about any awakening of Japanese nationalism fired up by football. England fans had more in common with our unfamiliar hosts than we might at first have realized.

Japan Today journalist Takanori Kobayashi questions the development of the 'Blue Heaven' fervour behind the national team. 'Where did all this patriotism suddenly come from? Other than during World War Two, the World Cup is one of the few times in Japan's recent history when men and women, both young and old, were singing the national anthem and waving the national flag free from care.' He believes the motivation arises from this need for Japan to assert itself as different from the rest of Asia and more than a match for American influence in the region. 'Many people, especially youths, are easily swayed toward nationalistic behaviour because they believe in the "uniqueness of Japanese".' But Takanori is unconvinced that too much concern over the consequences is required: 'There is always going to be a nationalistic fervour. In other countries, it would be called home support.' Or, where I come from, I-N-G-E-R-L-A-N-D. It wasn't just that the Japanese embraced us because we were so different, it was also because we were so very much alike.

*

If It Wasn't for the English

When England played South Africa in Durban in May 2003, we won 2–1. It was a friendly, the result didn't really mean all that much. But, for some of our fans at least, this trip represented the beginnings of the fan-friendly initiatives that have become increasingly popular and effective ever since.

And what better place to begin than football-crazy Chatsworth, a township fifteen miles outside of Durban. With the help of the local British Council office I had arranged for some England fans to be able to travel out there to a bar called Pub 501, where we would meet local South African fans. I thought we'd fill a couple of taxis, a minibus at best. Not a bit of it: two coachloads, everybody looking forward to a night out mixing with local fans.

Pub 501 is packed every time Man United or Liverpool, the two most popular Premiership clubs in South Africa, are on the box, but none of the locals had ever met England fans before. The BBC's Garth Crooks joined us direct from the team hotel with a message of support from David Beckham. Fans from South African league sides Kaiser Chiefs and Orlando Pirates swapped chants with England followers of Port Vale, Blackpool and Doncaster Rovers.

The next morning another large crowd of fans turned out as we left our hotels in an open-top double-decker bus covered in our England flags. Off we went to fit in as many township schools as we could visit in a day. Each stop was an unpredictable mix of bunfight and ceremony.

One of the fans joining in all of this was Tim Murray. By the end of the day Tim was pretty pleased with himself: 'I could have stayed on the beach today with my mates but I've had a great time, and they haven't had half the experience we've had, have they?' These kinds of activities continued to grow over the next couple of years –something of the sort is now organized on almost every away trip. Enjoying ourselves has remained one of our guiding principles. Any initiative would be centred on our contribution as fans, open to all and easy to take part in. Whatever we did would be as professionally organized as doing it all in our spare time would allow us, and aimed at enabling those joining in to get a taste of the country and culture we were visiting by mixing hosts and visitors up together.

Those South African kids could identify with us, finding what we were offering appealing and engaging, in the same way the crowd at Pub 501 had the night before. Getting a wider audience to take notice of our efforts would take time, but even on this very first venture there was at least the beginnings of others recognizing the value of what we were up to. The day after the schools trip, South Africa's *Daily News* splashed across their front page a photo of one of our visits with the caption: 'David Beckham might have met Nelson Mandela in Johannesburg yesterday, but the true meeting of the hearts and minds of Africa and England took place on a dusty schoolground in KwaMashu.'

In 1996 Turkey qualified for the European Championships in England. Dalston, just a mile from where I live, is home to the biggest single concentration of Turkish immigrants in England. With Turkey drawn to play all their games in Nottingham and Sheffield, each match day saw a huge exodus of cars and vans northwards, flying the red crescent and full of hopeful supporters. Their reward was a bit scant – three defeats and not a goal scored – but their fans were praised for their numbers, for entering into the party spirit of the tournament and their very obvious commitment to the team.

There were few anxieties about the presence of Turkey fans at Euro 96. They were just a bit of exotica, irregulars on the European or world stage; our attitude towards their team and fans was curiosity as much as anything else. While the Turkish national side failed to make much of an impact on the tournament, the improving standard of their club sides was more apparent. When Manchester United's 1994 Champions League campaign was ended by Galatasaray, even if it was only on away goals, this was an almighty shock. Worse was to follow; during the 1996 campaign it was Fenerbahce who inflicted on United their first-ever home defeat in European competition. And in 2000 Galatasaray topped all of this, defeating Arsenal to lift the UEFA Cup, the first Turkish club to win a European trophy.

However, it was what happened in that season's semifinal between another English club, Leeds United, and Galatasaray that has cast such a shadow over the emerging Turkey–England rivalry. On the eve of the match in Istanbul two Leeds fans were murdered. The precise details remain hazy; there has been a court case and convictions, but the entire story has never been fully uncovered. All that matters is that those two fans lost their lives and football was, in large measure, the cause of that loss. When Galatasaray defeated Arsenal in the Copenhagen final shortly afterwards, the fighting between some of those on both sides was clearly influenced by what had happened in Istanbul.

That same summer both England and Turkey took part in Euro 2000. Ours was a miserable campaign, made only momentarily tolerable by beating Germany. Turkey did much better than us. They made it through to the quarterfinals, eliminating in their group the co-hosts Belgium. The night of that match I was in central Brussels arranging to meet some friends as we looked forward to what we hoped would be an England victory over Romania the following evening.

With both Italy and Turkey winning earlier in the evening, first, second and third-generation migrants from both countries living and working in Belgium filled the Grand-Place area, running up and down the narrow side streets as the police struggled to maintain any semblance of order. The metro trains and buses brought more and more on to the streets. The crowd became intimidating, the intent of those joining in difficult to interpret. I don't mind admitting I was scared. I covered up my St George Cross T-shirt, placed my hand over my mouth as I spoke into my mobile so no one would overhear my English accent, and warned my friends to stay away. Nothing particularly untoward happened. Instead, two communities far from what was once their home country were making their presence, and their success, felt whether others liked it or not.

Italians: well, we're used to them doing well and making the rest of us aware of their footballing achievements. For the Turkish fans this was something new. Back home in North London something similar was going on amongst the Dalston Turks, and two years later during Turkey's even more successful World Cup 2002 campaign they would be doing the same all over again. We don't always find it easy to cope with others' celebrations, and when the celebrating is going on in our own backyard it can rankle more than a bit. Two world wars, an empire on which the sun never set, seeing off invasions, inventing and exporting a sizeable proportion of the world's sports: it can all add up to an unhappy tendency to sometimes be sore losers, jealous of the success of newcomers.

Can Abanazir is a Besiktas fan – he is also assistant professor in the Department of English Language and Literature at Hacettepe University in Ankara. Can translates for me a chant that is sung by the fans whenever Turkey, or one of their club sides, play in a European competition. 'Europe, Europe, Hear our voice. These are the footsteps of the Turks.' While in large measure we English define our nationalism by wanting out of Europe, for Turkey playing a game of football is a chance to remind the continent that for forty years they've been trying to join us. As Turkey's standard of football has improved the potency of the emotion has increased. 'On the pitch we lose any inferiority complex, at least by UEFA we are accepted into Europe. If we win then we prove how wrong the EU are to reject us.'

And, like the English, Turks have a past to resort to if self-doubt creeps in to present-day emotions. 'The Ottoman Empire, of course we don't forget our history.' The Ottoman Empire never achieved the same global scale as the British Empire, and dates back much further in their past than ours. Nevertheless, the magnitude of this empire, stretching from the coastal strip of North Africa to the edge of Vienna, isn't forgotten by most Turks in a hurry. 'Our football helps us to get over our national inferiority complex. We have this same mentality as the English. We are both too willing to have a go, stand and fight, to confuse playing football with waging war.'

Fearful of crowd trouble and the hugely expensive costs of expulsion from Euro 2004, the FA banned England fans from travelling to Istanbul for the October 2003 away leg of the tournament's qualifying campaign. I remembered those Turkish convoys from Dalston to Nottingham and Sheffield during Euro 96. Was there a way we could all watch this game together and prove the doubters wrong? If we couldn't do this in Istanbul, how about having a go here in London?

Taylan Sahbaz is an advice worker at the Day-Mer Turkish and Kurdish Centre in Dalston; he is also an Arsenal fan and manager of the champions of the Turkish and Kurdish London League, Gencligin Sesi FC. When he heard my idea he and his friends couldn't have been more enthusiastic. Within days we'd come up with a plan. Very quickly interest started to grow in what we were trying to do. Taylan got in touch with the Turkish-language newspapers which the Turkish and Kurdish communities over here read. Instead of running stories about us being banned from Istanbul they featured our effort at watching the game all together. It was the first time England fans had received any sort of positive coverage in these papers.

Taylan was as pleased as we were at the impact our initiative was having in his community, but he could hardly believe it when a BBC London TV crew turned up to film an interview with him, and the next day BBC Radio Five Live reporter Nigel Adderley arrived wanting one too. For twenty years this community has either been ignored or demonized by most of the British media. What do any of us know about why they're here, their culture, their beliefs? A match that had been presented as too dangerous to allow away fans to travel to was being turned into a symbol of how football unites almost as effectively as it can divide. And we were getting that message out, Turks to the English, English to the Turks, where it had never been heard before.

On the night of the game we packed tightly into a Dalston pub popular with the Turks. It was about one-quarter English, the rest Turkish. Just the right kind of ratio to create an away-match atmosphere, in fact. Most of us who turned up had travelled the world for England, some for a lot longer than me. We tied our flags up, the Turks tied up theirs. It was Turkish beer only, and sticky Turkish sweets were passed from table to table. The air was heavy with the smell of Turkish tobacco as fans pushed and shoved for the best view of the big screen.

The game finished a well-fought 0–0 draw, enough to see England through and leave Turkey as group runners-up, having to face a play-off to qualify for Portugal. But the best result was something we could all share. It was an evening of both hope and defiance.

*

If It Wasn't for the English

Munich, 1 September 2001, was an unforgettable night for any England fan. I spent the day of the match with Claus Melchior, co-editor of the German fanzine *Der Todliche Pass* (The Perfect Pass). The English possess this curious certainty about the Germans. They must surely know we're not very keen on them; we can never forget, or forgive, two world wars. On the pitch there is Mexico 1970, Italia 90, Euro 96 and the greatest insult of all, losing the final game at the old Wembley in October 2000 to them as well. So why would they possibly harbour anything but the same dislike in return for us? Claus's opinion of us is, I believe, fairly representative of mainstream German opinion. An unwavering affection for most things English, especially our football culture.

I quiz Claus about the whistling of the *Dambusters* theme tune. Row after row of fans with arms outstretched pretending to be Lancaster bombers. 'What is the *Dambusters*?' Claus owns and manages Munich's English-language bookshop – surely he'd know about this most famous of WW2 air raids, and the film made about it? Then I thought about this. I can't imagine whoever chooses the repeats to fill up any gaps in the German TV schedules would make this movie their first choice for its umpteenth showing. And no German beer is going to sell many extra pints, or rather litres, with an advert in between scenes of Barnes Wallis's ingenious bouncing bomb. Claus is nonplussed by the *Dambusters* and he's not much the wiser either after a few wisecracks about who gets the beach towels first, the Germans or the English. The joke clearly never reached Germany from the Costa del Sol.

Many will try desperately hard to offend, and some certainly succeed. But a fair proportion of all this just cheers us up and leaves those it is aimed at blissfully unaware of what we're getting up to. Our enduring inability to make ourselves understood can have consequences in reverse too. We're not always that clear about the meaning of what the other lot are saying about us. When England played Argentina at France 98 the entire Argentine end jumped up and down in unison. Very spectacular, bordering on the carnivalesque, and a few commentators remarked how jolly all this was, unlike the sour and bitter English chanting, 'You'll never take the Falklands.' The Argentinian football writer Marcela Mora y Araujo told me months later what her countrymen had been singing, 'If your mother's not an English whore, jump in the air.' Mmm, not much of the carnival in those sentiments.

Markus Hesselmann is the sports editor on the Berlin newspaper *Der Tagesspiegel*. He believes the English need to define themselves against the Germans in order to entrench their own identity. And this informs how the Germans react, 'Our response is never as dramatic as I suspect you expect it to be.' Nor does Markus consider England a serious contender as Germany's principal rival in football. 'Holland comes first, second and third for unpopularity, with Austria a distant fourth.' Austria, what had their near neighbours done to upset the Germans? 'Never mind your "Five-one". 1978 is our most iconic defeat.' West Germany, the world champions, lost 3–2 to Austria, the bottom team in their second-round group, and were eliminated from the World Cup in Argentina. As for England, 'Our good results against you of course affect how we view the rivalry, but the influence of your pop music on us Germans impacts on our attitudes too. Not just music either, but the high regard in which we hold your fan culture.'

At the Euro 96 semifinal the German fans at Wembley responded to our customary song-list by singing the chorus to 'Three Lions', 'Football's coming home', back at us in word-perfect English as a tribute to their own triumph, while in Germany the song 'Three Lions' topped their charts for most of that summer. Best of all, the Germans mooed. Yes, they aren't shy of a wind-up either, and instead of reaching back into their past they treated us to a tribute to England's latest contribution to European unity, Mad Cow Disease. And this lot aren't supposed to have a sense of humour?

Kevin Miles, provoked by our own lack of songs about football, and the enduring popularity instead of ditties like 'Ten German Bombers', wrote an impassioned piece in *Free Lions*, the England fanzine. 'Songs? We do not have many, and the ones we have contain very little to do with football. We have songs that are patriotic, and then some that are controversial – at best divisive, and at worst offensive. But precious few about football – which is after all what it's supposed to be all about.'

This lack says something about both our national identity and insecurity. Too often we feel we have to retreat into the comfort of the Second World War because we lack enough confidence in a more modern Englishness. We do now at least sing when we're winning. 'Ea-zee! Ea-zee!' In cod northern accents, arms clapping wildly and in unison above our heads, so maybe the odd victory might inject the celebratory yet into our national psyche. Meanwhile when England play in most other European countries, at some point a group of our fans, small or large depending on the mood, will chant, 'If it wasn't for the English you'd be Krauts.' Designed to offend and impose our assumed superiority, there is precious little sense of the mood of solidarity and celebration the liberation of occupied Europe provoked in 1944–5. Occasionally, though, the lines get rewritten and it's hard not to laugh. 'If it wasn't for the English you'd be Serbs' at Albania away at least suggested the lyricist had been consulting more recent history books, and more accurate accounts than the one that inspired 'If it wasn't for the English you'd be French' in the USA. What's a war of independence between transatlantic allies? There are almost limitless possibilities with the concept, though when we become aware enough of our own history to sing to the Scots, 'If it wasn't for the English you'd be Scottish' maybe we will be ready to sing more about our football rather than our history.

10

Keep the Flags Flying

Saturday 26 March 2005: eight o'clock in the morning, seven hours before kickoff, and fifty or so fans are gathering under the Munich clock at Old Trafford. It is the day of the England–Northern Ireland 2006 World Cup qualifier. All volunteers, for the next five hours we will be clambering over the East and West stands attaching thousands of flimsy plastic sheets to the seats with elastic bands. The initiative is called 'Raise the Flag'. When the national anthem starts the sheets, held up by twenty thousand fans, form two huge St George Cross flags. An extraordinary sight, created by the fans, and a new England tradition that is both effective and positive.

The inspiration for this dates back to the decisive match of the 1998 World Cup qualifying campaign in Rome. The game itself was one of those hard-fought goalless draws. Nothing spectacular, but England's job done nevertheless and, by topping our group, automatic qualification (against the odds) was secured. This was the first qualifying campaign for Anne and me, and a final weekend in Rome was a trip we had been looking forward to. Plenty of sights to see, pleasant weather, some magnificent food and drink to tuck into as well.

The press had been over the top with warnings of security cordons around the ground, body searches, passport checks, long delays and in-your-face policing. We weren't exactly seasoned England travellers but we knew enough not to take these warnings too seriously. The cordons were more chaotic than intimidating and we made it safely to our seats. The hugely impressive stadium was filling up quickly, the curved ends created an amphitheatre setting full of noise and colour, and our view of the pitch was excellent. To our right and left, though, we could see something nasty going on. The Italian police were wading into the England section, batons flying, spreading panic. Coins, bottles and punches were being thrown, as much from the Italians the other side of the crowd barriers as from our own fans.

We were grateful to be far away from where all this was happening and just hoped the trouble didn't spread. Thankfully, after the initial skirmishes both sides, and the police, seemed to decide they had had enough and retired bloodied if not unbowed. And then we saw it. The Italians, across one entire end, there must have been ten thousand of them at least, held up red, green and white cards to create a huge Italian flag. I'd never seen anything like it. This was fan power at its best. Supporters standing up for their country, making sure everyone could see their colours, but free of all the intimidation and prejudice that can too easily spill over into the violence and hatred we'd witnessed a few minutes earlier.

I had never been much impressed by the atmosphere at the old Wembley. A nightmare to get to, and get away from, a terrible view of the pitch, toilets overflowing with piss; what's more, the crowd more often than not seemed to lack the passion mixed with football wit and wisdom that our fans at clubs up and down the country are rightly renowned for.

What would Wembley look like decked out in one of these giant flags, thousands of fans holding up cards? At a fans' meeting with the FA I made the suggestion. I think they thought I was mad, but eventually they gave the go-ahead. The FA were anxious about it all going horribly wrong, but hands-off enough to let us just get on with it. Fans offered to help with the layout and the final home friendly before the 1998 World Cup in France was when we would see whether the entire enterprise would work.

Nothing like this had been tried before. We didn't want orchestration and instruction, that was the culture of the Italian and Spanish Ultras, and alien to our own more anarchic, individualized fan traditions. But if it worked we would have created a powerful symbol of our collective support for team and country. On match day a senior FA official collared me: 'Great effort, but they'll tear them up, burn them, won't hold them up, it won't work, will it?' I grinned – I had every confidence in our fans, but in reality neither of us knew whether he would be proved right, and me spectacularly wrong. When the first bars of 'God Save the Queen' began, one entire end of Wembley was covered in red and white. A St George Cross bigger than any flag that had been waved before in this stadium. From that game on Raise the Flag has become an England fixture.

This is why we are gathering outside Old Trafford at this most unreasonable hour. Sarah Rhodes, her partner Jon Cadden and their mate Ben Lindley are three familiar faces I recognize as I bark out the names on the register. The three of them have helped out at countless previous matches; Sarah explains why: 'We'd seen the appeal for volunteers on the englandfans website and it just seemed like something worth doing. It was a chance to be in the stadium early, seeing it all set up for the match, meet a bunch of fellow England fans, and be part of something bigger too.'

Like Sarah, Jon and Ben, hundreds of England fans have helped out with the preparation for Raise the Flag since 1998. Sticking a sheet of plastic over the back of a seat, fixing it in place with an elastic band, then doing the same again and again for the best part of six hours. It's hardly glamorous work but there is a strong sense of common purpose amongst everybody involved. For Sarah and everybody else who takes part there is one moment that makes all the work worthwhile. 'When the sheets are held up to form the St George Cross I feel a pride. In both the superb sight but also the fact that I helped make it happen.'

Hugh Tisdale has been involved with Raise the Flag from the start. A graphic artist by trade, together we had founded a small T-shirt company, Philosophy Football. With England games touring the country up to the 2006 return to the new Wembley, Hugh's first task is to visit the stadium England will be playing in to produce detailed plans for what rows of seats get which coloured sheets. 'What I like least about modern stadiums,' he says, 'is the way bands of executive boxes break up the previously uninterrupted terraces. Liverpool's Kop and Villa's Holte End are two of the few which haven't been affected; they are huge expanses just filled with fans.' Perfect for both the layout and impact of the flag.

Raise the Flag is structured but never orchestrated. Hugh believes this is the essence of its success. 'No one ever tells fans to hold these sheets up. They choose for themselves to take part.' There is a tangible sense of expectancy in the crowd as the opening bars of 'God Save the Queen' begin and this human mosaic takes shape. At first the flag is uneven and unremarkable. It isn't until almost every single one of these sheets has been held above the fans' heads that St George's four blocks of white with the vertical and horizontal strips of red takes shape. The process takes a matter of seconds. By the time we've sung the first line of the anthem the stadium is filled with two flags covering the entire stand behind each goal. And then, almost as soon as it forms, it is gone. The plastic sheets are chucked away the moment the anthem is finished.

In Hugh's opinion, 'the brevity contributes to the impact'. There is no rehearsal or long-drawn-out ceremony about it. We're here to see a football match. Raise the Flag is all of us doing our bit for pride in team and country, creating a spectacle that can be quite emotional. 'I've visited plenty of art galleries but I've never seen people moved by a picture in the same way our flag affects the fans in a stadium.' Raise the Flag works because it is done by the fans, for the fans, to lift the team (we hope) and say a big hello to all those watching the game on the TV.

When England hosted the World Cup in 1966 the tournament mascot was a cuddly lion named World Cup Willy. Nothing much wrong with that. The mix-up was what was sewn on to Willy's singlet. A Union Jack. Yes, the one and only time England has welcomed the greatest contest in world football to its shores and the organizing committee cannot even get the flag right. So not much surprise that when Bobby, Geoff and Nobby were parading the Jules Rimet Trophy around Wembley after the greatest game of football our country had ever seen, the fans were flying the wrong flag too. Not a St George Cross to be seen. Instead the flag that was everywhere was the one we share with Scotland, Wales and Northern Ireland, most of whose citizens couldn't give a flying wotsit when England beat anyone, and for whom England winning the World Cup was their worst nightmare.

No member of the Tartan Army would ever be seen carrying the Union Jack. It would be an unthinkable act. Their flag is the St Andrew's Cross. When England and Scotland played each other at

Euro 96 after a seven-year break, the St Andrew's flags the Scots flew were the same we were long used to see them flying. It was ours that had changed. During Euro 96, and afterwards, the St George Cross almost entirely replaced the Union Jack as the fans' flag. In football, England, Scotland, Wales and Northern Ireland are independent nations. No supporter would doubt this, even if the niceties of a constitutional settlement are yet to award the trappings of statehood to the four of us.

In 1996, thanks to an opening goal from Alan Shearer, a splendid penalty save by David Seaman and a moment of vintage Gazza, we beat the Scots. What would have happened if Shearer had missed, McAllister beaten Seaman, and Gazza collided with, rather than magnificently chipped, the hapless Colin Hendry? If, heaven forbid, Scotland had won, my bet is the next year they'd have voted for independence rather than the soggy compromise of devolution they opted for by a huge margin in the 1997 referendum. Scottish nationalism would have had its feel-good factor and we'd have been happy to bid the cocky so-and-sos a not very fond farewell from the Union.

This game in 1996, more than any other single event, sparked the visual realization of a process of separation. It wasn't that previous England–Scotland matches were any less partisan, far from it. But now the English flew their own flag rather than clinging to the Union Jack of an increasingly disunited kingdom.

In the 'We Are Not English' section of a Tartan Army website, Kenny Bell seeks to explain the reason why we compete separately. He makes a sensible case for why football helps us understand our differences. 'Football does not belong to politicians, it belongs to the people. Individuals, communities and societies have built human history, as they have built football – and governments. The modern European-style nation state only became dominant in the last century, and is disintegrating in some places. A footballing country is not the same as a political nation state, and both change over time.'

Never mind the politicians and passports, football is our nation, and if the English lack the customary trappings of statehood; our own parliament, borders, even an anthem to call our own, that is somebody else's problem. The Scots reached this conclusion first. As long as we flew the Union Jack, and for a century or more of English football this remained our flag of choice, we weren't facing up to our own nationhood in the way the Scots have.

Of course the Welsh fans feel much the same way about us as the Scots. Neil Dymock is the editor of the Welsh fanzine *The Dragon has Landed*. Would a Union Jack ever be seen at a Wales game? 'No, never. We have our own flag, why would we fly someone else's? It is nothing to do with any political argument, it's just who we are.' This common-sense approach to their nationhood is something the Welsh share with the Scots and leaves the English playing catch-up. St George might have a history stretching back to the Middle Ages – Richard the Lionheart, the crusades and all that – but it remains a remarkably recent choice to represent who we are. As we start to fly, wear and daub it as our national standard, however, it is wise to remember that a country's identity is never as simply packaged as might first appear.

Across the water, virtually the entire Catholic population of Northern Ireland support the Republic of Ireland rather than Northern Ireland, in football and just about everything else. Northern Ireland, despite the best efforts of the Irish FA (confusingly they regard their southern neighbours as a breakaway) is supported almost exclusively by Protestants. However, one rather significant detail serves to confuse everybody but the Northern Ireland fans. Their supporters all wear green, just like their team. A colour most would traditionally associate with the Republic of Ireland and Irish catholicism.

On the Northern Ireland fans' website, www.ourweecountry. co.uk, Jim Rainey explains the reason why. In 1978 Northern Ireland played the Republic for the first time ever, in Dublin, and the fans from Belfast, Londonderry and elsewhere travelled south to support their team. 'All totally pished and up to our necks with "Prodfest gear", no green in those days. The Northern Ireland support wore red, white and blue and each match was an excuse for denouncing all things republican and celebrating our Britishness.' The trouble was their next away match was against England at Wembley. The two teams had played plenty of times before, and the game was at the height of the troubles in Northern Ireland, yet the team's growing support spontaneously decided that, despite loyalism, their Irishness was more important to them than their Britishness. 'We felt we couldn't go to Wembley with our red, white and blue regalia. How could we differentiate ourselves from the smug English? Northern Ireland played in green so we should all bring anything green we could find.'

But wouldn't this mean they would look like the Republic's fans? Most of whom shared a religion and a republicanism that the North's fans had precious little affection for. 'We didn't want mistaking for "them uns". In those days there was no such thing as replica kits so we had to make our own colours. We bought Celtic hooped scarves and sewed small Ulster flags onto them.' Do-it-yourself national-identity making.

Three years later Northern Ireland made it to the 1982 World Cup. Wherever the Northern Irish went, everyone and everything was green, with a dash of white. Some back home still weren't so sure green really was their national colour. 'We had some convincing to do with the locals that Northern Ireland played in green and that nobody should be wearing red, white and blue to any of our matches in the future.' Any remaining arguments were settled by Gerry Armstrong's 47th-minute winner against the World Cup hosts and favourites Spain. An unforgettable match, and Northern Ireland fans have been known as 'The Green and White Army' ever since.

The pre-match pleasantries for England matches always follow the same procedure. The two teams line up, shake hands with a distinguished guest, some opera singer with an album to flog marches up to the microphone to provide lead vocals, we listen dutifully to their anthem, then sing ours as loud as we can muster. The Saturday in 2005 when we played Northern Ireland, though, these proceedings had to be rearranged. The Northern Irish, like us, don't have their own anthem. We both have to make do with 'God Save the Queen', which, until Scotland and Wales declare themselves republics, remains the official anthem of the United Kingdom. (If it was the Scots or the Welsh, of course, they'd have their own anthem to sing, and for us to jeer and whistle. Then they'd do exactly the same to ours, except it isn't just ours, it's theirs as well.)

We put all this to one side as the entire stadium gives the single anthem the usual tuneless ear bashing, strong in rousing volume if not in melody. Apart from Northern Ireland every other country has its own anthem, although Liechtenstein's song shares the same tune as 'God Save the Queen', which confused a fair few when we played them in the Euro 2004 qualifying campaign. Since we began doing Raise the Flag we have always laid out, in their own colours and with a welcome printed in their own language, our opponents' flag for them to hold up during their anthem. It is an initiative unique in world football, away fans arriving in a stadium to find something like this on their seats. Without exception they always join in. Yes, there are particular matches when our crowd boos and jeers the opposition's anthem, though we're hardly alone in this. At the Millennium Stadium when we played Wales in September 2005 each set of supporters did their best to drown out the other's anthem. But more often than not we listen in respectful silence and watch with pride as the flag we've provided for our guests is held up. And then finish with that wonderful moment of English applause, as much for ourselves and how we have changed as for those who have travelled to see their team play us, and who we hope will now get well and truly beaten. Our hospitality has its limits.

The Wednesday following the Northern Ireland match, another bunch of volunteers gathered outside Newcastle United's St James' Park to do the Raise the Flag layout for our game against Azerbaijan. Afterwards a load of us popped into The Strawberry, the pub right outside the ground, for a few well-earned pints. I had a copy of photographer Stuart Clarke's new book, *England the Light*, his brilliant visual record of Euro 2004. Most of us sat there had been to the tournament, and as we flicked through the pages the shots of Rossio Square, Estadio da Luz, beach football and Portuguese girls brought back plenty of happy memories.

Across the room a bunch of lads – Stone Island jackets, Burberry caps – recognized me and came over. I didn't know any of them. I'm ashamed to admit I was a bit wary. It turned out one of them had been stuck on the same Tube train as me when the line to Heathrow was shut down the night we were due to fly out to Vienna for the Austria match the previous September. Unlike me, he had a good memory for a face. Nothing to worry about, then. The next thing I know, this same guy has grabbed Stuart Clarke's book out of my hands. 'That's my flag! It's on the cover of this book, my fucking flag!' He insisted all his mates have a peek too. He was so proud, so pleased that it was his flag that had been photographed. Once they'd all finished having a look he passed the book back to me, treating it with a certain degree of reverence, and asked for details of where he could get his own copy.

*

Keep the Flags Flying

Stuart Clarke has been taking photographs of football for almost twenty years. Italia 90 was the first World Cup where he photographed England fans. His photos from Italy portray England supporters under siege, standing apart; English bodies being searched by heavily armed Italian policemen; security staff at the stadiums trying to make themselves understood by our fans, all sporting bulldog T-shirts; Italians keeping their distance from the English.

The results on the pitch were fantastic, our best performance since 1966, but off it Stuart's photos struggle to capture many happy memories. So why the shift? Where has this more recent visual culture of pride and fun come from? Stuart mentions four features that perhaps have always been there but only since Euro 96 have forced themselves into his pictures. 'The colours, the emotional energy, the camaraderie of the fans, the sense of wanting to state where we come from. Yes, there remains the unsavoury to photograph, but this is dwarfed by the absurdity and the humour of England fans abroad.'

The St George Cross dominates almost all of Stuart's photos of our fans, but what does it symbolize for him as a photographer? 'The flags don't come ready-packaged. They have been made, drawn on, added to. The flag-bearer needs this baggage, without it the fans are travelling light, stripped bare, unremarkable. They are saying, "I'm not just me, I am the flag."'

Our flag is remarkably unfussy. We are used to logos being plastered everywhere, official and unofficial sponsors engaged in a brand war to compete for our attention, custom and loyalty, policed by the commercial guardians of international football, who have sold advertising hoardings, banner space and retail rights to their favoured multinational corporations. The flags with which we redecorate stadiums are here not to sell fast food, a fizzy drink or a flexible friend. They are just saying we are here, we're part and parcel of this spectacle, and we're English. Stuart sums up expertly why his pictures of row after row of St George Cross flags strung out around a stadium have so much impact: 'The picture, as with the flag itself, provides a cool graphic. More so now, stripped away from the complicated Union Jack. It has a symmetry, an immediacy; it appeals to what is in most cases an untrained, unartistic eye.'

Daniel Campbell and Tim Weymouth are newcomers to flag-hanging. They have a problem, though – their huge Dagenham and Redbridge FC St George Cross is thirty-foot wide and twenty-foot deep. This won't fit just anywhere, so getting into the ground early is vital. On the 2005 USA tour they'd snatched the position behind the goal from the more experienced hands with their similarly huge flags. 'Back in Dagenham a great big roar went up at our local when the commentator for the game against USA listed the flags: "Blackburn, Burnley, Sunderland and – Dagenham and Redbridge." So now we've a reputation to maintain.'

Ged Sweeney is more of an old hand with his flag. 'We're Crewe Reds, Man United fans. Not many from United follow England away, so it was just a way of saying we're here.' Ged's now on his third flag; his first was a Union Jack, something hardly ever seen at England games now. 'France away, September 2000. I'd just finished putting my flag out in the Stade de France when these West Ham fans started on me, "What the fuck are you doing, we're not British, we're English." They were going to tear the flag down. I didn't want the argument so I just bundled it up and moved to somewhere else in the stand.'

Not many would react to Ged's flag with quite this degree of anger. The shift to St George has been more subtle, without any obviously nationalist overtones, rather an increasing awareness that the previous cosy coincidence of Britishness and Englishness won't do any more. Ged is in his mid-thirties: 'Growing up the Union Jack was everywhere. 1976 was when I first started going to football. You never saw a St George Cross in those days, always the Union Jack.'

Positioning is everything for the flag-hangers. Chris Radford managed to get his six-foot by ten-foot 'Chesterfield' flag right under the scoreboard in Niigata where England played Denmark in their World Cup 2002 second-round match. When Emile Heskey smashed home England's third goal of the night every camera in the stadium turned to the scoreboard. 'The *Sun*, the *Daily Mirror*, *Daily Star*, our flag was in the lot,' Chris proudly remembers. 'There's no feeling like it. My flag from where I live, lined up alongside all those others, thousands of miles from home. I've never quite understood why it's only the English do it, no other country has these flags with place, club, pub and family names stitched across them like us.'

Not many of those who carry their flags as they follow England do it for the publicity, rather it is a welcome consequence of their dedication in getting one of those prized front-row pitch-side spots. Few, though, will ever go home without some pictures taken of their flag in its place. 'Five hundred, maybe more,' is how many snaps Tim Murray has taken of himself with his 'Monks Brook' flag. When Tim first followed England, to Italia 90, he took a Union Jack. 'Not many bothered, just a few of us. And hardly any had stitched or painted where they were from across the flag. It was completely different to what it's like now.'

Tim likes his beer. When he was getting his flag organized for the trip to Japan he thought he would put the name of his local, The Monks Brook, on his flag along with where he lives, Chandlers Ford. 'Everywhere me and the flag goes I pin it up, hotels, bars, beaches, buses even, not just the match, then take a snap for everyone back at the pub.'

Tim's local paper, the *Southern Daily Echo*, ran a big feature on his flag under the title 'Flag of Friendship'. In the piece Tim explains what his flag means to him: 'The flag is not there to say we've conquered anyone or anything like that. It's there to say come and join us. Come and have a party.' Tim doesn't make a big deal about any of this, but at his pub, the snooker hall where he plays, and on his work notice board, those who know him have proudly pinned up the article about their mate. His flag has helped them to be a part of following England. Spotting it in a stadium on the big screen or TV back home, and knowing their pub, their town, is a part of that match.

During World Cup 2002 Jonathan Glancey, architecture and design editor on the *Guardian*, attempted to explain the artistic appeal of the St George Cross. 'A striking and memorable pattern or logo, that unlike the union flag, even an idiot can paint across their face. It does look good. Which hugely paid advertising agency or design consultancy could come up with a more powerful logo?' Glancey was coming round to the argument that there was something even dyed-in-the-wool liberals could savour in St George: 'The fact that so many people from so many different backgrounds can wrap themselves in this antique emblem shows that there might – might – just be a little chivalry behind the effing, blinding, beery bravado after all.'

The editor of the indelibly liberal *Guardian* clearly agreed. Accompanying the paper on the day before our quarterfinal with Brazil was a free cut-out-and-keep St George Cross. The paper's liberal tendencies couldn't, however, be kept fully in check. In case readers might get the wrong idea, in the top-left corner of the flag a flash read: 'No ugly connotations. No white van required.' The humour was laid on thick with a degree of pomposity the political class is recklessly good at. Nevertheless, just ten years previously the very idea of a St George flag free with the *Guardian* would have led to angry splutterings over middle-class breakfast tables the length and breadth of England.

Tim Vyner is a professional artist, and Derby County fan. The Professional Footballers' Association has never before appointed an official World Cup artist, but after being approached by Tim they agreed to his proposal and funded Tim's trip out to Japan in 2002. Most of his paintings feature the fans, with the St George Cross everywhere: 'The flag is both discreet and overt,' says Tim. 'In Sapporo's Odori Park before the Argentina game there were thousands of England fans just doing their own thing. Each little gathering was acting slightly differently but all together, and the flags are central to this. They help create an atmosphere and define the landscape we find ourselves in.'

Tim went to Euro 2004. 'I saw this one flag in Rossio Square, Lisbon, with "We Still Believe" written across the St George Cross. No club or place, just a simple declaration of why we put ourselves through all this, and keep coming back for more.' Tim has turned that flag into a painting with 'We Still Believe' emblazoned on the cross and the four white background spaces filled with 'Ozzy and Jax, Bev and Lol, Me and Me Dad, Toffo, Mike and Deb, Club and Country' and many more of the messages he had seen across other flags out in Portugal. The picture is a simple one, it lacks the intricate detail of much of Tim's work, but it remains, like the flags themselves, hugely effective. 'The fact that it seems almost hand-made and lacks obvious sophistication makes it loyal to its inspiration.'

After World Cup 2002 Tim's paintings from Japan were exhibited in a London gallery. One particular painting of his caught my attention. The delicate watercolours picture the aftermath from Shizuoka following England's defeat by Brazil. In the background is the stadium where our hopes had been finished off by Rivaldo and Ronaldinho. The foreground is filled by fans streaming away through the carefully manicured parkland and forest in which some half-crazed Japanese architect had located this huge sporting arena, miles from anywhere, not a house – or pub – in sight. England fans carrying their flags, Japanese supporters sitting on the grass looking almost as dejected as us, but proud to be wearing their Beckham number seven and Owen number ten shirts.

And in amongst us, Brazilians. Over to one side is a guy in a St George Cross tabard. He looks like one of Richard the Lionheart's Crusaders. (He's been at almost every England World Cup game I can remember, always happy, whatever is happening on the pitch, and waving above his head as he dashes up and down the aisles this huge plastic replica World Cup.) And right slap-bang in the middle of this evocative picture is me, and my flag for the day.

There is a story behind my flag. Trevor Ballance, who Anne and me were staying with in Tokyo, had come to the match. Trevor's Japanese wife Kinuko Fujii is a calligrapher. I'm no artist, but with Kinuko's help I had carefully written down on a scrap of paper in Japanese characters, 'Thank you Japan! *Arrigatoh Gozaimas Nippon*'. I'd never taken a flag to an England game before but, like so many others, I had been overwhelmed by the way the Japanese had received us. I knew I was unlikely to get a prime position behind a goal, or anywhere in full view of the TV cameras, and had too much respect for the flag-hanging regulars to even try to nick one of their spots. And what if we upset the odds and actually won? Then the flag should surely wait for the semi-final.

For all these reasons my flag had to be something I could roll up and bring out only if the worst happened and we lost. Why 'Thank you'? Because after the Japanese side were knocked out by Turkey in the previous round, the entire squad stripped off their shirts to reveal vests with 'Thank you Japan' and paraded around the stadium to show their fans the gratitude they rightly deserved even at this moment of defeat. It was a great gesture and as I watched it on TV it got me thinking whether there was something similar to be done to show both pride in our performance and thanks to the Japanese for having us.

Kinuko's script helped, but it was a heck of a long passage when spelled out in both languages. Anne and me had stopped in Kyoto for a couple of days sightseeing before the Shizuoka game. In a traditional Japanese clothing store I found the ideal material for my flag. An 'obi' is about ten yards long, one yard deep, made of white linen and is normally wrapped round and round a petite Japanese woman's waist as part of her Kimono outfit. Perfect for scrawling in huge red letters my bilingual message. I laid my obi out along a quiet side road and carefully did my best to copy Kinuko's Japanese characters. By the time I'd reached the end of my material and added an exclamation mark to my 'Thank you Japan' the first few letters had dried nice and hard under the baking-hot Japanese sun. Thankfully this meant I didn't have to endure the curious stares of passers-by for too long. 'Ah-so, crazy Englishman, practising his Japanese handwriting,' they were no doubt thinking.

When the match was over and England's campaign finished, Trevor held one end of the flag, myself the other and we marched out of the England end. As we emerged through the exit the Japanese stopped, stared, read my script, nodded approvingly at my spelling and applauded. And they kept applauding; in fact they clapped this flag for our entire walk back to the coach park. It still gets my tears of emotion welling up years later just thinking about it.

Tim had caught the scene perfectly. He had thrown into this clash of cultures a little bit of public diplomacy, inspired by our unique culture of daubing where we come from across our flag, paying due respects to our host's language, and utilizing a part of their national dress.

Stand-up comedian and novelist Rob Newman was perplexed by the absence at France 98 of a giant St George to unfurl and pass over our heads at the start of a match. Writing after the tournament, Rob theorized the meaning of this absence: 'Foreign fans have more fun. Apart from England, the only other country not to have a hundred-foot flag or silky banner passed overhead is the USA. This is because Anglo-Saxon capitalism does not encourage collective life, nothing is owned collectively.'

I have no idea whether Darren Pullen or Gavin Morton-Holmes are dedicated to the overthrow of capitalism. But they have each done something about this 'lack of a giant flag' situation Rob puts down to free-market economics. Gavin's flag is a twenty-foot wide, thirty-five-foot high portrait of Bobby Moore on the shoulders of his England team-mates holding the Jules Rimet trophy aloft. 'I was inspired by Italian football, all those huge banners they have.'

The flag first went to Albania away in March 2001 where Gavin faced a rather severe problem. 'There wasn't much lighting in the stands where all the England fans were. We unfurled the banner and passed it up and down our section above our heads. But of course in the sixty-six final the team were wearing red, so the banner is mainly red too. When you are under the flag it isn't that easy to make out what's on it, the image is for others to see. The poor lighting made this even worse and a few idiots couldn't make out the image properly, saw all this red and thought it was an Albanian flag. First they tried to set fire to it, and then they chucked it from the back row right out of the stadium.'

Gavin retrieved his banner, asking the confused Albanian stewards who had hauled it out of the puddle far below where it had landed, 'Can I have my banner back, please?' The next few England matches were played in daylight. Everybody could make out Bobby, Geoff and the rest on the flag and Gavin's banner became a widely welcomed feature of the build-up to kick-off.

It was the excitement of Beckham's last-minute equalizer in the final World Cup 2002 qualifier, against Greece at Old Trafford, which caused the greatest trauma in the short life of his flag. 'After I'd recovered from that free kick I looked around and my flag had gone. By now it was really rather popular amongst a decent number of fans. I got in touch with the ones I knew. Could they help me get it back?' Within twenty-four hours the BBC sport website had been bombarded by over 400 emails seeking support in launching a nationwide hunt for the flag.

'The BBC called me: "Are you the man responsible for these hundreds of emails we have received?" an official-sounding voice asked.' The BBC wanted to help and Gavin was invited on to *Football Focus* to launch what he called the 'Can I have my Bobby back?' appeal. 'There I was sitting on the TV sofa next to Mark Lawrenson talking about what this flag meant to me and loads of others.' A few days later, with the agreement that no names would be involved, Gavin got his flag back.

Darren Pullen, meanwhile, has in his possession the biggest England flag of the lot. Safe in the knowledge that it would take three or four excessively burly individuals to do a runner with it, he isn't expecting to have to endure the sort of angst Gavin had to go through when he lost his. 'Mark Robinson, a Middlesbrough fan, first got me thinking about a huge flag. He'd mentioned that Boro have the biggest fans' flag in the Premiership, and as we're both England fans we thought it was only right England should top even that.' One hundred foot by sixty foot is what their huge flag measures. They call it a 'surfer flag', inspired like Gavin by the choreographed carnival that the Italian Ultras organize in their stands before every match.

'It's a flag for the fans, funded by the fans. We've a website where fans can donate money. The finished article cost over three thousand pounds to make. It had to be fireproofed, the material used is impossible to tear, insurance and transport had to be organized. Most importantly it is so big we have to secure permission to get it into the stadium.'

This is a seriously collective business, quite contrary to the self-ish individualism that Rob Newman believes so many of us prefer. 'More than two hundred and fifty fans have donated money, and we all voted on what we would have written across the flag,' says Darren. The basic design was easy enough to decide upon, a St George Cross with nothing provocative or negative. The message chosen to paint along the enormous crossbar? 'We Still Believe'. It's the same phrase Tim Vyner had spotted in Rossio Square on another flag, and then used to create his painting. Darren reminds me where it came from: 'It's a line from "Three Lions". Those three words explain why we follow our country. Even after all those disappointments, never quite finishing the job, we still do it. Our faith is never broken.'

Singer Billy Bragg moves in similar political circles to Rob Newman. They are both regulars on the left-wing benefit circuit, using music and comedy respectively to promote a variety of worthy causes. His politics remain unwaveringly socialist, combined with a belief in what it could mean to be English. 'It's a certain kind of Englishness I've always been interested in, the coming together of ordinary people to survive, fight and win World War Two. The ideals that founded the Welfare State in the late 1940s. The sense of community which today is constantly under threat.'

Billy's England is a country of Ovalteenies, dunking biscuits, blue collars and flat caps, William Blake and his green and pleasant land under the shadow of dark satanic mills. His English imaginary, however, surpasses simply nostalgia for a bygone age. 'The Right purposefully want to write off pop music. Their history stops at the 1950s.' On Billy's bookshelf in his Dorset home are recent books on Englishness that I've read too: Simon Heffer, Roger Scruton, Peter Hitchens and others. 'None of them write about the Beatles, and everything they came to mean. What were those four guys doing? They listened to black American music, or white Americans trying to play like black Americans, and were inspired to create some of the most influential and long-lasting music of the twentieth century.' Billy locates the success and popularity of the Beatles in the capacity of Englishness to listen, learn, adapt and reproduce.

For Billy, football, St George and an emerging English nationhood are all connected. 'We all want some sort of sense of belonging, usually to a sort of combination of nation or society. We can't talk about the popularity of the St George Cross, Scottish Saltire or Welsh Dragon in a vacuum. The architecture of Britishness has changed, for good.' The era of devolution has coincided with the successive tournaments England qualified for: Euro 96 followed by France 98, Euro 2000, World Cup 2002, Euro 2004 and World Cup 2006. This is what has fired up the popularity of St George, something that fills Billy with hope for the future. 'The flag is synonymous with Englishness; the confusion with Britishness which the Union Jack causes is coming to a close. St George is like a blank canvas, it is much more neutral than the Union Jack. It is there for us to write what we want on it.'

He identifies three elements of decline which will settle the fate of Britishness and create the conditions in which Englishness will begin to be defined in its own right. 'The empire has gone. The monarchy don't inspire the loyalty and unquestioning respect they once did. The rise of St George is eclipsing the ubiquity of the Union Jack. Once that flag starts to be replaced by our own, an English one, then the fundamental structures of the nation state start to crumble. And we are left wondering what it means to be English.'

Football, for Billy, has been a vital part of all this. 'It enables our national identity to waver between the belligerent and the celebratory.' The belligerency is what he has a problem with. The celebratory he seeks to foster. 'Those fans' flags. They're a visual celebration of all these places coming together and calling themselves a nation.'

If St George is our visual celebration, then *The Great Escape* and 'Football's Coming Home' provide the soundtrack. No one would ever accuse England fans of being part of that much-fabled English tradition, a tendency to be a bit on the mild side. We chant, cheer, jeer and sing out of tune. The musical accompaniment, of sorts, is provided by John Hemmingham on trumpet, Steve Wood on euphonium and Steve Holmes on snare drum. These three are the England band regulars, sometimes swelling to near orchestral proportions with a trombonist, saxophonist and bass drummers joining in.

In 1996 newly appointed England manager Glenn Hoddle and David Davies from the FA were at Highbury when Arsenal were playing Sheffield Wednesday. John and his band are all Wednesday fans. When their team went 1–0 up, Steve Holmes began to make an almighty racket on his drum, and the rhythm never stopped, not even when Arsenal scored their fourth in the 4–1 thrashing. 'The FA wanted to know if we would consider playing for England. It has to be the best thing that's ever happened to me. I told them, of course we'd bloody play, when can we start?'

None of the band would make any claims to be skilled musicians. 'We're fans who happen to have a musical instrument in our hands. We couldn't get away with what we do if there was any falsehood about us. We go everywhere, paying for our tickets and travel out of our own pockets.'

Their first game as a band was Poland at home in 1996. England went behind and John was wary of striking up a tune. 'If we became associated with losing we knew that would be the end of us before we'd hardly started.' They needn't have worried. Shearer scored twice to keep our 1998 World Cup qualifying campaign on a winning run and the band haven't stopped playing, whether we're winning, losing or settling for a draw, ever since.

Their repertoire, they would be the first to admit, is limited. Most of the time they simply provide the backing music to England's favoured terrace anthems. 'Football's Coming Home', 'Keep Me English', 'On the Ball', and 'Ingerland! Ingerland! Ingerland!' But their special achievement lies with making one particular tune England's own, the theme to *The Great Escape*. It appears a strange choice. The film was released way back in 1963, so the music can hardly be accused of being faddish and fashionable. The composer, the late Elmer Bernstein, is American. And the film, while heroic, ends eventually in tragic defeat. Just a solitary Aussie, a claustrophobic East European of indeterminate nationality played by Charles Bronson, and Willie 'The Tunnel King', who if my memory of endless repeats serves me well was Scottish, actually succeed in escaping the POW camp. And the only sport played in the entire movie is Steve McQueen catching his baseball.

But it is also a tale of pluck in the face of overwhelming odds that, notwithstanding the multinational make-up of the escapees, we like to think of as peculiarly English. And most important of all was the fact that, as John Hemmingham points out, 'It was a tune everyone would know and could join in with.' In Rome, October 1997, when England played Italy in the final, and decisive, qualifier for World Cup 98, *The Great Escape* echoed around the Olympic Stadium.

John accounts for the success of the tune that night, and ever since: 'There's a good melody to it. The fans clap along to form the rhythm section, and their voices supplement the brass.' None of this was probably quite what Elmer Bernstein had in mind when he composed his most famous musical score. Though when the film critic Philip French described it in Bernstein's obituary as 'far from triumphalist, it is the music of jaunty defiance, of grace under pressure', he rather neatly summed up the reasons why it has become an England fan anthem.

Apart from *The Great Escape* many England fans would list 'Rule Britannia' amongst their favourites for the band to belt out and the rest of us to join in with. 'God Save the Queen' has also become established as the fans' unofficial way to welcome the start of the second half, unprompted by the pomp and circumstance of officialdom.

There's more than a few sentiments in the lines of these songs that I find disconcerting and unappealing. 'Britons never, never, never shall be slaves' rings a bit untrue when the ancestors of a high proportion of the team line-up found themselves in precisely this awful predicament during the age of Empire. But then maybe the song is saying to Rio, Jermaine and Ashley that we wouldn't stand by and let such a sorry situation happen again. As for 'Happy and glorious, Long to reign over us' raucously sung at the top of their voices by one of the most anti-authoritarian crowds Englishness ever gathers together, where's the sense in that? The 1977 Sex Pistols version of 'God Save the Queen' might have more obvious appeal, and for some of those old enough to remember, possibly did. But 'God Save the Queen' is what gets sung, the authorized edition. Except it's not our anthem is it?

You don't have to want the heads of the Windsors on a stake to sign up to the opinion that it's about time England had an anthem of its own, rather than having to make do with the British version. The prime candidate for an English national anthem is usually William Blake's 'Jerusalem'. It certainly fulfils one of the criteria that Billy Bragg demands for a song to qualify as an anthem: 'How can you have a national anthem that doesn't even mention the country we're singing in praise of?' 'God Save the Queen' fails on that count. It is a hymn to the house of Windsor rather than Blake's lyrical focus on 'England's mountains green'. 'Jerusalem' is stirring too – anything that can rouse the WI from their knitting patterns and flower arranging scores highly in that department.

The hit comedy double-act of the '50s and '60s, Flanders and Swann, weren't convinced. In one of their sketches they ask, 'What national song do we have?' They pause for dramatic effect, before answering their own question: 'Jerusalem?' This is followed by prolonged guffaws from the audience. Agreed, Jerusalem, a divided city in the faraway Middle East, might make for a strange title for an English anthem. It's not a place that alongside Sheffield, York or Bradford will be painted across one of our St George Cross flags. Of course, Jerusalem in the song represents not a place but an idea. The idea that our anthem is about both the country we are from and the something better we'd like it to become, is surely part of the song's appeal. Written in religious language, there is nothing uniquely Christian, or political for that matter, about the ambition for England that Blake's script describes; it is the basic human emotion to desire a better lot for ourselves, and others less fortunate than us, that he so powerfully depicts.

In April 2005 Nick Griffin, leader of the far-right, racist British National Party (BNP) was charged at Halifax police station on four counts of inciting racial hatred. His supporters protested outside waving their St George Cross placards with 'England our England' neatly printed across them and singing 'Jerusalem'. The Jerusalem they dream of is an all-white and unpleasant land. Does this mean the flag, the song, and all the associated accessories are indelibly stained with the mark of racism? Of course not. When those like Brian Viner in the *Independent* declare, 'It certainly appears fortuitous for the BNP that the election is so close to Euro 2004; in the run-up to polling day their symbol is everywhere,' they award the symbol, our St George Cross, to the BNP simply because it seems they don't want anything to do with it themselves. According to Viner, flag-flying is 'not something educated, reasonable, broad-minded people do'.

Ravi Deepres takes photographs of black and Asian England fans. What does he think of this argument that St George is best left to the BNP? 'My photos of Asian England fans wearing the flag, this represents inclusion, and the adaptability of cultural identities.' Ravi recognizes the obvious tensions that remain. 'There is a level of discomfort, feeling out of place, being a minority, but there is also this powerful experience of adoption; the shirt, the badge, the flag and the team.'

After World Cup 2002 the photos Ravi took in Japan formed an exhibition he called 'Patriots'. 'It was so important to get my pictures of England's increasingly multiracial support, and others like them, into the public domain. We must prevent it just being an individualized experience. Once people see one of these pictures they don't need any explaining. It is so obvious what is going on.' Ravi singles out the symbolism of black and Asian fans wearing and flying the flag as crucial in this process: 'That image is so much more powerful than any words that could ever be written.'

Most of those who criticize all this flag-waving justify their dissatisfaction by convincing themselves that we're either all right-wing nutters or else so stupid to be the dupes of these extremists. Of course, the overwhelming majority of us are neither. Nor are we on some sort of political mission to reclaim the flag. St George can't be made to belong in this simple sense to left or right, and nor should it. But the flag is not just another team badge or corporate logo either. It has a meaning beyond what the eleven blokes we're flying the flag for get up to. What precisely? Well, we're not quite sure. When two million marched against the war in Iraq, one couple carried their St George Cross instead of a banner or placard. In the four corners they had written, 'Not in our name'. At Edgware Tube station, alongside the flowers and wreaths after the horrific 7 July terrorist attack, another St George Cross appeared. In this flag's four corners were the words, 'Bombed but never beaten'.

At Glastonbury, St George Cross flags appeared in front of the main stage where previous generations of festival-goers had satisfied themselves with 'Where's Wally' or 'Hello Mum' daubed across their bed sheets. When an overtaking car, van or lorry has in its window a St George Cross, can we really be certain what the driver's views are on race, immigration, the European constitution? Not any more we can't. All we can be certain of is that he, or just as likely she, is hoping for an England win.

St George can mean almost anything. Stained red with centuries' worth of empire, plunder and war, its early twenty-first-century surge of popularity symbolizes the break-up of Britain into its historic constituent parts. Worn by black and Asian fans it is a celebration of our modern multicultural national mix. The flag we will all wave when Becks, or his successor, finally lifts the World Cup once again for England. Most England fans would settle for the last one. Proudly claim the flag as where we come from, and argue the toss over the rest.

*

At the Parken Stadium in Copenhagen in August 2005, the night England played Denmark, I was hard pushed to spot a single Danish flag tied up like ours were, covering the section where the England fans had been put. The Danish fans are known as 'Roligans' – a loose translation would be 'friendly fans'. They know how to have a good time, they're rightly renowned for it. Never any trouble, they put on their plastic Viking helmets, add a pair of dodgy blonde pigtails, dress uniformly in their national team colours of red, drink themselves stupid and give the Dutch and the Scots a run for their money in claiming the title 'friendliest fans in the world'. However, Kenn Ronning, one of the leaders of the Roligans, points out to me one thing the Danish fans lack: 'We don't do flags like you do. You cover the stadium, not just your end, the whole place. And on each flag is written where you come from.' It has taken a foreigner to remind me just how impressive a sight this is, and the fond regard others have for the sight we create.

The pre-match entertainment for the Denmark game features a squad of nimble cheerleaders. They march around on the pitch without sparking very much interest. Apart from when they bounce past our end to the usual catcalled invitations to get a particular part of their anatomy out for the lads. Smiling, the girls shake their pompoms at us. The one at the front is clearly in charge, she has a Union Jack on a mini-flagpole to wave. Wrong flag.

It's a mistake easily made. Which is the only team to compete in European Championships and World Cups that does not qualify as a nation state? Easy! Easy! England. Tiny Luxembourg, Andorra, and Liechtenstein have all the necessary qualifications. Their own parliament, borders, passport, national anthem. And since 1997, even Scotland has its parliament and first minister, Wales and Northern Ireland something similar. England is alone in having none of the constitutional trappings of nationhood. Yet in football we are treated as if we amount to more or less the same as every other country on earth.

It leaves the Danes, and a good part of the rest of the world, confused. They only know the Union Jack, the British prime minister, the British Embassy, the British royal family, the British Army. Who does this team they're playing represent and to which country does the flag the fans fly belong? It helps that we've won the World Cup, our league is one of the most famous in the world, and a handful of our players are globally branded superstars. But in terms of our nationality others remain almost as confused as we are.

It is these travels with I-N-G-E-R-L-A-N-D as our football nation, whether sat in an armchair in front of the TV or in some corner of a foreign stadium decked out with St George Cross flags, that have helped establish who and what the English are. It is a relatively recent process. Until 2002 there was hardly a speck of red on England's first-choice kit of white. Instead it had all sorts of splashes, stripes and other devices in varying shades of blue. But since the hugely popular strip with a red stripe down one side hinted at a St George Cross, all the subsequent kits have incorporated something similar. Another sign of this collision of football and our emerging nationhood.

The process of defining what our Englishness means to us remains a contest. The crowd shifts from one extreme to the other, while the majority remains content stuck in the middle ground. Our do-it-yourself Englishness has flirted with a hardcore nationalism that detests all things overseas. Today it is increasingly a soft patriotism that is favoured. Those who dress up as chain-mailed Crusaders, or don bowler hats and bash a briefcase in their hand with a rolled-up *Financial Times*, are the minority. But just add together the thousands who will join in a conga in Niigata, raise the flag at a home game, pack a floppy St George jester's hat in their hand luggage, or simply rub up against fans of another country and not get all bitter and twisted. The soft patriots are approaching a majority.

Tanked up on hope, pride and commitment, the support for hatred, prejudice and confrontation is emptying. Not gone entirely, but on its way out. The flags say it all. A patchwork of cities, towns, villages, clubs and pubs, families and mates; from here, and now we're there. Our history is unchanged; we can do nothing to alter it. The St George Cross will always be bloodied. It is the resources of inspiration that have been reinforced. A little bit of a *Carry On*, Pythonesque absurdity, the hapless leadership of Captain Mainwaring, the stoicism in defeat of Hancock, matching Shakespeare's Falstaff pint for pint and laughing off the after-effects with the same good humour. The hearts of oak that meant Nobby and Bally ran all over the Wembley pitch in 1966 now beat just as strongly inside Rio and Ashley. Marching tunes from the Second World War at the game, home-grown garage and rap blaring out the car stereo system on the way home. And before the journey is over, a curry or a kebab to replenish the calories we lost as we sweated over whether Becks would put that last-minute free kick past their keeper – Yesssss!

All this and more; not everyone joins in, agrees with, or even welcomes every bit of it. But most will cheerfully admit to celebrating some part of these different expressions of what our Englishness means to us.

Ninety-minute patriots? Not bloody likely, the passion doesn't come off in the wash. Glory-hunters? One trophy, and nothing much else after four decades of trying to win another one has never dulled our support. Xenophobes and racists? Don't inscribe your narrow-minded prejudices onto our painted faces, thank you very much. Football and nation: it is impossible to think of

Keep the Flags Flying

England without accounting for the relationship between this pair. We're hopelessly in love with both of them. And like all the best relationships, we forgive the disappointments, forget, hope for a better result next time and come back for more. Win, lose or draw, we keep the flag flying.

Extra Time: Further Reading, Websites and Contacts

My effort with *Ingerland* has been to foreground the various ways in which our support for the England team, home and away, has helped construct a variety of different ways of 'doing' Englishness. Four books tackling this subject of our national identity in very different ways are:

Kumar, Krishan (2003), *The Making of English National Identity*, Cambridge University Press, Cambridge

Paxman, Jeremy (1999), *The English: Portrait of a People*, Penguin, London

Sawyer, Miranda (1999), *Park and Ride: Adventures in Suburbia*, Little Brown, London

Weight, Richard (2002), *Patriots: National Identity in Britain 1940–2000*, Macmillan, London

Of course, the bulk of *Ingerland* is about the football. Books that tell the story of some of England's more successful campaigns with a style and context which examines more than just who scored what include the following. Incidentally, *All Played Out* is regarded by many, including myself, as amongst the finest of all football books. Chris England's hilarious book is about World Cup 2002, in case you hadn't guessed.

Hill, Dave (1996), *England's Glory: 1966 And All That*, Pan, London

Dawson, Jeff (2001), *Back Home: England and the 1970 World Cup*, Orion, London

Davies, Pete (1990), *All Played Out: The Full Story of Italia 90*, Mandarin, London

England, Chris (2003), *No More Buddha, Only Football*, Hodder & Stoughton, London

Ingerland

Books on the background to today's England fan culture vary from academic analysis by John Williams and others of the World Cup 1982 and Euro 88 campaigns to Kevin Miles' fan activist's account of Euro 2000 and various self-published fan diaries.

Johnson, Colin (2000), *St George in my Heart: Confessions of an England Fan*, Terrace Banter, Lockerbie

Miles, Kevin (2000), *An English Fan Abroad: Euro 2000 and Beyond*, Rebel Inc, Edinburgh

Williams, John, Dunning, Eric and Murphy, Patrick (1985), *Hooligans Abroad: The Behaviour and Control of English Fans in Continental Europe*, Routledge, London

Williams, John, Dunning, Eric and Murphy, Patrick (1990), *Football on Trial: Spectator Violence and Development in the Football World*, Routledge, London

There are few books which detail the experience of women, black and Asian, or family fans; amongst those which do are:

Back, Les, Crabbe, Tim and Solomos, John (2001), *The Changing Face of Football: Racism, Identity and Multiculture in the English Game*, Berg, Oxford

Coddington, Anne (1997), *One of the Lads: Women Who Follow Football*, Harper Collins, London

Williams, John (2001), *Football and Families*, University of Leicester, Leicester

There is a huge literature on what creates football hooliganism and its impact on public disorder. The best analysis I have ever read is by Gary Armstrong, while various authors have written books from the inside to uncover the causes of England fans' violent reputation.

Armstrong, Gary (1998), *Football Hooligans: Knowing the Score*, Berg, Oxford

Brimson, Dougie (2000), *Barmy Army: The Changing Face of Football Violence*, Headline, London

Brimson, Eddy (2001), *God Save the Team: Fighting for Survival at Euro 2000*, Headline, London

Buford, Bill (1991), *Among the Thugs*, Secker & Warburg, London

Mash, Jamie and Bazell, Matthew (2000), *Invasion and Deportation: A Diary of Euro 2000*, Terrace Banter, Lockerbie

Extra Time: Further Reading, Websites and Contacts

Following in the wake of Simon Kuper's superb book on the global culture of football there are now an increasing number of books on how, in other countries, the game has contributed towards the framing of national identity.

Black, Ian (1997), *Tales of the Tartan Army*, Mainstream, Edinburgh
Hesse-Lichtenberger, Ulrich (2003), *Tor! The Story of German Football*, WSC Books, London
Kuper, Simon (1994), *Football Against the Enemy*, Orion, London
Winner, David (2001), *Brilliant Orange: The Neurotic Genius of Dutch Football*, Bloomsbury, London

Not many authors have tried to explain the particular relationship between football and Englishness. I have edited a collection of essays on the topic, David Winner and Dave Russell take a lengthier historical look at the subject, while Stuart Clarke has produced a thrilling visual insight into England at Euro 2004.

Clarke, Stuart (2005), *England the Light: Euro 2004*, Giant Step, Ambleside
Perryman, Mark, Ed. (1999), *The Ingerland Factor: Home Truths from Football*, Mainstream, Edinburgh
Russell, Dave (1997), *Football and the English*, Carnegie, Preston
Winner, David (2005), *Those Feet: A Sensual History of English Football*, Bloomsbury, London

Of course nowadays there is a huge variety of useful information to be found on the Internet, plus, from fan groups to the Football Association, almost everyone has their own website.

England supporters' band: www.englandband.com
England supporters' huge flag: www.fansflag.com
Policing and football-violence researcher Clifford Stott's website: www.footballfans.org.uk
International network of fan groups: www.footballsupportersinternational.com
Football Supporters Federation: www.fsf.org.uk
Football photographer Stuart Clarke's website: www.homesoffootball.co.uk
Campaign against racism in football: www.kickitout.org
LondonEnglandFans (includes reports on fan forums and fan-friendly events): www.londonenglandfans.co.uk
Exhibition space for football photographer Mark Leech: www.offsidebar.com
Pioneers of 'soft patriotism' T-shirts: www.philosophyfootball.com
FA website for all the latest news on the England team: www.theFA.com

Ingerland

Official England supporters club, including how to join:
www.theFA.com/englandfans
When Saturday Comes, the monthly football magazine web edition:
www.wsc.co.uk
Independent England fans website and message board:
www.365englandfans.com

Index

Index

Index

Index

Index